The
Railways of Dundee

by

Peter F. Marshall

THE OAKWOOD PRESS

© Oakwood Press and Peter F. Marshall 1996

British Library Cataloguing in Publication Data
A Record for this book is available from the British Library
ISBN 0 85361 482 2

Typeset by Oakwood Graphics.
Repro by Ford Graphics, Ringwood, Hants.
Printed by The Witney Press, Witney, Oxon.

Coal wagons await collection from the quay between Earl Gray and King William IV Docks on the Harbour branch. *Author's Collection*

Front Endpaper: Ward station in the 1850s, the original Dundee and Newtyle Railway terminus. The incline rose beyond the station and the Harbour line crosses Ward Road in the foreground. *Dundee Courier*

Rear Endpaper: Caledonian Railway '125' class 4-4-0 No. 126, a Brittain 'Dundee Bogie' at Dundee West. These locomotives hauled local goods trains between Dundee and Perth around the turn of the century. *HMRS/Vintage Collection*

Published by
The Oakwood Press
P.O. Box 122, Headington, Oxford OX3 8LU

Contents

Tay Bridge station looking west around the turn of the century.   *Author's Collection*

VIEWS IN DUNDEE.

An engraving of Dundee streets in the 19th century.

Author's Collection

Chapter One

The Growth of Dundee
1027-1890

'A very large place, the situation is very fine, but the town itself is not so'
Queen Victoria, on her visit on 11th September, 1844.

There are few towns or cities in the British Isles with a more attractive location than the City and Royal Burgh of Dundee. Situated on the northern shore of the estuary of Scotland's longest river, the River Tay, the earliest settlement on the present site took advantage of a natural harbour provided by both the indented coastline between St Nicholas Craig and Castle Rock and a sandy bar at the narrow mouth of the estuary between Tentsmuir Point and Buddon Ness, a few miles downsteam towards the North Sea. The protection provided by Castle Hill and Corbie Hill to the north meant that the settlement was able to grow, safe from either sea or land attack.

The earliest habitation at Dundee was around the area now known as Seagate between Scouring Burn and Dens Burn, the two streams which flowed into the Tay a quarter of a mile apart and which later supported the great textile mills which gave the town its prosperity. It was logical that the growth of the settlement should be along the shore of the river. The slightly sloping beach would have been most suitable for fishermen to haul up their boats and the rocky outcrops offered protection against the erosive effect of the tides. The inhabitants of this early hamlet were engaged in fishing and farming - primarily for their own use. However a hoard of English coins, buried in 1027, has been found upstream of Dundee, revealing that a trading pattern had emerged even then.

By the 12th century Dundee had become an urban and market centre able to support the King and his court when it toured in the area. As recognition of this, the town was raised to the status of a Royal Burgh during the reign of King William I around 1190. Alexander Scrymgeour was appointed Constable of the Castle of Dundee in 1298 bestowing some autonomy on the Burgh, and by the 1360s a tron, or public weigh beam, was erected in the market, emphasising the town's importance as a trading centre. King David II granted a Charter in 1359 prohibiting the neighbouring settlements of Coupar Angus, Kettins, Kirriemuir and Alyth from holding markets, as Dundee held that privilege. This meant that the produce from the rich hinterland beyond the Sidlaw Hills had to be brought to Dundee if it was to be sold.

Dundee became recognised with Aberdeen, Edinburgh and Perth as 'one of the four great towns of Scotland' by the traders of Bruges. A visitor to the town observed that 'the habourage within the shelter of Castle Rock was as safe as the medieval mariner could reasonably expect'. The earliest exports included wool, sheepskins and hides, contributing 10 per cent of the annual duty paid to customs in Scotland around that time. By the 17th century the port was receiving flax, iron and timber from the Baltic and wine from France, all indicating an improvement in the standard of living and the beginnings of the textile industry, so important to the burgh's fortunes in future years. The town grew steadily along the river shoreline and also inland up the 25 ft and 50 ft raised-beaches behind to the cluster of cottages that was Hilltown.

The port increased in importance but the quality of the harbour facilities was deteriorating, Daniel Defoe, the author and traveller describing them in the 18th century as 'indifferent'. Dundee had a population of 19,329 by the time of the first Statistical Account, a parish by parish survey of the whole country, produced by The Church of Scotland. That for Dundee was prepared in 1792 by the parish minister, Dr Robert Small. In it, he locates with a confident accuracy the 'principal' pier at 56 .27'.23"N and 3 .2'.55"E. A later observer commented that there was 'one small pier and two or three clumsy erections in a state of dilapidation.'

Indifferent could well have been used to describe the quality of the buildings in the town, many of which were built with frames of wood imported from the Baltic. In the typically east coast style of 'crow step' gables, few stone-built houses lasted into the '19th century, although, one, Gardyne's House still stands behind the High Street. So at the end of the 18th century, the magistrates and council embarked on a programme of improvements, opening up new streets in the town, including one down to the shore, and built new piers and generally improved the harbour. No less than 116 vessels were operated from the port at that time, 34 in foreign trade, 78 in coastal trade, which included coal from the Forth, and a further 4 in whaling. The first whaling company, The Dundee Whale Fish Company was formed in the middle of the 18th century and, in 1814, eight whalers sailed regularly from the port to the whaling grounds. Naturally, in such a significant port, there was also a shipbuilding industry with two yards employing 31 men in all.

The principal product of Dundee at the time of the first Statistical Account was coarse linen cloth called 'Osnaburghs', 4,242,653 yards being woven and valued at a total of £108,782 14s. 2d. In 1778, there were 2,000 looms in Dundee dedicated to the weaving of linen while a quarter of the cloth was brought to the town from neighbouring parishes to be sold. The importance of the linen trade brought about the formation of the British Linen Bank, which in turn gave added strength to banking in Dundee during the late 18th century. Cotton was a less important fibre and was sold as 'callicoes, handkerchiefs and coarse waistcoats.' Around the end of the century, £14,000-worth of leather was tanned, £7,000 of footwear was exported, and there were 1,700 employees in the thread industry. Although sugar, glass and soap-making were all in decline and buckle-making was destroyed by the shoelace industry, such variety shows the growth of the Dundee as a prosperous trading and manufacturing town.

The second Statistical Account was published in 1833 and reveals a very different burgh, growing in confidence and becoming an even more significant port. The population had grown to 45,355 in 1831 and the linen industry had expanded through the determination of the manufacturers to adopt new machinery which both reduced labour costs and improved the quality of the finished product. Advantage was taken of a bounty payable on linen exports and millowners set the price of Osnaburghs at the lowest in the class for which the highest bounty was paid.

Finance in the town had the support of several local banks during this time.

As well as the British Linen Bank, there had been a branch of the Bank of Scotland since 1696 and, in 1765, George Dempster founded the Dundee Banking Company. The enterprise of the linen manufacturers was shown again when raw flax imports became more expensive. In 1824, they had brought a parcel of jute fibre from India to experiment with in their mills but met with resistance from the spinners. Commercial spinning of this new fibre did not begin until 1832 when a better treatment for the yarn ensured a better spinning process. Coincidentally, the bounty had ceased to be payable on linen exports on 5th January, 1832. Meanwhile, the port had grown to handle this increase in trade. Plans to extend it had been passed by Parliament in 1815, when the management of the port was vested in commissioners selected from magistrates and other public bodies.

At a cost of nearly £250,000, new docks were created near the original outcrop of St Nicholas Craig. In 1815, the foundation stone was laid for the new works which were set out to the design of Thomas Telford. Beginning with the tidal harbour and West Graving Dock in 1820, and followed by King William IV Dock in 1825 and the Earl Grey Dock in 1834, the expansion brought an increase in shipping resulting in a rise in income from harbour dues from £4,096 in 1815 to £10,802 in 1830. The continued success of Dundee as a port soon meant that even these facilities were insufficient and further harbour Bills were sought in Parliament, and obtained in 1836 and 1843, to extend the works eastwards. Whereas 116 vessels operated out of Dundee in 1792, there were 259 in 1831, the harbour handling 2,921 movements that year. The Dundee, Perth and London Shipping Company (DP&L) had been formed in 1798 with four ships plying to London. By 1801, two more ships began the Glasgow trade and the company bought out the four vessels which had been operated in competition to the Thames. Traffic for Perth was transferred to lighters and towed up river by a steam tug. The DP&L continued to expand, operating a virtual monopoly from Dundee throughout the early decades of the 19th century.

The steady expansion of the harbour accompanied the building of a new Customs House at the foot of Trades Lane in 1843. Designed by James Leslie and John Taylor, this was the largest Custom House in Scotland. By 1848 the rough protective walls of Victoria Dock were in place alongside the recently built Dundee & Arbroath Railway terminus. Both these works resulted in the shipbuilding industry, already established in the area, being relocated further east. Amongst the better known companies which had yards at Dundee around this time were Gourlays which was established in 1790, and Alexander Stephen, both constructing whalers. The rapid expansion of the jute trade from India was hampered by difficulties encountered during the creating of Victoria and Camperdown Docks which were not finally completed until 1865 and 1875 respectively. By then, a fleet of between 70 and 80 fully rigged vessels were engaged in transporting the raw jute to Dundee. Wharves and quays had to be constructed along the river side to handle the larger ships.

The whaling fleet, in contrast, was in decline by 1832, due to the introduction of gas as a means of public and domestic lighting (candles were made from whale fat), but the arrival of jute gave the trade a much needed fillip through the use of whale oil mixed with water in the spinning process. As a result, by

1872 Dundee had become the focus of 19th century whaling in Great Britain. In 1867, 2,000 tons of oil was refined from whale blubber landed at Dundee, by boiling it in nearby yards then storing it in tanks around the East and West Whale Lanes in the Seagate area. The oil was then used in the jute mills of the town. One of the primary customers for jute yarn at this time was the Dutch government which used it for bagging coffee in the East Indies, thus opening up seaborne trade with that part of the world. The other important centre of the whaling industry was Peterhead, and, before the fall in whaling activities in the 1880s, special trains carried whale oil to Dundee from the north-east port for use in the jute industry.

The Crimean War of 1854-6 brought an interruption of supplies of flax from Russia boosting the jute traffic even more. From April 1861, the American Civil War and the imposition of the Merrill Tariffs - a 20 per cent duty on the importation of jute goods to America - brought about a reduction in supplies of cotton. This simply worsened an already depressed home market, and when the United Kingdom almost joined the American War Dundee's trade was virtually at a standstill. However the demand from both sides in the USA for large supplies of linen and jute restored traffic with the US as the mills in Dundee could provide all the cloth that was required.

Raw jute imports grew from 37,000 tons in 1860 to 277,000 tons in 1895. This, then, was the golden age of jute production. Sadly the price of whale oil had collapsed by the 1890s and so brought about the final demise of whaling. In due course, the jute industry, like the cotton industry in Lancashire, found that manufacturing was more efficient when taken back nearer to the source of its raw material. As a result Dundee's foundries, which had provided the town's mills with their powered machinery, began to export this equipment to India. The jute industry continued into the 20th century as a backing for linoleum and carpets but demand for the rough cloth declined steadily after World War I.

The layout of the town was greatly improved with the opening up of new roads and better access from the High Street to the harbour area and Craig Pier. In 1877 the first public tramway was opened by the Dundee Tramway and Omnibus Company Limited. A double track line was constructed from the Head Post Office to the west end where large terraced houses were being occupied by the newly emerging middle classes of the town. The first trams were horse drawn and ran down Reform Street, through High Street and Nethergate to Perth Road at Dalhousie Terrace.

When A. & K. McDonald were contracted to extend the new docks they employed a Barclay locomotive on the works, completing this in 1875, but by 1890 a report from the Harbour Master showed both that large jute steamers were being held up in the river because of the lack of accommodation and that nearly every ship had to be lightened before entering the docks.

A new wharf and sheds were erected to the west of the cattle market and work began on the Eastern Wharf, originally constructed of timber but rebuilt in concrete early in the 20th century. The last dock to be opened was the Fish Dock in 1900, but a further wharf was opened east of Camperdown Dock and named after King George the Fifth in 1915. Recognising the importance of Dundee, Queen Victoria had granted a Charter in 1889 raising the burgh to a city.

When Charles Dickens paid a visit to the town in 1858, he described it as, 'an odd place, like Wapping, with high rugged hills behind it.' He went on, 'We had the strangest journey by bits of sea and bits of railroad alternately, which carried my mind back to travelling in America.' He had clearly experienced the difficulties which all northbound travellers from Edinburgh had to endure before the estuaries of the Forth and the Tay were bridged.

Therefore, both the port, with its associated industry, and the geography of Dundee between hills and water dictated the way in which transport and, specifically, the railways were to grow. In an industrial town with a comparatively small middle class, the development of the many individual railway schemes extending outwards from the town illustrate how the enterprising townsmen exploited this new means of transport to expand their trade. With support and finance from landowners, local banks and the Town Council of Dundee, these railway schemes (some of which did not succeed, as we shall see) provided Dundee with a series of local railway enterprises which came together to produce a transport network which, when eventually joined with the rest of the country, formed an important part of the national system we know today.

ANNO SEPTIMO

GEORGII IV. REGIS.

****

Cap. ci.

An Act for making a Railway from the Royal Burgh and Port of *Dundee* in the County of *Forfar*, to *Newtyle* in the said County. [26th *May* 1826.]

WHEREAS the making and maintaining a Railway with inclined Planes, where such Planes are necessary, for the Passage of Waggons or other Carriages, from the Royal Burgh and Port of *Dundee* in the Parish of *Dundee* in the County of *Forfar*, or near to such Royal Burgh and Port, to the Valley of *Strathmore* in the said County, passing through Part of the Parishes of *Dundee*, *Mains* and *Strathmartin*, *Auchterhouse*, *Tealing*, *Caputh*, and *Newtyle*, and terminating at or near to the Farm-stead of Mill of *Newtyle* in the Parish of *Newtyle*, in the said County, will be of great local and public Utility : And whereas the several Persons herein-after named are desirous, at their own Costs and Charges, to make and maintain the said Railway and other Works ; but such Purpose cannot be obtained without the Aid and Authority of Parliament : May it therefore please Your Majesty that it may be enacted ; and be it enacted by the King's most Excellent Majesty, by and with the Advice and Consent of the Lords Spiritual and Temporal, and Commons, in this present Parliament assembled, and by the Authority of the same, That the Magistrates and Town Council of *Dundee*, Subscribers J   A   Stuart Wortley, George Kinloch, Peter Wedderburn, David incorporated. *Jobson*, *Patrick Anderson*, *David Nairne*, *Alexander Clayhills*, *David Brown*, *Patrick Kirkaldy*, *Andrew Dalgairns*, *James M'Nicoll*, *Hugh Watson*, *Alexander Balfour*, *David Miln*, *Thomas Bell*, *George Gray*, *David Rankin*,

[*Local.*]   31 R   *John*

Act of Parliament for Dundee and Newtyle Railway.   *Dundee District Libraries*

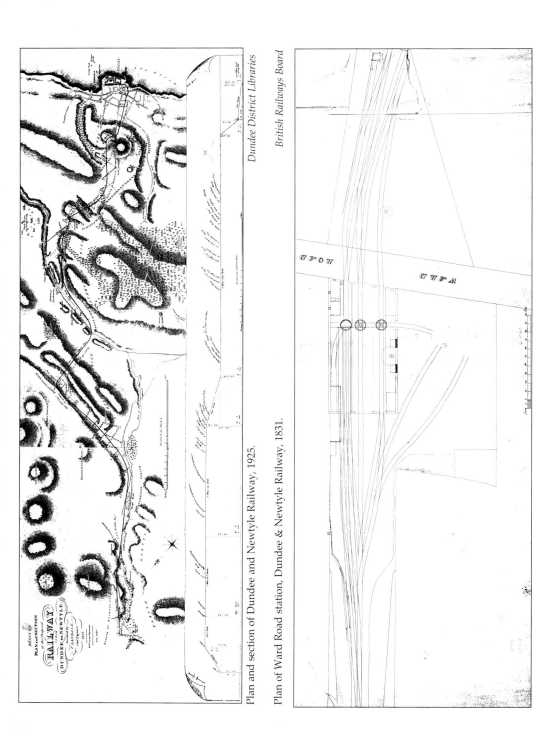

Plan and section of Dundee and Newtyle Railway, 1925.

Plan of Ward Road station, Dundee & Newtyle Railway, 1831.

Chapter Two

The Dundee & Newtyle Railway
1825-1868

'A Private Enterprise for the Public Good'
translation from the Seal of The Dundee & Newtyle Railway

With the ease of communication, presented by the flat and rich agricultural land of the Carse of Gowrie to the west and the gentle slopes of the Angus coast to the east, it was strange that the first railway to be constructed from Dundee should be to the hilly north and that it should try (and succeed) to cross the Sidlaw Hills which rise nearly 1500 feet behind the town. However, there had been several early attempts to bring the rich hinterland of Strathmore into closer proximity to the coastal markets.

Strathmore had been a popular, but an unavailing, territory for the promoters of canals in Scotland since 1760. In 1767, George Young, a merchant from Coupar Angus, submitted a plan to the Earl of Findlater for a canal eastwards along the length of the fertile plain from Perth. Another local, William Keir, showed that the level of water at Coupar Angus was only 97 ft above the Tay at Perth and estimated that the intervening 20 miles could be crossed by canal for £20,000. Smeaton and Brindley were each approached to engineer the route but both refused.

James Watt was asked in January 1770 to come from Glasgow to survey a possible route, but, at first, he too declined saying that he was busy with the Monkland Canal, near Glasgow. However, on 15th April, 1770 he wrote to suggest a week's viewing before beginning a full survey. His report, for which he charged £211 4s. 4d., advised that a canal be constructed from Kinnoul Hill, near Perth, to Forfar without locks. Had it been made, it would have been 16 ft wide creating a channel three feet deep capable of carrying boats 56 ft long with cargoes of 20 tons.

Although a turnpike existed north of Dundee, a further canal project was mooted in 1810, when Robert Stevenson, a civil engineer of Edinburgh, was asked to carry out a survey for a canal to link Forfar to the coast at Arbroath and to Perth in the west, but that too was never built. A 'terraqueous undertaking' had been advocated as late as 1817, when correspondence in the Dundee press had proposed a canal be built from Strathmore to the town. A fresh scheme was suggested and abandoned in 1825, but by then a more significant proposal had been made.

The first positive signs of improved communications to the Strath came when the Town Council of Dundee met on 5th January, 1825 and set up a committee with the purpose of arranging the construction of a railway from Dundee into Strathmore. The Town Council also approved a sum of £100 towards a survey of the possible route. A long prospectus was produced in the local newspapers inviting 'gentlemen of the county' to a meeting in Dundee on 1st February for those wishing to subscribe to the survey for the building of a railway, 'for the expeditious and economical transport of merchandise, grain and all descriptions of farm produce; and of manure, stones, lime, coal and other heavy and bulky articles'.

The meeting was chaired by George Kinloch, a liberal minded landowner from Meigle, who was known as the 'Radical Laird'. He did not support the idea of a canal but preferred, instead, to explore the benefits to be gained from a railway link from Strathmore through a break in the Sidlaw Hills to the improved harbour facilities at Dundee. The meeting agreed that they wanted a survey to be undertaken and Charles Landale was commissioned to carry it out. Landale, who has been described variously as a civil engineer, an architect, and an apothecary, was the fourth son of Charles Landale of Craigmill, a Burgess of Dundee and architect of the Town House. Landale, too, had designed houses in the town and had patented a central heating apparatus. More importantly, in 1821 he had engineered Lord Elgin's Railway, a coal waggonway with two inclined planes which he had arranged ingeniously to allow wagons to roll downhill between them in either direction. This early line ran from Dunfermline to the banks of the Firth of Forth at Charlestown. In the same year, he also redesigned the Tranent Waggonway, one of Scotland's oldest.

Landale examined two possible routes over the Sidlaws, both beginning at the northern boundary of Dundee but with alternative routes dividing before crossing the high ground, one ending at Douglastown near the county town Forfar and the other in a field 'at or near the farmstead of Mill of Newtyle'. Prior to the arrival of the railway, Kirkton of Newtyle consisted of a church, a smithy and a handful of cottages in addition to the farm. It can only be surmised why the latter route was selected in favour of that to Forfar. Perhaps it was to divert trade away from that town or perhaps it was because a major shareholder was the Honourable J.A. Stuart Wortley, later to become Lord Wharncliffe, a leading land owner through whose Belmont Estate the Newtyle route was to pass. An improved access to the markets in Dundee would give him an advantage over his neighbours as well as ensuring the provision of coal from the port of Dundee, since the supply of Strathmore peat had dried up around 1800.

Kinloch and Landale as Chairman and Engineer respectively of the newly formed Dundee and Newtyle Railway company went up to London to ensure the passage of the Bill through Parliament. The Dundee and Newtyle Railway Act (7 George IV cap. ci) was given Royal Assent on 26th May, 1826. An estimate of £26,000 had been made of the cost and annual running expense was estimated at £3,400. The Act authorised capital of £30,000 in joint stock of 600 £50 shares and a loan of £10,000 was drawn through a mortgage from the Dundee Union Bank at 4½ per cent. The major shareholders were Dundee Town Council, The Earl of Airlie, Lord Wharncliffe, the Rt Hon. William Ogilvie and George Kinloch, who each subscribed £1,000. There were 187 initial shareholders mostly local and amongst these first shareholders were two Dundee engineering companies keen to benefit from railway expansion, the Dundee Foundry Company and J. & C. Carmichael of Ward Foundry who subscribed £500 and £100 respectively. The Act, among other items, stipulated the conditions which had to be observed including maximum fares to be charged for passengers and freight and the nature of the level crossings, along with the need to erect screens where the railway crossed a turnpike road to ensure that horses would not be startled by the passage of trains!

The initial line of railway which was settled upon was from a depot on the north side of the town at the Hospital Ward, through School Wynd and West Chapel Shade. From there, a stationary engine would haul the wagons up a 1,060 yds-long inclined plane of 1 in 10 gradient to the Law (the hill dominating the town). It went on for 4¾ miles by level plane to Strathmartine, a textile village to the north, where the route turned west, crossed the Dighty Burn and, at Rosemill Quarry, headed north once more up a second incline, almost a mile long of 1 in 25 (with a second stationary engine) towards the farm at Pitpointy. Here the line turned west again for another 4¾ miles on a second level plain, passing through Auchterhouse and Millhole farm before descending by means of a third stationary engine, past Hatton Farm and down a 1 in 13 slope, 1,000 yds-long, through a gap in the hills, and into Newtyle.

Landale at first recommended that horses be used to pull the wagons along the two level planes which he proposed, but pointed out that 'in the long term, there is reason for believing that machines will work at much less expense than horses.' He also believed that a satisfactory locomotive had not yet been produced, but that there was justification for believing that such a mechanical perfection was sure to come. By the creation of the three inclines within such a short length of railway (it was only 11½ miles-long), and by inaccurate estimates, Landale had condemned the line to an unprofitable existence.

Tenders for the preparatory works were invited by the beginning of 1827, the earthworks being assessed to cost as little as £356. Landale had allowed £18,216 for the track which was of malleable iron fish-bellied rails weighing 28 lb. to the yard, placed in 7 lb. cast iron chairs on stone sleepers at a gauge of 4ft 6½ in. The rails were manufactured by Longridge and Company of Bedlington Iron Works in Northumberland, being delivered by sea from Blyth.

An order was placed with J. & C. Carmichael at their foundry in Dundee for the three stationary steam engines at a price of £3,700. The dimensions of these engines were:

Incline	HP	Piston	Pressure	Drum	Gears	Load
Law	40	21 in. x 60 in.	40 lb.	12 ft	3:1	24 tons
Balbeuchley	20	27 in. x 54 in.	4½ lb.	12 ft	2:1	16 tons
Hatton	20	27 in. x 54 in.	4½ lb.	12 ft	3:1	16 tons

The Law incline was clearly the steepest with the most powerful engine, although it is believed that an engine from Maudslay of London was installed in place of Carmichael's. Here the rails were laid out differently to the other two, being single track at the bottom where it left the Ward station, then double track in the middle as a passing place and three rails at the top with a centre rail shared. Each train on this incline had a four ton ballast wagon fitted with a brake and clutches on the rope which was 7½ in. in circumference. The journey time on all three inclines was between four and seven minutes. In each month of operation, the engines consumed 85 tons of coal from Preston Grange Colliery near Edinburgh, once again shipped to Dundee, and delivered for 10s. per ton.

Although it was not indicated on the original survey by Landale and his assistant William Corsar, a tunnel was formed at the top of the Law incline, thus avoiding a further detour around the hill. Costing £5,000 to dig out, it was 10 ft 2 in. high, 10 ft wide and 300 yds long with a single track through it. The construction of the Law tunnel produced early problems, for, in December 1828, having expected to cut through a solid volcanic plug, the contractors found loose rubble, a fall of which caused a fatal accident to one of their workmen. There was a further rock fall in March 1829, although the work had been completed on 21st January.

Costs continued to rise, typical of many lines in the early days of railway building when estimating was far from exact. As an example of the inaccuracies to be found in estimating, in the Parliamentary submission Landale had estimated £25,600 for the line, excluding land acquisition, but Matthias Dunn, when he was invited to comment on the railway proposals, felt this was low. David Jobson, the company treasurer, resigned 'in a bad humour' in April 1829 because he feared that the alleged incompetence of Charles Landale could make him personally liable for the resultant losses. Under clause 83 of the company's Act, debts could be recovered by 'the Sale of the Goods and Chattels of the Treasurer'. The need to line the tunnel and the extra expense in compensating farmers, plus other unforeseen expenses led to criticism in the local press that 'this useful undertaking was nearly at a stand' for the want of funds.

A shareholders' meeting on 16th June, 1829 levelled the blame at Landale. Ten days later, he rebutted the charges that he had mismanaged the construction, pointing out that agreed compensation was running at four times the original estimate. As the principal landowners were also major shareholders, it was hard to argue against his defence, but yet within two months Landale had been relieved of an additional post he held, that of superintendent of the line. He had, at that meeting, threatened to leave the work incomplete if he was not paid.

A further Act was sought and passed on 29th May, 1830, authorising the issue of shares to the value of £10,000, as well as allowing borrowing up to a maximum of £20,000. This second share issue was taken up by only 25 subscribers including four of the original main shareholders. In 1831, Dundee Town Council also offered further security of £2,000. By December 1831, the line was virtually ready to open. So keen were the company to begin revenue earning operations that they had started a limited service at the beginning of the month. A poster announced 'A coach will be started on Friday, 16th December to run between the Engine House at the Law of Dundee and the Engine House at Hatton Mill near Newtyle. The coach can carry twelve inside and twenty-four outside'.

It was not until the beginning of April 1832 that all the inclines had been brought into use and a full service could be operated. The company set down clear rules for the operation of the inclines. No more slack rope than necessary was to be used, and no unnecessary jerks created. Heavy passenger trains were to be lowered on the east rope of the Law incline, six passenger carriages at a time with the 'breaks' manned. The limit for ascent was only five carriages and only 18 tons of goods could travel on the incline using either rope. On Balbeuchley 24 tons could ascend and up to 30 tons descend, but all trains had to be slowed to 5 mph when they were 60 yards from the switches at the lower end. The time taken for this incline was seven minutes. The weight limit at Hatton was 20 tons and the time to be taken there was four minutes.

Signalling on the line was comparatively sophisticated. The signal at the foot of the Law was a white board with a black centre which was turned to face the engineman five minutes before the advertised departure. He had to wait for the board to be turned before commencing the ascent. A bell was rung in fog and red and white lights were employed at night. Elsewhere, the signals showed the traditional red for danger, green for caution and white for all clear. The first coaches were two old Tally Ho! coaches which had been employed on the Dundee to Perth turnpike road and which were bolted on to a wagon chassis. The fare charged was 1s. 6d. inside and 1s. outside for the whole journey which took one and a half hours.

Stations were of very poor quality although built of stone and wood. They were built at:

Ward station, Dundee
Off-set at back of Law later known as the Cross Roads
Off-set at Flour mill, St Mary's Road, later Baldovan
Off-set at Baldragon
Foot of Balbeuchley incline
Top of Balbeuchley incline
Off-set at Auchterhouse
Newtyle Depot

The decision to terminate the line at Newtyle did little to promote the range of traffic which the railway needed. Since before 1832 only a small settlement existed at Newtyle, further development was needed and the principal landowner, Lord Wharncliffe, agreed not to grant any further leases near to the railway. Rather, he decided to invite the submission of plans for a new village with a prize of ten guineas for the best by 20th February, 1832. The winning plan from George Mathewson of Dundee was implemented between 1832 and 1838. Advertisements for the sale of leases in the new settlement made great play of the fact that the terminus of the railway was adjacent. In the six years from the new village being planned, £1,053 was spent on the provision of roads, water and drainage. However, the growth of the village did not produce a large enough expansion of traffic to provide a profit for the railway company.

The Dundee and Newtyle (D&NR) called in Nicholas Wood, the mining and civil engineer from Killingworth and former judge in the Rainhill Trials. He was known for his views on the benefits of stationary engines compared with the use of locomotives, and was asked to advise on the line and its possible extension further into Strathmore. In his report to the Directors on 23rd February, 1832, he was able to make a number of observations about the layout of the tracks, 'there is a trifling error in laying out the engine planes (inclines) in not providing sufficient room for the landing (stopping) of the trains of carriages.' He suggested that the siding at the top of Balbeuchley ought to be extended to allow for the 'flattening' of the rails before descent. Wood did not believe that the 28 lb. rails were heavy enough but, as they were now installed,

DUNDEE AND NEWTYLE

Railway.

THE COACHES on this Road will, on *Tuesday first*, commence running *Three Times a-day*, starting from each end at the following hours—namely, at Eight Morning, half-past Ten Forenoon, and Four o'clock Afternoon. Parcels will be received and booked at the Depots at Dundee and Newtyle.

The WAGGONS will also start from both ends at Eight Morning, half-past Ten Forenoon, One o'clock, and Four Afternoon.

Carts with Goods for the Waggons will require to be at the respective Depots at least one hour before the Waggons start.

Railway Office, Barrack Street,
March 31, 1832.

D. HILL, Printer, Dundee.

Notice of the full service on the Dundee and Newtyle Railway, 1832.
Dundee District Libraries

light use might not damage them, and he criticised the quality of the buildings, thinking them to be insufficient for the expansion of traffic, although the Newtyle depot was suitable for lime, coals etc. On revenue, he commented that the cost of transporting goods and produce to Newtyle from bigger settlements around the village was a deterrent to generating traffic, and an extension to the line into the wider region was desirable. The D&NR was in no position to finance new lines so this development fell to two smaller companies, more of which later.

Amongst other recommendations, he suggested a method of carrying freight traffic. He reported:

> The great bulk of traffic is coal, lime and flax outwards from Dundee, Grain in sacks, potatoes in sacks or in bulk and stone inwards from Newtyle. Coals and lime may be carried in the same two ton waggon with bottom doors. Potatoes, flax and grain require a larger waggon with end doors carrying 1½ tons. It is recommended that some coal and lime waggons have both end and bottom doors. Waggons for coal and lime should be fitted with case hardened iron wheels and be made of wrought iron.

Initially goods receipts were poor, but passenger traffic exceeded even the most optimistic estimates, and day excursion tickets were soon being offered, along with season tickets and workmen's fares with sheep shearers at half fare! Although the railway had opened just over a year after the Liverpool and Manchester and only a couple of months after the Glasgow and Garnkirk, which used locomotives from the start, it was not until 1833 that locomotives replaced the horse traction engaged on the level stretches between the inclines on the Dundee and Newtyle.

The first locomotive was No. 1, an 0-2-4 named *Earl of Airlie*, which was built by J. & C. Carmichael (*see Chapter Seven*) who had previously built a stationary engine for the Edinburgh and Dalkeith Railway. It had vertical outside cylinders 11 in. x 18 in. driving 4 ft 5 in. wheels through push rods and bell cranks pivoted behind the cylinders. Such an elaborate method may have been simpler than that of *Puffing Billy*, but did not take full advantage of the direct drive demonstrated on Stephenson's *Rocket*. The *Earl of Airlie* was delivered to the line on 20th September, 1833 and entered service nine days later on the Law to the foot of Balbeuchley section.

No. 2 also from Carmichael's was identical, being named *Lord Wharncliffe* and delivered on 25th September, 1833, and destined to work the section between Balbeuchley Top and Hatton. Both locomotives operated at 50 lb. pressure and weighed 9 tons 10 cwt. An entry in the company's cash book for 31st October, 1833 reads 'To James and Charles Carmichael, for supply of 2 Locomotive Engines and other machinery supplied from 1st May to this date. £1,402 17s. 3d.' A third engine, No. 3, named *Trotter* smaller and mechanically different to the first two, was built in March 1834 by the Dundee Foundry to Carmichael's design, although this is by no means certain.

A fourth locomotive was ordered for the line from Robert Stephenson & Co. of Newcastle. It was named *John Bull* and was the first four-coupled engine, the driving wheels being 4 ft 4 in. in diameter. No. 4 was an 0-4-0 with inside cylinders 11 in. x 16 in., entered traffic in April 1836 and was for coal trains only. Fuelled by coke it cost £1,137 10s. Early services were far from intense, with passenger trains leaving both Dundee and Newtyle at 8.00 am, 10.30 am, and 4.00pm and goods trains leaving at exactly the same time (presumably combined) with an additional service at 1.00pm each way. To accommodate locomotives, an engine house was constructed to the north of the Law incline.

Several tales exist about the comments of local worthies who experienced railway travel for the first time. Sandy Gaul, from Auchmithie, was disgusted when he observed a train at the Law tunnel. He described it as 'a perfect humbug. It puffed, it puffed, and it came, and it came and when it saw me, it ran into a hole in the hill and hid itself.' Another story tells how a guard stopped his train at Balbeuchley when he saw an old woman hurrying over adjacent fields, but was less than pleased when his potential passenger simply asked, 'Could ye change a shilling?'

By 1836, the company found itself in more financial difficulties, with interest charges of £1,200 annually and unpaid accounts for the rails. Further share capital of £100,000 was authorised by another Act on 4th July, 1836, but this was not so well subscribed as previous issues, even at a discount of 40 per cent, with only 1,534 of them taken up, mainly by creditors. It was even reported in the local newspapers that shares could change hands for 'a tumbler of toddy'.

The 1830 Act also empowered the extension of the line at the Dundee end through the streets to the Harbour, although work had already begun without Parliamentary approval. The company could 'treat and agree for the use of a branch railway to facilitate communication with the Harbour of Dundee'. The group of shareholders called themselves 'The Trustees of the Harbour Branch Railway', and began to buy up property between Nethergate and the river's edge at Yeaman Shore.

Plans were drawn up in 1834 at the time the town's new docks were being formed and, after several meetings, the Town Council gave permission for rails to be laid through the streets, from the Ward station down Lindsay Street, across Nethergate to Yeaman Shore, where the line turned east to join up with the railway created by the Harbour Trustees at Earl Grey Dock. Both the management of the Dundee & Newtyle Railway and the engineers of the Dundee & Arbroath Railway (see Chapter Three) who were the well known partnership of Grainger and Miller, were consulted about the proposals. Miller recommended that the line be built and operated with horse traction and restricted to two goods wagons at a time due to the steep inclines encountered (1 in 24 and 1 in 37).

The line was completed and in operation by February 1837. The property at Yeaman Shore was transferred to The Dundee & Perth Railway in 1846 (see Chapter Four), but the Harbour branch continued to function until the closure of Ward station in 1861. The section along the public highway at Yeaman Shore was discontinued in favour of a stretch through railway property in 1847.

Extensions to the line at the northern end of the D&NR were built to alleviate the difficulties encountered in transporting goods and produce to Newtyle. The Newtyle and Coupar Angus Railway was incorporated by an Act on 21st July, 1835 followed by the quaintly spelled Newtyle and Glammiss Railway on 30th

July, 1835. The Coupar Angus branch was opened in February 1837 and that to Glamis was opened for goods traffic during 1837, but not until 4th June, 1838 was it open for passengers. Neither line was deemed to be successful in bringing in new business.

To encourage through traffic, both new lines were built to the same 4 ft 6½ in. gauge as the D&NR and made a connection at the northern end of D&NR near the Newtyle terminus. The routes shared the line northwards for the first mile or so then diverged west for Coupar Angus and east to Glamis. Despite both railways being separate companies, they shared the services of the same Engineer, William Blackadder of Glamis, and were to all intents and purposes, simply branches of the D&NR. Traction was initially by horse but, although the Coupar Angus line did not possess its own locomotives, the Glamis railway is recorded as having borrowed *Victoria*, an 0-4-0 built by Stirling of Dundee for the Arbroath and Forfar Railway.

The Coupar Angus line was about 5½ miles long and relatively level for the most part. This enabled the return coach to Newtyle to take advantage of the stiff wind that can blow along the broad vale of Strathmore, and consequently, on windy days, a tarpaulin was erected at the rear of the coach permitting speeds of between 10 and 20 mph to be attained from Coupar Angus and Ardler. William M'Intosh of Meigle recalled this enterprising technique being in use between 1837 and 1841. The horse would trot along behind, ready to take over if the wind dropped.

Major General C.W. Pasley, who was Inspector General of Railways at the Board of Trade, examined all three lines on 18th February, 1842, and reported to Lord Rippon, Chairman of the committee of the Privy Council. The inspector reported that he was accompanied by the manager, Mr Baird, the motive power superintendent, a Mr West, and one of the Carmichael brothers who represented the shareholders. He commented on the light rails as Nicholas Wood had done, as well as the 'injudicious curves' in particular that at the top of Balbeuchley incline, which he remarked was only 173 ft in radius.

He commented also that he was informed of the practice of making the engine wheels travel on their rims round the outside of the sharpest curves. His observations on the use of inclined planes were also a condemnation of the engineering of Charles Landale, for Pasley suggested that Balbeuchley incline could have been dispensed with completely by the use of a shorter route and gentler curves. Pasley also reported on the need for gates at the crossing by Baldovan station, where a woman had been killed in January 1842 by 'imprudently walking on the line.' There were no other gates missing at any other crossing but the 'side fences were not complete throughout the whole extent of the railway.'

From the D&NR, he went on to inspect the branches on board one of the D&NR locomotives which had been 'obligingly ordered for the purpose'. The Glamis route was in such disrepair following the collapse of some of the embankments that traffic had been temporarily halted and he did not proceed further with that line. His examination of the Coupar Angus branch revealed that it was in good order. Pasley also commented on the one continuing aspect of the Dundee and Newtyle which was already well known to its shareholders

- it had never paid a dividend. Despite the success of the line in the carriage of freight, the cost of the frequent change of motive power with the additional cost of maintaining the stationary engines and regular replacement of their cables was draining any cash surpluses.

The railway had been successful in a number of ways. It had opened up the countryside to the north of Dundee by replacing a twice weekly unreliable coach service from Blairgowrie with a four times daily railway service carrying around one hundred people per day in the early years. The line had also provided the increase in the carriage of goods to and from the port which was originally intended, carrying coal and lime inland as well as many thousand tons of manure annually. The return traffic was again as anticipated, mainly agricultural produce, especially potatoes for the London markets. From the point of view of those over whose land the line passed, there had been a very definite advantage. A Director of the company wrote to Sir Neil Menzies on 20th February, 1838, 'though the Shareholders have never received any dividend whatever, yet all the Landowners and not a few of the Tenants acknowledge, that they have been great gainers. Their properties have been increased in value far beyond the money they have sunk in the railway.'

The rates charged varied from 3*d*. to 6*d*. per ton per mile with special rates as low as 1½ d. per ton per mile for cinders, hay and manure. The revenue from goods had always exceeded that from passengers, but none of this had produced enough profit to cover the running costs and the passenger duty on travel. This tax, which was introduced in 1836, was based on the number of passengers carried and was levied at a rate of ½*d*. per mile for every four passengers carried. The Dundee and Newtyle, like most other Scottish railways, elected to pay a composite sum which was 23.3 per cent rather than the calculated amount. The duty ranged from £10 in 1834 to £150 in 1838 and it still had to be paid out of the company's capital rather than revenue because the increase in fares to cover it had resulted in a drop of passengers, and so in the income. The ability to pay a lump sum was ended in 1838 and the amount to pay was dramatically increased to £243 in the next year. The following table shows the traffic returns and the effect the tax had on the year from April 1836.

Date	Passengers	Goods(tons)	Costs £
Dec. 1831-Mar. 1832	7,075	1,564	400
Apr. 1832-Mar. 1833	31,264	24,393	3,320
Apr. 1833-Mar. 1834	34,057	33,879	4,764
Apr. 1834-Mar. 1835	51,366	38,323	4,719
Apr. 1835-Mar. 1836	57,141	43,824	4,931
Apr. 1836-Mar. 1837	48,444	37,097	5,220
Apr. 1837-Mar. 1838	55,650	41,231	5,587
Apr. 1838-Mar. 1839	61,169	47,929	6,342

By the 1840s the situation had become very difficult indeed. In 1841, the company had an income from passenger travel of £2,937 and paid £290 in tax. Passenger revenue dropped over the next three years, giving an income of £2,651, although by then the tax had been reduced to 5 per cent.

The Board were most concerned at the lack of profitability of the operation and relied upon its new Chairman when giving evidence to the Select Committee on Railways on 27th May, 1840. The Chairman was George Kinloch, son of the founding Chairman who had died in 1833, and he revealed that the affairs of the company were so desperate in 1839 that the creditors had proposed to liquidate the company, with the Board offering no opposition. Indeed, the Chairman admitted that 'it is a very bad concern; it has never paid a farthing.' The need to foreclose was nevertheless averted by the infusion of a loan of £40,000 in return for stock of pretty doubtful value.

The situation had been bad enough for some time and the board met at Ward station on 10th April, 1838 for the purpose:

> . . . of considering articles of roup* prepared by the Committee for a lease of the railway: for receiving the resignation of such members as may wish to decline continuing in the Committee, and, if the meeting sees fit, appointing others: or, if the meeting think it more desirable, appointing DIRECTORS to manage the affairs of the Company.

Following this meeting, a notice appeared on 13th April, 1838 in the *Dundee Perth and Cupar Advertiser* intimating 'To be exposed to Public Roup on Wednesday 2nd May, the Dundee and Newtyle Railway on a lease of three years', but this offer was unsuccessful. Despite the parlous state of the company's finances, the Coupar Angus branch was leased from its owners but the D&N Directors pointed out on more than one occasion in 1841 that they would be unable to pay the rent.

Some of the Directors were forced to resign in that year by the Union Bank which was also pressing for payment. The outstanding amounts were not, in fact, paid to the Coupar Angus company until May 1844 by which time the lease arrangement had been ended by mutual agreement. The shareholders lost all interest in a railway company which was not paying them a dividend, the Directors having been unable to hold a half-yearly meeting of the company in March 1842 until, at the fourth attempt, sufficient members could be found.

A further opportunity to lease the company was offered on 2nd December, 1842 and yet another on 11th January, 1845 when the following appeared in *The Railway Times*:

RAILWAY TO BE LET

> To be for a period of three years, to commence on 2nd February next or such other day as shall be agreed upon, The Dundee and Newtyle Railway, including under that general term the engines, coaches and the whole conveniences and other plant to the concern and also the extensions of that Railway to the Harbour and Docks of Dundee. The draft or lease containing the terms and other particulars will be ready for being exhibited on or before Friday 10th January.

As local businessmen and landowners, the Directors were determined that the line should be kept open for traffic, since no doubt their trade benefited from it. This time the offer was accepted by the promoters of the Dundee & Perth Railway (D&PR), determined to prevent a rival scheme (called the Dundee and Strathmore Junction Railway and promoted by the Scottish

---

* Roup = Auction (Scots)

Crossroads station house seen here in 1982, on the original D&NR line. It is now a private house. *Author*

The point on the Newtyle line where the Lochee deviation met the line of 1831 to the right. A local freight returns to Dundee in the 1960s. *Dundee Courier*

Midland) from entering Dundee by way of a line from Perth via Coupar Angus. The prospectus for this northern approach to Dundee showed grandiose hopes for a line to supplant the D&NR altogether and develop new traffic between Dundee and the rest of Scotland and even England. The Dundee and Perth successfully negotiated for the lease through an Act of Parliament dated 27th July, 1846 (9&10 Vic. cap. ccxxviii) to operate the line and its branch for 999 years for a guaranteed £1,400 per annum. The new arrangement took effect from October 1846.

This union brought about some measures for improvements to the line, with the widening of the gauge to 4ft 8½ in. a high priority. Among the improvements were minor alterations to the course of the line at Baldovan station, where a reverse bend to the north of the station was straightened out, and a further easing was carried out at Baldragon where the station was relocated by a few yards on the new line of track. The whole line was closed for the month of October 1849 to allow the gauge change-over to take place.

Three locomotives, *Earl of Airlie*, *Lord Wharncliffe* and *Trotter* were converted but *John Bull* was sold to contractors on the Perth line. *Wallace*, the original locomotive on the Dundee and Arbroath, was transferred to the Newtyle line in 1852 by the Dundee and Perth and Aberdeen Railway Junction (D&P&ARJ),* as No. 8. No. 1 was eventually withdrawn as No. 10 in 1854 and spent its last days as a pumping engine on the Dundee and Perth line at Errol.

Alexander Allan, locomotive engineer with a later owner, the Scottish Central, is thought to have restored the *Earl of Airlie* around 1859 since a photograph shows up-to-date shanked buffers replacing the dumb buffers which were originally fitted. No. 2 was employed similarly as a stationary pump at the Seabraes works of the D&PR in 1854 having become No. 11 in the meantime. *Trotter* was withdrawn around this time but there is no detailed record of the fifth locomotive built by Roberts & Co and named *Dundee*.

Three second-hand locomotives of the Bury type were purchased from the southern division of the London and North Western Railway in October 1853 to replace the Carmichael engines. They were numbered 10, 11 and 12, this design of locomotive being known in the area as a 'Tod'. They were named *Balbeuchley*, *Hatton* and *Law*, one later working unsuccessfully on the Carmyllie branch of the Dundee and Arbroath. Nos. 13 and 14 were acquired from George England in 1855, both being 2-4-0s and named *Scorpion* and *Spitfire*. Two further locomotives were obtained from Stephensons in 1860 (Nos. 16 and 17) being 0-4-0s and costing £1,900 each. They were later renumbered 72 and 73 and one is believed to have worked the Broughty Ferry Pier branch in 1887, continuing as a shunting engine in the goods yard at Broughty Ferry after the branch closed.

Other improvements were approved through these measures, The Dundee & Newtyle Railway (Widening, Altering & Improving) Act of 2nd July, 1847, including opening out the Law tunnel, and a deviation avoiding Balbeuchley incline from Rosemill to Auchterhouse. The Law tunnel was never opened out and the Balbeuchley avoiding line was not built until a further order in 1859.

The Eassie to Glamis section of the Glamis branch was closed in July 1846, the remainder of the line following in October 1847 with the Coupar Angus branch

* The Act joining the Dundee and Perth with the Dundee and Arbroath created the unusually named D&P&ARJ.

closing shortly afterwards in November of that year. The Scottish Midland Junction line from Perth to Forfar was opened on 2nd August, 1848 and a curve was re-established on a partial new line between Meigle station and Newtyle, being replaced in August 1861 with a curve from the west on the line of the original Coupar Angus railway from Ardler to Newtyle.

An Act for the improvement of the Dundee & Newtyle line was promoted in the 1850s and authorised on 21st July, 1859. This permitted the removal of two inclines, at Balbeuchley as mentioned above and, more significantly, the Law incline. The former was opened on 1st November, 1860 with new stations at Dronley and a relocated Auchterhouse. The Lochee deviation, as the other route was called, opened on 10th June, 1861 between Ninewells Junction and Fairmuir Junction. It took the line from south of Baldovan station on a long sweep to the south-west through the important industrial suburb of Lochee before swinging south and then east to join the Dundee and Perth line, facing towards Dundee at Ninewells Junction. This led to the closure of both Crossroads (although it was not used from 1858) and Ward stations, the Law incline and tunnel and the opening of new stations at Lochee, Lochee West and Liff. The horse-drawn route through the streets of Dundee to the Harbour branch was also closed at this time, the new link to the Harbour and the Dundee and Arbroath line being further south through the DPR station in Union Street.

On 26th July, 1863, the Scottish Central Railway (SCR) became the new landlords of the D&NR, having taken over the Dundee and Perth and Aberdeen Railway Junction, this being the re-formed Dundee and Perth Railway. Powers were obtained by the SCR in 1864 to make a divergence from the last of Landale's inclines at Newtyle, with a sweeping curve to the west of Hatton incline to a new station on the north side of Newtyle, replacing the original which was retained as the goods depot alongside the Newtyle Chemical works. The work was not completed on this deviation until 31st August, 1868 under the aegis of the next owners, the Caledonian, who took over the SCR in 1865. The Dundee and Newtyle Railway, however, existed as a separate leased company until the grouping in 1923 when it was absorbed into the LMS.

Although it was neither a profitable railway nor an integral part of some future national network, the Dundee and Newtyle Railway has commanded a place in the history books as one of the earliest railways in the world. The unusual nature of its three incline planes and the advanced design of its early locomotives added to the distinctiveness of this minor line, but the history of the other lines to Dundee will put it into a clearer context.

Chapter Three

The Dundee & Arbroath Railway
1836-1863

'The promised returns are but as glittering baubles'
Francis Whishaw on the Dundee & Arbroath Railway 1840

The port of Arbroath is well known historically for being the location of
Robert Bruce's signing of Scotland's Declaration of Independence which took
place at Arbroath Abbey in 1320. The town is now a seaside resort and
industrial centre as well as a fishing port famous for its 'smokies' or smoked
haddock.

Situated 18 miles east of Dundee, Arbroath displays an independence of its
own but has always been closely linked with its larger neighbour. With toll
houses at Balmossie, Ardestie and Muirdrum, the road from Dundee to
Arbroath was one of the busiest turnpikes in the country by the end of the 18th
century for, as well as the local traffic between the two ports, this route carried
the important coaches between Edinburgh and Aberdeen.

All the coaches on the route were acknowledged by travellers to have a high
standard, both for a smart turn out and for all important punctuality. Amongst
the well known names given to them were 'The Highlander', 'The Commercial
Traveller', and 'Hope and Industry'. However, the best appointed of them all
was the 'Defiance' which ran from Edinburgh to Aberdeen by way of Brechin.
Good timekeeping was perhaps not so difficult along the coastal route, for the
countryside was generally flat between Dundee and Arbroath but the terrain
was less easy further north, giving uncertainty to the traveller.

There was sizeable coastal shipping along the North Sea coast but there were
clear advantages in a new railway to the local communities such as Monifieth,
Carnoustie and especially Broughty Ferry. It might be seen in retrospect as
cynical to suggest that the proposers of a Dundee to Arbroath line were actually
set on a more convenient route than that offered by the Dundee and Newtyle
Railway to the eastern parts of the county. However, there was little doubt at
the time that the traders of Angus were seeking a more direct route to the coast.

William Blackadder had surveyed a possible line between Forfar and
Arbroath with Stevenson in 1826. Later, Grainger and Miller were employed by
William Fullerton Lindsay Carnegie, a well known Angus landowner, to survey
a route between those two towns. They had, in fact, previously surveyed a line
on behalf of the two town councils of Brechin and Montrose, but were never
paid for this work. Carnegie became Chairman of the Arbroath and Forfar
Railway, being the biggest influence in its creation, and also helped to promote
the line from Dundee to Arbroath together with another local landowner, Lord
Panmure.

Previously, George Matthewson, winner of the competition for the best
planned layout of 'the novel manufacturing village' of Newtyle, had been
approached in June 1834 by a Mr Hunter of Blackness in Dundee with the
intention of railway expansion along the coast. Matthewson was invited to

survey the lands along the northern shore of the Tay estuary between Dundee and Arbroath with the purpose of identifying a suitable line for a railway between the two ports. His findings were favourable, indicating that for a capital outlay of £45,000, a railway could be built and produce an annual revenue of £6,000 with dividends between 8-10 per cent.

This brought about a burst of local press enthusiasm both for the scheme and the advantages of railways in general. A meeting of supporters was held on 12th October, 1835 at the Woodhill Inn, east of Ardestie Toll and appropriately half-way between Dundee and Arbroath. William Ramsay Maule, (1771-1852), who was the first Lord Panmure, chaired the meeting and a committee was formed to promote a Bill both in Parliament and amongst the local population. They also agreed to ask Grainger and Miller to make a full survey of the possible line of a railway. This was speedily done by Miller (while Grainger, his elder partner, was engaged on the Forfar line) and completed in three weeks. John Miller reported at a public meeting that the cost of constructing a 16½ mile double line would be £58,635 which would increase to £85,000 when land and rolling stock was purchased, with a provision of another 10 per cent for unforeseen eventualities. He estimated the revenue at £10,708 and running costs at £3,569 producing a return of 7½ per cent.

Those attending that meeting were so keen on Miller's proposals that £94,000 was promised there and then, leaving many potential investors grumbling that they had lost an opportunity. Lord Panmure offered £2,500 and to meet the demands of the unhappy subscribers, the total was increased to £100,000. The Trustees of Dundee Harbour and both Dundee and Arbroath Town Councils were quick to support the Bill which became an Act (6-7 Will. IV cap. xxxii) on 19th May, 1836, the same day as the Arbroath and Forfar Railway (A&FR). The Act enabled the £100,000 to be raised as joint stock capital in £25 shares and a further £40,000 could be sought in loans.

Dundee textile engineers were keen to encourage this new form of transport in the vicinity of their works with both James Stirling and James Steel buying £100 worth of shares and Peter Borrie and Peter Kinmond £500 each. In contrast to the Dundee and Newtyle subscription list 10 years earlier, there were almost twice as many local investors, at 343, providing 89 per cent of the capital. Also, there was a high proportion of subscribers with a substantial stake in the proposed undertaking. Eight-four shareholders, each holding over £500 worth of shares, provided 60 per cent of the Dundee and Arbroath's share capital whereas, on the A&FR, 15 shareholders with a similar investment produced 40 per cent of the share capital in that company. It is, nevertheless, significant that a modest port and market town such as Arbroath could provide such financial support for two new railway ventures at the same time.

Officers of the Dundee and Arbroath Railway (D&AR) were appointed at a further meeting, held in Dundee Town Hall, on 8th June, 1836. Lord Panmure was elected Chairman, with a 20-strong council of management including the Provosts of Dundee and Arbroath, Alexander Kay and William Anderson, as well as Dundee engineers, Peter Borrie and James Stirling, and John Miller.

Lord Panmure was a substantial landowner in the county of Angus, so, his consent to allow construction of the railway was essential, since two-thirds of the proposed line passed over his land. However, his generosity was beyond reproach, for he feued* between 50 and 60 acres to the company at a nominal rent of only £40 per year, mainly as compensation for his tenants. This 'truly liberal conduct' kept land purchase costs at £340 per mile and enabled the estimated construction costs to be very low at £5,500 per mile. John Miller had presented an estimate on 9th February, 1836 of £99,844 including £7,545 for land, £32,427 for earthworks, £52,034 for the 56 lb. rails and £7,839 for engineering. Miller's estimates were, sadly, on the optimistic side, like many at the time, the total costs of the line eventually coming to £107,272 with an additional £36,281 for rolling stock, stations and other expenditure.

Included in the estimates was a £12,054 contribution to a link with the Arbroath and Forfar Railway, a figure which was later reduced to £8,400, but at a meeting of the Committee of Management on 3rd September, 1836 it was agreed not to contribute to the link with their neighbouring railway. An element of rivalry and animosity between the two companies was revealed at this meeting, although this later improved when a connection was made through the streets of Arbroath by a horse-drawn carriage.

The near level course of the D&AR was to be from a new station at Lady Loan, close to Arbroath harbour, and a few hundred yards from the terminus of the A&FR in Kelpie Street. Following the shoreline on a gentle curve, the line went through East Haven, where there was a station, and then West Haven, both small fishing settlements, before entering the first town on the route, Carnoustie, although then still a village. This was the next station described as a 'small cottage, a building suited to the traffic of the place'. Cutting across sandy promontory of Buddon Ness, the line then reached Monifieth, the third station, where it rejoins the coast. At Broughty Ferry there was a further station and then the line passed through West Ferry, before entering Dundee. The railway initially terminated at Craigie but eventually crossed a causeway over the mud flats to the east of the town to a terminus at Trades Lane.

When Francis Whishaw examined the line in the late 1830s, he counted ten overbridges, five underbridges and nine level crossings. There were 40 occupation crossings between fields on the route. He noted that the line was laid on stone blocks and cross sleepers. The rails, according to Whishaw, were flat bottomed with straight profile top weighing 48 lb. per yard and fixed in 14 lb. chairs by wooden keys. The rail joints were made on 20lb. chairs.

The Directors of the company expressed themselves satisfied with the work performed by Miller who was recognised as one of Scotland's leading railway engineers. With his wide knowledge of railway construction, he was able to recommend in the summer of 1837 that the company buy from ironfounders at the bottom of the market when prices had reached as low as £7 15s. per ton for rails, around half previous contract prices. Chairs were also purchased at a bargain price of £7 per ton compared with £9 the previous year.

The track was built throughout to a different gauge to the D&NR, being 5 ft 6 in., the same as the A&FR. This was primarily because Grainger and Miller could not envisage their lines becoming anything more than local to Angus and the coast and certainly not part of a national network. Grainger also believed that the 'English' gauge of 4 ft 8½ in. was too narrow and the Great Western's

---

* to lease land on a perpetual lease at a fixed rent

7 ft 0¼ in. too large, his compromise gauge permitting larger locomotives and comfortable coaches. The space between the tracks was also generous at 6 ft 5 in. with 6 ft 3½ in. for the cess on either side of them.

The line was divided into eight separate contracts, and tenders accepted for them all. Construction, however, was not without trouble, for in July 1837 Brotherton and Macpherson, winners of four of the contracts, became insolvent and could not pay wages to their men. The contracts had to be re-let, but even then there was a strike four months later provoked by one of the replacement contractors. Hunter, the contractor for 25,000 stone blocks, failed to deliver both the quantity and the quality required. A court judgement ruled that the company could obtain them from another supplier and pass the additional cost on to Hunter.

A delay of a different kind was encountered in March 1837 near Broughty Ferry, where Pictish skeletons were unearthed during the creation of the permanent way. The bodies were inside stone coffins lying in varying positions and states of preservation. At the same place a grave carved from solid rock was uncovered, but these events did little to set back what was a straightforward programme. By the next year, the line was completed from Arbroath as far as Craigie crossing, two miles from Dundee, at a cost of £6,000 per mile compared with £54,000 for some English railways.

The opening ceremony of the line, on Saturday 6th October, 1838, was typical of the grand affairs held on these occasions. At 11.15 am six horse-drawn omnibuses departed from the railway offices in High Street, Dundee, with the guests and officials of the company and made for Craigie where the inaugural train was waiting with the locomotive, *Wallace*, at its head. The first train on the Dundee and Arbroath Railway departed at noon from the temporary platform at Craigie, and comprised five first class and five second class coaches with 400-500 people. A brass band was installed in the leading coach and Lord Panmure was seated in the coach named *Panmure*. Amongst the other dignitaries present were George Kinloch, Chairman of the Dundee and Newtyle and William Carnegie, Chairman of the Arbroath and Forfar Railway as well as both Grainger and Miller.

The trip to Arbroath took 45 minutes with a stop *en route* to oil the axles, hundreds of people lining the way to cheer the spectacular cavalcade. However, the civic authorities of Arbroath were conspicuous by their absence at the end of the first leg of the trip. The return journey was undertaken at an average speed of 26 mph in 43 minutes. A second ceremonial train left Craigie after the arrival of the first and took 36 minutes to reach Arbroath, returning in approximately the same time.

At a dinner that evening in the Hall of the Seamen Fraternity, the Chairman, Provost Kay of Dundee, acknowledged the great support received by the line's patron, Lord Panmure, and hoped that other proprietors of the railway would follow his example in recognising the benefits to their properties and not make exorbitant claims for compensation. He declared that he was 'sure that the inhabitants of the district would not rest until they had made Glasgow to the right and Aberdeen to the left of Dundee'! During the many toasts and cheers throughout the evening, much was made of the absence of Provost Allan, and the Town Councillors of Arbroath, and William Carnegie, as a Freeman of the Burgh, responded to the generous toast to the town of Arbroath

Wallace, the first locomotive on the line, was one of three engines built in 1838 by Kinmond Hutton and Steel, of the Wallace Foundry, Dundee. They were 2-2-2s with driving wheels being five feet in diameter, and outside horizontal cylinders, of 13 in. diameter and 18 in. stroke. Weighing 12 tons 3 cwt, they cost £1,012 each including tender. The second and third engines were named *Griffin* and *Fury* respectively. Two further engines, *Rapid* and *Dart*, were delivered by Kinmond, Hutton and Steel in 1839 with larger driving wheels of 5 ft 6in. and costing £1,370. The *Railway Times* reported that these locomotives gave 'great satisfaction but . . . the Rapid . . . is improved in appearance and speed.' The locomotives were transported from the Wallace Foundry by road to Broughty Ferry, where they were put on rails for the first time. This was where the D&AR had its early workshops. The same company delivered another engine similar to *Rapid* and *Dart* to the line in February 1840, its first journey being later that month on the day of Queen Victoria's wedding to Prince Albert, giving rise to its name, *Queen*.

As was traditional, the carriages were also given names. On 13th April, 1838, a meeting of the committee of the company recorded that two carriages, named *Panmure* and *Broughty Castle* had been received and a month later, on 7th May, *The Fair Maid*, *Golfer* and *Mercury* had been delivered. Built by two coachmakers, Messrs Cuthbert and Son of Dundee and Wallace of Perth, they were joined by others called *The Antiquary*, *Patrick Robertson*, *Dolphin*, *Eagle*, *Stag*, *Mucklebackit*, and *Ochiltree*, which were delivered subsequently, the latter two being third class.

According to the report of the opening in the *Dundee Courier* of 9th October, 1838, the first class carriages were 'fitted up in a most comfortable and elegant style, with plate glass windows and sides, and cannot be surpassed by any description of carriages. The second class carriages are also exceedingly comfortable, and are supplied with hair cushions, and in every respect as easy as the first class, only they are open at the sides.'

Constructional difficulties were not limited to the financial security of the builders. The causeway along the final stretch of the line to Dundee presented a headache to the company. Here, the margins of the River Tay were a series of muddy pools and shallow beaches near the small harbour known as Carolina Port, the adjacent land being occupied by several businesses. The line was intended to pass in front of these sites, cutting off the concerns from the river. The problems over these frontages were resolved by many frontagers having to transfer their businesses across the line and to the east to ensure they retained access to the river. There were objections from the Dundee Gas & Light Company and several others but the Dundee and Arbroath Railway Company is reported to have come to 'an amicable arrangement of all the points in the dispute and the adoption of a greatly improved line at the western end, satisfactory to all'.

One of the provisions of the railway company's Act was that this proposed section of line, within the bounds of the harbour, should be under the ownership of the Trustees of the Dundee Harbour which was being considerably extended. This was to prove an advantage for both the railway company and the harbour since the extension of the docks would bring much new business. The Trustees were at first also reluctant to allow the creation of an embankment along the river frontages to the east of Dundee, but eventually they agreed. This section of the line was known as the Trades Lane and Carolina Port Railway and was leased back to the D&AR under agreements of 10th and 12th October, 1838, and remained under the ownership of the Harbour Trustees until 1907.

A temporary terminus was built and brought into use in June 1839 once the construction reached Roodyards, 1½ miles from the projected end of the line in Dundee. This remained the nearest point of the railway from Dundee until the final stretch was built on the disputed new causeway alongside the Harbour Trustees' dock expansion the following year. On Wednesday 1st April, 1840, the line was opened the final ¾ mile to Trades Lane giving a total length of 16 miles, 5 furlongs and 90 yards from Arbroath. The first trains ran to the new terminus from the next day and the temporary Roodyards station was closed.

The modest station building constructed at Trades Lane was adjacent to what was to become one of the most architecturally imposing new buildings in the town. The Custom House was built from 1842 to 1843 and was situated between King William IV Dock and the incomplete northern quay of the forthcoming Victoria Dock, then under construction. However, there was no splendour about the nearby terminal station which was erected for the newest railway in Dundee. Being 320 ft long by 30 ft wide and made of wood planking with a conventional pitched roof, it very soon became the subject of much criticism, particularly from William Thoms, one of the company's own Directors. He described it as 'a wooden shed containing two lines of railway with no waiting room and no convenience for the passengers. I have not seen anywhere so inconvenient a station'.

Also there was a small single road engine shed which was to be found off the main line, alongside the western of the two new docks. Whishaw had referred to the intermediate stations as being 'of neat appearance, in the Gothic style of architecture', and gave a full description of the terminus at Arbroath. However, of the Trades Lane terminus he made no comment. It was apparently not yet completed when he surveyed the railway.

During this period of completion of the line, the services increased from the initial timetable of 1838 of two return trips daily on Monday, Tuesday and Thursday and an additional train each way on Wednesday, Friday and Saturday. By June 1839, trains were providing a service of three return journeys every weekday with a fourth on Saturdays. A special service was put on to Broughty Ferry on Saturday evenings to accommodate those who wished to take the air along the Tay estuary. On 19th August, 1840, the Church of Scotland Presbytery remonstrated on behalf of the Presbytery of Dundee with Directors of the company over their proposals for Sunday trains.

Fares from Dundee to Arbroath were 2s.6d. (12½p) first and 2s.(10p) second class. Children under 10 travelled for half fare. Season tickets became available from the main stations on the route. There was no third class at the outset, but covered coaches were introduced in 1839 to provide for the third class passenger. So great was the demand for this additional facility that soon extra uncovered carriages had to be obtained by the company, bringing complaints in turn from those passengers who were not quick enough to get a seat in the covered coaches. They had to suffer the unpredictable Scottish weather in the poorer open conveyances which were more akin to goods wagons.

As with the Dundee & Newtyle Railway, there was a excited response from the local population to the new experience of travelling by train. The stations along the line were all on the coast and the towns which they served offered the Victorian excursionist a range of facilities. There were beaches at Broughty Ferry, Monifieth, Carnoustie, and East Haven as well as at Arbroath itself where the cliffs were a particular attraction in comparison with the flat river valley, further up stream. Thus passenger returns quickly became the greater part of the company's income, providing 66 per cent of the 1843 income of £12,943.

Like the Dundee and Newtyle, the Dundee and Arbroath had to pay the Passenger Duty which was introduced in 1836. It paid a total of £29 in the first year but a revision in the method of calculating the amount due left the company with a bill of £879 in 1840. Grainger complained to Lord Seymour's Select Committee that the charge was unfair and proposed a tax based on a percentage of gross receipts. George Duncan, a Director of the D&AR, complained that the full tax could mean the railway might have to abolish third class since the company was, like so many of its Scottish counterparts, reliant on the third class passenger for a high proportion of its receipts. This dependency meant that they would be unable to put up fares without a significant loss of custom.

The location of the Trades Lane station alongside the proposed dock development was an advantage for the transport of goods from the rapidly increasing shipping generated by the port. Arbroath, although a port itself, was content to allow the import of raw jute through Dundee for convenient trans-shipment by the D&AR to the mills being established there. However, the Harbour Trustees were reluctant to either sell or lease land for the provision of a link to the west to the Harbour branch off the Dundee and Newtyle and so on to Perth. Instead they preferred the convenience of the ships which berthed at the recently completed Earl Gray and King William IV Docks to unload straight on to the quayside.

The lack of a connection in the centre of Dundee was a disadvantage for years and could arguably have denied Dundee the opportunity of being on the only route from Aberdeen to Edinburgh, Glasgow and to England. Equally the absence of a connection between the Dundee and Arbroath and the Arbroath and Forfar simply compounded the difficulties which the traveller encountered on his journey northwards. The dream of an integrated network on the east coast was further encouraged during the early years of the Railway Mania.

Once they had appreciated the advantages of a continuous line from Dundee to Aberdeen, the Directors of the two railways met with the newly formed Dundee and Perth to overcome the two short stretches in both Dundee and Arbroath which stood in their way. At this meeting in London on 19th May, 1845, it was agreed that the two Arbroath railways would alter their gauge from 5 ft 6 in. to 4 ft 8½ in. This would be done with the creation of a connection in

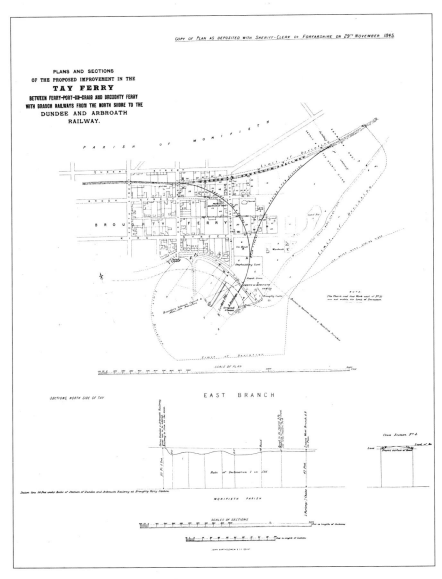

Plans and sections of proposed branch to the pier at Broughty Ferry, Dundee & Arbroath
Railway, 1845.   *Scottish Records Office*

Arbroath, linking the line from the south with both the Arbroath & Forfar Railway and the Aberdeen Railway Co. (AR) and so encourage through services from Dundee, Perth and Edinburgh.

A new Act, The Dundee and Arbroath Extensions Act (9-10 Vic. cap. cxxxiii), was passed on 3rd July, 1846 leading, amongst other things, to the creation of the short link between Almerieclose, an expanding textile suburb north of the town on the Forfar line, and to Geordiesburn on the Dundee line. This left the original stations at Catherine Street on the A&FR and Lady Loan on the D&AR at the end of short branches on their respective railways.

The Junction Line, as it was called was opened for goods traffic on 23rd December, 1847 and for passenger trains on 1st February, 1848, when a new joint station was also opened and the horse-drawn connection abandoned. The joint station buildings were deemed at the time to be temporary, but lasted until May 1853 when a more permanent structure was opened. An agreement had been signed by the Directors of the A&FR on 1st January, 1846 leasing their railway to the Aberdeen Railway Company to the north. Approved by an Act of 26th June, 1846, this arrangement came into effect, after much wrangling over finance, on the day that passenger services began over the new linking line.

At an open meeting in October 1846 for interested parties, the Dundee and Arbroath sought to raise £50,000 for a number of important projects including the regauging of the line, at £5,000. Amongst the other aspects to be paid for were the new line in Arbroath, and the adaptation of the rolling stock to suit the new gauge. Four new and more powerful locomotives were also proposed to replace four of the six originals, the other two were to be rebuilt. £10,000 was considered sufficient to pay for these improvements to the motive power since the company hoped to sell the four locomotives which it was discarding.

Almost as significant a facet of the 1846 Dundee and Arbroath Extensions Act was the authorising of a branch from the main line near Broughty Ferry to the pier at Broughty Harbour. This was sought because the Directors:

> . . . were aware that the Edinburgh and Northern Railway Company had also given notice and lodged plans for the line but the Directors considered that it would not be expedient to allow any other company to come across the water and acquire a footing on the north side of Broughty Castle; certainly no company could work that small branch so advantageously as the D&A.

The Broughty Ferry branch opened in May 1848 to coincide with the completion of the Edinburgh and Northern Railway line through Fife to Ferry-Port-on-Craig and the ferry crossing to Broughty Pier. Traffic consisted initially of passenger services, but goods trains followed in 1850. The size of the harbour at Broughty Ferry remained modest because of the importance of Broughty Castle as a strategic look-out at the mouth of the Tay. A condition of the Harbour Act was that no edifice was allowed to protrude out into the river from the high water mark and obscure the garrison there. This limited the size of the pier and the harbour. The branch originally had a junction with the D&AR, facing Dundee, leaving the main line near the workshops just east of Broughty Ferry station before describing a very sharp curve towards the pier. A later realignment, opened on 1st May, 1851, gave the branch a connection facing Arbroath which avoided the need for the original sharp curve but meant a reversal of trains to and from Dundee.

The D&AR continued to provide a substantial service for the local population while these works were being considered and built. The reported income for the week ending 21st June, 1846 was £312 10s. 2d. This was made up of £100 11s. 7½d. from 373 tons of goods and £211 18s. 6½d. from the ticket sales to 10,382 passengers. The railway was yielding a return of 6 per cent by 1847, but despite this in January 1847 the company entered into a formal arrangement with the Dundee and Perth whereby the latter would take over the operating of the D&AR from 30th April, 1847. The Dundee and Perth had not yet opened their own line by this time and were keen to control the Arbroath line. The amalgamation, although short term, was to be an involved arrangement, accompanied by several Acts of Parliament.

An essential ingredient of this association was to have been a line unifying the eastern and western arms of the new combined railway. Such a joint line, planned to cross the middle of Dundee between the two railways but never constructed, was enacted by the Dundee and Perth Railway (Dundee Junction) Act 1848 (11&12 Vic. cap. lii). A full and specific outline of the proposal was placed before the Town Council for their consideration and comment. It listed in great detail the impact the high level line would have upon the centre of Dundee, its shoreline and harbour enabling the civic representatives to make an accurate judgement of the value of the connecting line.

The line would leave the D&PR on a 1 in 100 incline to Yeaman Shore north of the existing station and gaining 14 to 16 feet in height. It would sweep north with 'considerable curves' and cross Union Street by an arched bridge of a 30 ft span with two side arches of 7 ft, all at a height of 16 ft. The proposed line would then cross Green Market with a single span of 35 ft, and Tyndal's Wynd on an 8 ft arch. Castle Street was the highest point on the line and would be crossed in a similar way. The descent would then be a gentle 1 in 140 to Trades Lane, passing over Commercial Street in a single 30 foot span, Gellatly Street in 25 ft, Candle Lane 11 ft and Trades Lane itself in a 30 ft arch with two side spans of 7 ft each.

The descent would increase to 1 in 100 to join the Dundee and Arbroath Railway at Peep o' Day Lane east of the Trades Lane station on a low bank, which would run 50 yards north of Dock Street for 300 yards until it reached the Dundee Foundry's works. Intervening narrow lanes down to the shore would be stopped up. The Magistrates and Town Council of Dundee deliberated on this wealth of detail and issued a pointed statement on the 6th January, 1848 rejecting the proposal for this connecting line. This expressed their concern that the 'smoke and noise will be an annoyance to the inhabitants'. The 'lighted furnaces' of the locomotives would also be dangerous.

Regardless of the failure of this connecting railway proposal, the Dundee and Arbroath Railway Lease Act 1848 (11&12 Vic. cap. cliv) was sought and passed on 31st August, 1848 to enable the formal leasing to take place and change the name of the company to The Dundee and Perth and Aberdeen Railway Junction Company. The lease was, however, not put into action and a disagreement over its terms arose the following year when, on 10th November, 1849, a proposition was made to reduce the 8 per cent return to 6 per cent for five years. The Directors felt that due to the depression and an expensive dispute with the Caledonian Railway they would be unable to maintain the higher return. This was investigated by the D&AR and reported as being unsatisfactory at a meeting on 26th December, 1849.

The wrangle continued, and on 9th March, 1850 the Dundee and Arbroath separated itself, by mutual agreement, from the arrangement with the Dundee and Perth, returning equipment worth £20,000 and giving an undertaking to work the Arbroath line until a formal break could be made. A report of even better terms was put before the company on 6th June, 1850 and a new Act, The Dundee and Perth and Aberdeen Railway Junction (Additional Capital) Act, (13&14 Vic. cap. xxxix) was passed on 15th July, 1850 to terminate the lease from the previous March. Through services were maintained to the Harbour branch.

The truce was an uneasy one for before too long the company was grumbling about the loss of traffic to the D&P&ARJ. At a meeting held on 7th June, 1854, the Board noted that there was a diversion of traffic from the Edinburgh Perth and Dundee Railway which had agreed to sent its goods to Dundee via Perth rather than across the Tay by way of the ferry. In order to make up for this, the company announced that it had entered into an agreement with Lord Panmure who was promoting a new line to be opened about two miles from Arbroath into the Angus countryside at Carmyllie. The new railway, it was believed, would be able to take advantage of the rich agricultural and mineral resources of the district and act as a feeder to the main line.

The independent Dundee and Arbroath existed in its new form for another 12 years, and in order to re-establish rules for the running of the railway, the Board of the D&AR agreed to use those employed by the Dundee, Perth & Aberdeen Railway Junction Co. By simply substituting the company's name for the previous one and making minor alterations, a new rule book was established, probably typical of many railway companies of the time. Three hundred copies were printed for the 'guidance and instruction of Officers and Men. Every person do keep a copy under penalty of 5/-'. The General Regulations were:

1. Each person to devote himself exclusively to the company's service, attending during the regulated hours of the day, and residing wherever he may be required.
2. He is to obey promptly all instructions he may receive from persons placed in authority over him by the Directors, and conform to all the regulations of the Company
3. He will be liable to immediate dismissal for disobedience of orders, negligence, misconduct or incompetence.
4. No instance of intoxication on duty will ever be overlooked; and, besides being dismissed, the offender will be liable to be punished by a magistrate.
5. Any person using improper language, or cursing or swearing, while on duty will be liable to dismissal.
6. No person is allowed to receive any gratuity from the public, on pain of dismissal
7. Any instance of rudeness or incivility to passengers will meet with instant punishment.
8. Every person receiving a uniform must appear on duty clean and neat; and if any

COUNTY OF FORFAR

PLAN

PARISH OF DUNDEE

DUNDEE AND ARBROATH RAILWAY

(DUNDEE STATION ENLARGEMENT &c)

PLAN SHEWING THE GROUND TO BE TAKEN IN THE
Parish and Royal Burgh of Dundee in the County of Forfar,

for enlarging the

Dundee and Arbroath Railway Station at Dundee.

AND THE

PROPOSED DIVERSION OF A PART OF DOCK STREET THERE.

WITH SECTION THEREOF.

As described in the Parliamentary Notices thereof Published in November 1850.

CHARLES OWER, ENGINEER.

C. CUNNING, ENGRAVER, DUNDEE.

RIVER TAY

TIDE HARBOUR

VICTORIA DOCK

PROPOSED DIVERSION OF DOCK STREET

PROPOSED STATION ENLARGEMENT

KING WILLIAM
THE FOURTH DOCK

RATE OF INCLINATION 1 IN 1728

Plan showing the diversion of Dock Street, Dundee to expand East station, Dundee & Arbroath Railway, 1850.

article provided by the company should have been improperly used or damaged, the party will be required to make it good.

9. No servant is allowed, under any circumstances to absent himself from his duty without the permission of his superior officer.

10. No servant is to quit the Company's service without giving 14 days notice; and in case he leave without such notice, all pay then due will be forfeited. On leaving the service, he must deliver up his uniform.

11. The company reserve the right to deduct from this pay such sums as may be awarded for neglect of duty such as fines and for rent, when the servant is a tenant of the Company.

12. Should any servant think himself aggrieved, he may memorialise the Board, but in any such case, the memorial must be sent through the head of his department who will then send it through the Manager.

During this period of uncertainty of ownership, further improvements had been undertaken. The line was regauged along with its neighbour, the Arbroath and Forfar, and the more usual left hand working was introduced, although no specific Parliamentary approval was given for this. A newer heavier rail of 72 lb. was introduced and the track at the Dundee end of the line was relaid, from Carolina Port to Broughty Ferry. Later, from early in 1852, the rails between Broughty Ferry to Arbroath were relaid at a rate of 3 miles per year. In 1850, land was taken for the enlargement of the frequently criticised Trades Lane station and the re-routing of Dock Street to permit this expansion. Some of this land was occupied by the Dundee Gas Light Company and the Dundee New Gas Light Company. By the Dundee and Arbroath Railway (Dundee Station) Act (Vic. cap. lxiii) of 3rd July, 1851 authorisation was given to build a new terminus station adjacent to and north of the existing station. There was a junction with the original line at what became Camperdown Junction, but the part of the line between there and Carolina Port to the east remained the property of the Harbour Trustees. The original terminus was removed in January 1858, although the rails were kept to maintain the single track connection to the Dundee and Perth line in the west, with trains limited to three coaches or four wagons drawn by horse.

Known initially as Dock Street station until 1858, Dundee East was a more accommodating structure than its predecessors. The arched roof curved from platform level at both sides and was graced by a glazed screen, in the form of petals, flanked by two modest stone columns topped by a pair of Grecian urns. The station buildings themselves were more utilitarian, being situated on the northern side of the 200 feet long and 56 feet wide train shed, and providing all of the usual basic requirements of a terminal station. There were four platforms, numbers one and four beyond and two and three within the protection of the arched roof. The station was six years in construction, but on its completion on Monday, 14th December, 1857, the *Dundee Courier* felt that at last a presentable terminus had been built for the town. The opening was 'to the great comfort of all travellers from and to Dundee on the line.' The Directors, they reported, were to be congratulated on 'the handsome building and general accommodation.'

Also incorporated in the improvements at Dundee East was a new goods

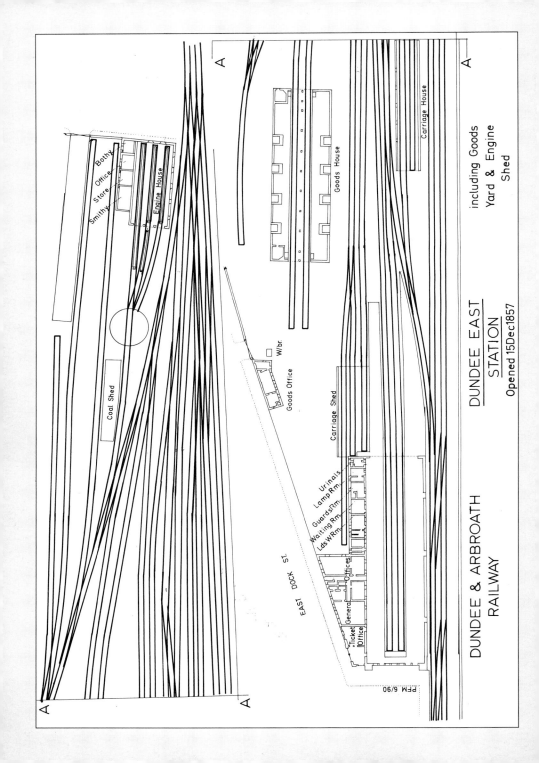

DUNDEE & ARBROATH RAILWAY

DUNDEE EAST STATION
Opened 15 Dec 1857

including Goods Yard & Engine Shed

Bothy
Office
Store
Smithy
Engine House
Coal Shed
Goods House
Carriage House

W/br.
Goods Office
EAST DOCK ST.

Carriage Shed
Urinals
Lamp Rm
Guards Rm
Waiting Rm
Lds W Rm
Offices
General
Ticket Office

PFM 6/90

depot and, a couple of months later, the company moved its locomotive shed from the earlier site to the south of the line to its new location in the triangle formed by the repositioned Dock Street. The facilities here were also improved and a three road shed over 80 feet long was constructed with access across a small turntable. There was a full blacksmith's shop, coaling shed and offices.

A new station at West Ferry, a few hundred yards to the west of Broughty Ferry was opened in 1859. By this time, through connections between Aberdeen, Edinburgh and Perth were commonplace. However, it was not a simple journey for passengers intending to travel beyond Dundee as they had to book to Arbroath and then re-book for their destination. Trains left Arbroath at 8.30, 9.05, 11.05 am, 1.15, 2.45, 4.41 (London mails), and 7.50 pm and from Dundee at 1.40 (London mails), 6.45, 10.50 am, 1.30, 3.15, 4.45, and 8.30 pm. Additional trains ran between Dundee and Broughty Ferry in connection with the services from Edinburgh. The link between Dock Street and Union Street stations in Dundee continued to be by horse-drawn coach. Special fares were available by the services advertised in 1858, for example the third class fare to London from Arbroath and Dundee was 37s. (£1.85) and return fares from Dundee to the coast at Monifieth, Carnoustie and East Haven for 'Pleasure Parties of not less than six' were granted at the single fare.

The frenzy of activity that was to be found amongst Scottish railway companies in the late 1850s and early 1860s did not miss the Dundee and Arbroath. A new company, the Scottish North Eastern (SNER) was created from the merger of the Aberdeen Railway and the Scottish Midland Junction Railway (SMJR), through an Act of 29th July, 1856. The Directors agreed to vest the Dundee and Arbroath into this new company from 31st January 1862, ratified in the Scottish North Eastern Railway Act of 28th July, 1863. This also transferred ownership of the company to the SNER and brought about the end of the independence of the Dundee and Arbroath. When the Caledonian Railway spread its tentacles outwards in 1866, it in turn took over the SNER and so the Arbroath line united with one of the leading railways of the country. With a principal position on the entry to Dundee for trains from both the north and the south (via the ferry crossing), it would therefore shortly find itself centre stage in the battles fought between its new masters and the North British Railway.

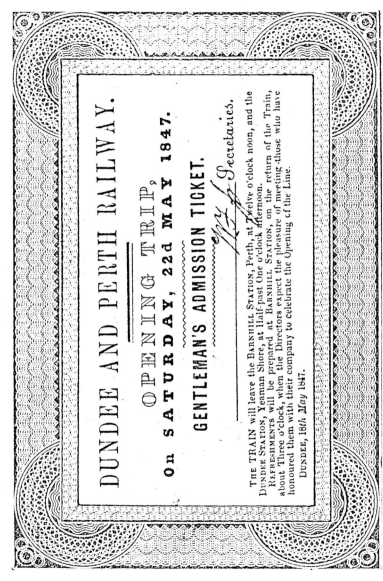

DUNDEE AND PERTH RAILWAY.

OPENING TRIP,

On SATURDAY, 22d MAY 1847.

GENTLEMAN'S ADMISSION TICKET.

Secretaries.

The TRAIN will leave the BARNHILL STATION, Perth, at Twelve o'clock noon, and the DUNDEE STATION, Yeaman Shore, at Half-past One o'clock afternoon. REFRESHMENTS will be prepared at BARNHILL STATION, on the return of the Train, about Three o'clock, when the Directors expect the pleasure of meeting those who have honoured them with their company to celebrate the Opening of the Line.

DUNDEE, 18th May 1847.

Opening Day ticket, Dundee and Perth Railway, 1847.

Chapter Four

The Dundee & Perth Railway
1835-1863

'Between Dundee and Perth, man, I stepped upon an iron rail,
A railway did it call, man'
Charles Balfour, Dundee and Perth Railway Guard, 1847

The strategic and political importance of the City of Perth, 20 miles to the west of Dundee, could not be ignored by the promoters of railways in central Scotland. Positioned at the lowest crossing of the River Tay, guarding the main road to the Highlands and surrounded by rich agricultural land, this former meeting place of the Scottish Parliament and one-time home of Scottish kings made an attractive goal for lines from all directions. John Knox delivered his first rousing sermon of the Reformation at St John's Kirk in the city, and the burgh was pillaged by the resulting flare-up leaving few of its original buildings standing. The prosperity of the area has always depended on the surrounding farm land and the county was well endowed with castles and substantial houses.

As with both the Arbroath and Newtyle railways, it was a major landowner who, in 1835, first advanced the idea of a railway from Dundee to Perth. George William Fox Maule, a relative of Lord Panmure, succeeded to the title of ninth Baron Kinnaird in 1826, and set about ameliorating the lot of his tenants through education and agricultural improvement. He applied steam power to the work on the farms around his family home at Rossie Priory by Inchture, midway between the two towns.

In spring of 1835, he invited James Rattray Findlater to survey the Carse of Gowrie, the rich farm lands on the north bank of the Tay west of Dundee for a line of railway. Findlater, a civil engineer who had an office at 15 Castle Street Dundee and in 1834 had prepared a plan for supplying Dundee with water, arranged a full report offering several alternative routes across the flat countryside and an assessment of the construction costs and returns. His report, dated October 1835 and published on 11th November, was submitted to interested parties at a meeting, called by Lord Kinnaird, in Dundee (*see Appendix Two*). It gives an interesting reflection on the way that new railway projects were assessed by their promoters at that time. Findlater's findings were supported by George Buchanan, an Edinburgh civil engineer with an interest in railway construction, who had made his own observations of the country in June 1835 and subsequently commented on the former's report.

In his submission, Findlater pointed out that the population of Dundee had doubled in the previous 20 years and so great was the commercial importance of the town that there were currently six large mills or factories in the course of erection. The significance of Dundee as a port with sailings to Hull, London and Leith, he felt, made it necessary that lines of railway stretched out in all directions. He believed that there was considerable traffic to be gained from the port of Dundee to Glasgow because of the trade in Baltic produce on the Forth and Clyde Canal and from Ireland through the River Clyde. However, Findlater was less than complimentary about the recently established Dundee and Newtyle Railway, noting that it was 'so defectively designed and executed, carved through insurmountable country, that it was no criterion of the advantages of railways.'

He offered reassurances about the speed of the proposed trains, suggesting that an hour would be sufficient for the 20 mile journey. His notes, taken from George Stephenson's Glasgow and Garnkirk Railway on 6th September, 1831, showed that a train covered the first mile of that line in 68 seconds, the second mile took 66 seconds and the third took 59 seconds, this equating to 53 mph, 54¼ mph and 61 mph respectively. Also, he believed, there would be no loss of tolls on the Dundee turnpike, opened as recently as 1790, because the returns on the Glasgow to Airdrie Turnpike had been greater since the opening of the Glasgow and Garnkirk.

The several routes which James Findlater submitted all began at the Harbour in Dundee and made a level connection with both the D&AR and the D&NR which would be subject to an arrangement with the Harbour Trustees. An embankment or bulwark was to be constructed westward along the northern bank of the river at designated distances from the shore line. The route would then touch land at Magdalen Yard Point, a rocky outcrop near Perth Road, before following the edge of the river and crossing Invergowrie Bay again on an embankment. West of Invergowrie village, three differing routes were proposed, all meeting at Inchyra.

The southern line took a south-western course close to the river bank as far as Inchyra, while the northern option headed due west to the Dundee to Perth turnpike keeping nearer to the hills before reaching Inchyra. A third route, which Findlater favoured, followed a line very similar to today's railway before assuming the north route to Inchyra. Two options were put forward for the next part of the line, passing either side of Seggieden, before sharing the route to Perth. The entry to the town was to be by a wooden bridge over Willowgate, the narrow eastern channel of the Tay between the shore and Moncrieff Island, along the eastern side of the island and then back across Willowgate to the eastern side of the river to a terminus at Commercial Street, Bridgend.

The railway was thereby left on the opposite side of the river to the centre of Perth, and would have necessitated passengers crossing the Perth Bridge to reach the town. This arrangement was explained by the need to keep the main channel of the river clear for the construction of Perth Harbour. However, on the completion of these works, a connection could be made with the proposed Dunkeld and Crieff Railways. Lord Kinnaird's first meeting was followed by a public announcement in the Perth press on Friday 13th November, 1835 by the clerks to the company, Shiell and Small of Dundee, who proclaimed that 'The Dundee and Perth Railway Company has now been formed and the most sanguine hopes are entertained that they may this season be able to bring an act of Parliament. Only one-fortieth of the stock has as yet been subscribed by the city of Perth. The whole capital of £160,000 might soon be raised in Dundee alone.'

The announcement went on to express the hope that there might be a junction with the line being proposed to Glasgow.

However, the Dundee and Perth Railway of 1835 was a railway which was destined not to be built. Lord Kinnaird had not been successful initially in gaining the support of some of his neighbouring landowners who were far from favourable to building a railway near their property. Even amongst those who supported the idea, there was dissent over which of the routes should be adopted, particularly where the line crossed their land. Hay, the landowner of Seggieden, wanted exorbitant recompense for traversing his unavoidable strip of land near Perth. Lord Gray of nearby Kinfauns Castle also disputed the line passing his property. On 6th July, 1836, a report in *The Perth Constitutional* announced:

> The latest proposal is for the line to cross the River Tay near Inchyra by a swing bridge and come into Perth on the south side of the river avoiding expensive interference with the pleasure grounds of Seggyden, Kinfauns and Barnhill. It would be convenient for Newburgh, giving a branch off the Edinburgh line to Newburgh which must surely be built. It is to be hoped that the River Commissioners offer no objections.

The trustees of the Dundee to Perth turnpike were not appeased by Findlater's confident statement about the improvement in traffic on the Airdire turnpike, for they also wanted adequate compensation of £10,000 for the debts which had accrued on the road. The railway's proposers assumed, as others had done in the past, that the two termini would generate most of the traffic and that the rural nature of the intervening country would sustain the stops *en route*. The only significant settlements in the Carse of Gowrie were Errol and Inchture and neither of these were to be served directly by the railway.

Despite announcements in the press at the same time that the 'want of money is no longer likely to be an obstacle', most of the capital remained unsubscribed. In May 1836, by which time the opportunity for a Parliamentary submission was lost, only £55,000 had been offered for the £160,000 share capital, and this had risen to just over half the total by the following year. Additionally, unlike both the Newtyle and Arbroath undertakings, there was not the expected financial support for the Dundee and Perth from the local community. A number of subscribers were from England but their investments were at risk from the forthcoming recession and when they became aware of the disputes amongst the Perthshire landowners, these distant supporters withdrew from the scheme. By June 1836, the buttress of English money was all but removed. The project was wound up in 1837.

However, Lord Kinnaird did not give up on the possibility of a railway between Dundee and Perth. Economic times had been difficult at the end of the 1830s and it was not until 1844, in the years of Railway Mania, that the scheme was resurrected. The prospect of this new railway raised a heated debate in Dundee. The local press voiced its astonishment at any opposition to the proposed railway and the possibility of a connecting railway along the North Quay of the harbour in Dock Street, Dundee. Provost James Brown expressed the view of the Chamber of Commerce that the line should be built, with the link to the Dundee and Arbroath being subject to some restrictions such as a ban on steam locomotives and limitations on the haulage of passenger carriages and goods wagons.

A public meeting was held in Dundee in January 1845, when those attending expressed their approval of a new scheme and formed a 'vigilant' committee to oversee its promotion in Parliament. The response was better this time and on 27th May, 1845, the press was reporting that:

> A good deal of interest has been felt in the town with regard to the fate of the Dundee and Perth Railway Company's Bill in Parliament - a serious opposition having been threatened by the Scottish Midland Junction Railway. We observe that the preamble of the Bill has been approved by the Committee of the House of Commons.

This 'threat' was provoked by the possibility of the Scottish Midland Junction Railway absorbing the ailing Dundee and Newtyle Railway as part of its progress through Strathmore from Perth towards Aberdeen. The D&NR had been offered for let on 10th January, 1845 and had the SMJR been successful it would have gained access to Dundee from Perth via the north. The Committee referred to was Lord Dalhousie's Board which had been set up by Gladstone when he was President of the Board of Trade. In order to reduce the amount of time spent by the Select Committee examining each of the proposals set before Parliament, this new group advised on questions of public safety, any likely amalgamations, comparisons between different routes, and spoiling schemes.

The Dundee and Perth Act (8 & 9 Vic. cap. clvii) passed through all stages without delay and received Royal Assent on 31st July, 1845. Among the Directors named was at least one fellow landowner of Lord Kinnaird, namely Sir Patrick Murray Thriepland who owned Fingask Castle, situated at Rait overlooking the Carse of Gowrie. The authorised capital was £200,000, made up of eight thousand £25 shares raised in £5 calls with further borrowings of up to £66,600 permitted when all the capital had been subscribed and half of it paid up.

John Miller, the company's Engineer, selected a line similar to Findlater's central route. From the Harbour at Dundee the line formed a junction with the other Dundee railways and was made up initially of an embankment over the river bed a few yards out from the shore. From there, the route westwards was along the shoreline to Invergowrie where the route crossed Kingoodie quarry (now flooded) and struck a straight line across the flat Carse of Gowrie to Inchyra, and then along the river's edge past Seggieden and round the bend in the Tay and across the river at Moncrieff Island to a terminus at the South Inch. As with the 1835 proposal, this route brought protests from the many vested interests along the river. From the bathers at Magdalen Yard Point to the salmon fisheries of Lord Gray at Kinfauns, objections meant that the railway company had to alter its plans to accommodate a variety of opposition. A costly extension to the embankment was made to permit a 15 ft gap to be left for the river to flow in near the outdoor bathing at the Magdalen Green, and Lord Gray was paid £12,000 for the right to skirt his lands at Kinfauns.

The Navigation Commissioners and the Admiralty opposed the lightweight bridge at Moncrieff Island and the Town Council of Perth were unhappy about the new station at the South Inch. As neither of these difficulties had been reconciled satisfactorily by the time the Act was passed, a temporary terminus was established at Barnhill on the Dundee side of the river. The first meeting of the newly formed company was held at the Royal Hotel, in Union Street, Dundee on 28th August, 1845, by which time tenders had been advertised for 4,400 tons of iron rail, 900 tons of cast iron sleepers and 50,000 wooden sleepers. The contractors began on 18th September, 1845. and early the next January, *The Dundee, Perth and Cupar Advertiser* reported that the line was:

> . . . making rapid progress. Nearly 1,000 men are employed by the contractors. The bulwark in the River Tay is in an advanced state and will be carried past the Magdalen Yard. The permanent rails are in course of being laid at different places. . .
>
> The engines will be of the most modern and powerful construction, capable of performing the entire distance between Dundee and Perth in twenty minutes.

At a meeting of the company on 28th August, 1846, Lord Kinnaird proclaimed that the whole of the line had been contracted, and works were going ahead satisfactorily.

Stations were planned at Glencarse, Errol, Inchture, and Invergowrie, although Lord Gray was unhappy about the position of the platform at Kinfauns. The Dundee terminus was originally a long narrow wooden shed with open sides at a timber yard in South Union Street adjacent to the Harbour. It was considered inferior even to the temporary terminus at Perth where the home of the former proprietor of Barnhill had been converted into a station and the grounds opened for the use of passengers. Stations were later built at Longforgan and at the popular meeting ground at Magdalen Green, where George Kinloch had addressed 10,000 townsfolk in 1832.

The Dundee and Perth successfully prevented the Scottish Midland Junction Railway from entering Dundee via the Newtyle line, with powers to lease the D&NR. The Dundee and Perth Railway (Amendment) Act dated 27th July, 1846 (9&10 Vic. cap. ccxxviii) was passed to permit this leasing for 999 years at £1,400 per annum and to purchase the Harbour branch. These arrangements were completed by the 6th October, 1846 when Lord Kinnaird also told an extraordinary general meeting that the intended station across the river at Princes Street, Perth 'would not do' and that a plan to move it west of the town had been conceived. This would enable the railway to connect with both the Scottish Central and the Edinburgh and Northern at a cost of £33,000.

The Directors were in an expansionary mood at that time for the same meeting was informed of a proposal to build three short branches from the main line to secure agricultural, coal and lime traffic in the Carse. Two of the lines were to run inland, one to Inchture, 1¼ miles long and the other to Inchmichael, 2¼ miles, and the capital was to be increased by £4,000 to cover their construction cost. These lines were authorised in 1847 along with a third, only three-quarters of a mile long, to Powgavie, nearer the river.

Of these three, only the Inchture branch was completed, perhaps understandably when the destination was only a few hundred yards from the gates of Rossie Priory, home of Lord Kinnaird who had insisted that the main line be built at some distance from his family seat. The lightweight 'T' section wrought iron track was laid from the rear of the station at Inchture to the east side of the road to the village, which it followed for the mile and a half to a terminus at the crossroads on the turnpike, and was opened on 1st February, 1848. Regular transportation for the lifetime of this service was a horse-drawn carriage. At first an old four-wheel composite coach bought from the Dundee and Arbroath Railway was employed to be replaced in 1865 by the later owners, the Scottish Central, by a four-wheeler from the main line. On 15th April, 1890 an individual coach, known locally as the *Dandy*, was ordered from St Rollox. This vehicle was painted in Caledonian livery and offered both first and second class seats. There were six return journeys daily, taking about 25 minutes each way.

Locomotive-hauled coaches were said to have traversed the line, called the 'Lang Cassy', (Long Causeway) on occasions in the early days to save passengers from changing at Inchture, particularly at harvest time. The practice was not continued after the Caledonian Railway took over, due to the lightweight rails. A short goods extension was constructed half a mile north-west to a brick works, with a spur to a clay pit. When this was closed, a pug locomotive still reached Inchture with horse manure wagons from Dundee for local farmers. The line closed on 1st April, 1916.

The Inchmichael branch was to be constructed from Errol station north past the village of Inchmichael into the Sidlaws near Fingask Castle, home of Sir Patrick Murray Thriepland. However, the cost of the works was high and the likely return low so, following a committee of inquiry, the Directors agreed to terminate the line at the turnpike in 1850, before it was completed but not before a cutting had been created to the north of Errol station. A road now passes through this minor engineering feature, the branch being closed on 30th November, 1852. The branch to Powgavie which would have run south from Inchture station was never built, but a short branch was constructed from Errol station to Ninetree Brae, to the north east of the main line. Later, short narrow gauge lines were constructed to Pitfour Brick and Tile Works by Glencarse and to Errol Brick and Tile works at Inchcoonans. Near Kinfauns Castle, a short tramway was constructed in later years for the Tay Salmon Fisheries. The extension of the line from Barnhill through Princes Street station to Perth General station was also authorised in 1847.

By this time the mood of railway entrepreneurs had turned from the promotion of local lines to the advantages of a national network. The North British Railway had opened from Edinburgh to Berwick the previous June as part of a main line from Scotland to London, and the Caledonian Railway (CR) which was incorporated on the same day as the D&PR was nearing the completion of the first stage of its line from Carlisle as part of a future west coast route through Scotland. This would reach both Edinburgh and Glasgow in 1848 linking with the Scottish Central to make a continuous line to Perth and onwards to Aberdeen. The Dundee and Perth Railway was keen to take advantage of the potential traffic which could be generated from the south and take it to Aberdeen via the Dundee and Arbroath Railway. The newly formed Edinburgh and Northern Railway was approaching Dundee through Fife and the crossing of the Tay would bring a major competitor for the east coast traffic.

In January 1847, the Directors concluded an agreement with the D&AR to lease that railway from 30th April, at a guarantee of 8 per cent. As recorded in Chapter Three, the D&AR was to construct a railway through Dundee from its terminus at Trades Lane and join the D&PR at a point to the west of the town. The Arbroath company would make representations to Parliament but the expenses would be met by the Dundee and Perth and then repaid out of new stock. The line would be operated by the Perth company for a maximum of 37½ per cent of the gross revenue. No less a personage than Isambard Kingdom Brunel would be the arbiter of any dispute.

Delays in completing the line were attributed to bad weather over the winter of 1846/7. The Chairman, Lord Kinnaird, at a meeting on 26th February, 1847 expressed his regret that the line was not yet open, due to these delays. He also announced an arrangement whereby the Dundee and Perth would become part of the route via the SCR, CR, and LNWR to London forming 'a continuous line between 400 and 500 miles long, without interruption from ferries.'

By May, the line was complete and a grand Opening Trip was arranged for the Town Councils of both Dundee and Perth as well as the gentry of the Carse. This was held on Saturday 22nd May, 1847, and *The Dundee Courier* reported the ceremony:

> The train from Perth started about twelve noon and as it proceeded along the line was joined at different stations by parties from the Carse. It arrived at Dundee shortly after one o'clock and was loudly cheered as it approached the station at Yeaman's Shore, Dundee. The band, which occupied an open carriage in front struck up the air of 'Bonnie Dundee'. The Dundee Party, who were then to join the party from Perth and accompany them from Dundee on the return journey to Barnhill had previously taken their seats in the carriages provided for them.
>
> A short time was occupied in arranging the entire train, consisting of thirty carriages which presented a most imposing appearance.
>
> Four of the splendid locomotives which do so much credit to our enterprising townsmen, Kinmonds, Hutton and Steel, were now in readiness: three of them were placed in front of the train whilst the fourth was dispatched as a pilot. All parties having taken their seats, the shrill whistle sounded the signal for departure a few minutes past two o'clock, and immediately the truly magnificent train was in motion.
>
> The train proceeded onward at a cautious speed, seldom exceeding 25-30 miles per hour, and, after stopping at several stations, reached Barnhill exactly at three o'clock.

All along the way crowds gathered and cheered as the procession of locomotives and carriages passed along. Even Lord Gray joined in the celebration by dressing Kinfauns Castle with bunting and firing a salute of 19 guns from the castle as the inaugural train passed. The line was opened for public service on the following Monday.

The locomotives employed on the line comprised four 0-4-2 tender engines from Kinmonds, Hutton and Steel, three 2-2-2 types numbers 5, 6, and 7 named *Vulcan*, *Lucifer* and *Dundee* and a Crampton 4-2-0 from Tulk and Ley of Whitehaven. This latter locomotive, named *Kinnaird* after the company Chairman, was taken to Hull and transferred to a ship for the journey to Dundee. Two more tender engines were acquired from Stirling and Company

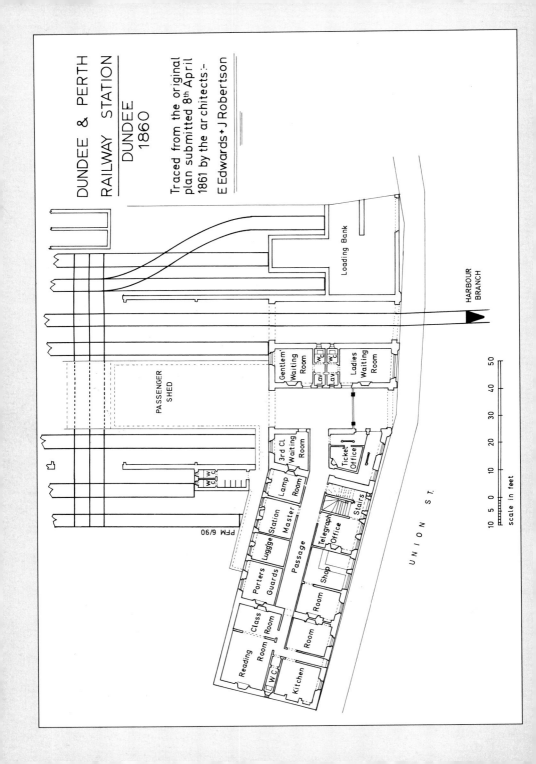

DUNDEE & PERTH RAILWAY STATION

DUNDEE 1860

Traced from the original plan submitted 8th April 1861 by the architects:- E Edwards + J Robertson

Loading Bank

HARBOUR BRANCH

PASSENGER SHED

PFM 6/90

W.C.

Gentlem' Waiting Room

Lav. W.C. W.C. Lav.

Ladies Waiting Room

3rd Cl Waiting Room

Lamp Room

Station Master

Luggage

Porters Guards

Passage

Reading Room

Class Room

Room

Room

W.C.

Kitchen

Room

Shop

Telegraph Office

Stairs

Ticket Office

UNION ST.

scale in feet

10 5 0   10   20   30   40   50

in Dundee. They were named *Caledonia* and *Gowrie* and were delivered in 1847 and 1848 respectively.

The Dundee and Perth Railway was an immediate success. Its first special excursion was held during the first week of public service to acknowledge the efforts of the contractors and their workforce. Around 700 men from works in Dundee and Perth were given the afternoon off and marched to the South Union Street station to join a train of 23 carriages pulled by two of the Dundee-built locomotives. There were six trains each way at first leaving Dundee at 7.45, 10.00, 10.45 am, 1.15, 3.45, and 7.30 pm, with return trains from Perth at 7.00, 8.30, 10.30 am, 12.30, 3.00, and 7.15 pm. All trains took an hour and stopped at Invergowrie, Errol, Glencarse and Kinfauns. The 8.30 am and 3.00 pm trains from Perth offered a connection in Dundee with trains for Arbroath, as did the 8.30 am, 12.00 noon and 6.00 pm trains from Arbroath in the other direction. Fares between the two ends of the line were 3s. First, 2s. Second and 1s.6d. Third. The trip from Barnhill station into Perth was by horse-drawn omnibus but only for first and second class passengers. A more convenient booking office was opened in the centre of Perth, at 23 South Street.

The Dundee and Newtyle (Widening, Altering and Improving) Act, 1847 gave the Dundee and Perth Railway powers to upgrade the quality of the Dundee and Newtyle line in the somewhat vain hope of making this ailing line more profitable. However, with the approaching completion of the Caledonian and entry of the Scottish Central Railway into Perth in May 1848, not to mention the opening of the 32 mile-long Scottish Midland Junction Line from Perth to Forfar on 11th September, 1848, the Dundee and Newtyle had to be able to compete with the improving access to Strathmore.

The single track bridge across the Tay at Perth was opened on 8th March, 1849. This structure was primarily of wood, erected on a tight curve of 330 feet but with an iron swing bridge opening to clear 50 feet over the navigable channel of the Tay. Its construction damaged a fresh water pipe which lay on the river bed and carried water to Barnhill from Anderson's water works, still visible today to the south of the site of Princes Street station at the Perth end of the bridge. The Water Commisioners demanded that a new pipe was laid to ensure a continuity of supply, to which the railway company somewhat reluctantly agreed.

The original bridge was replaced by a stone and iron structure, designed and built by the Caledonian Railway in 1863 at a cost of £27,000. Still with a single track, it was constructed with five spans to the west of Moncrieffe Island and seven spans to the east, crossing the island itself on 10 stone spans. The span nearest Tay Street on the western shore was able to open but remained in use for only 20 years. A footbridge was added to the northern side providing access to the island from both sides of the river. The Perth Harbour Commissioners became disturbed at the railway's success and planned to improve the harbour facilities, since the regular steam boat service between Dundee and Perth had been withdrawn due to the cheaper, faster and more convenient railway service.

Success came at a price for the railway as this series of expensive improvements left it in a financially straitened position by the end of the 1840s.

Receipts were falling from passenger traffic and the Directors sought loans and increases in share capital, even holding discussions with the Caledonian Railway with a view to leasing the line to the more powerful neighbour. An internal report was put to the Board by newly appointed Directors in July 1850, suggesting amendments to give the company more financial stability.

Servicing facilities for the railway were at Dundee, or more specifically, Seabraes, the reclaimed and dried up river margins to the west of the town centre. There the Dundee and Perth constructed a coaling stage, joiner's and blacksmith's shops and an engine shed fed by a fan of five tracks from a small turntable. With land so plentiful here, there was also room for a large engine shop and a manager's house.

The company found it necessary to raise additional capital and at a meeting on 17th October, 1859 the Board resolved to raise £70,000 by the issue of 7,000 £10 stock with 'all the priorities and privileges conferred by the Dundee and Newtyle Act of 1859. Further capital was sought by an Act (25 Vic. cap. xxxv) of 3rd June, 1862, this time for £60,000 in 5 per cent shares and a loan of £20,000 for the Dundee and Perth, as well as £19,000 5 per cent shares and a £4,900 loan for the Dundee and Newtyle.

Unlike its contemporaries, the D&PR attracted fewer passengers than was originally hoped, carrying over 200,000 in 1851, mostly in third class, but rising to 300,000 by 1858, a figure still below Miller's estimates. Goods, however, were the company's success with 81,857 tons conveyed in 1851 and double that within five more years. This accomplishment did not escape the attention of the Scottish Central Railway with its established Perth base. Having a direct route via the Caledonian to Glasgow and England as well as to Aberdeen over the Scottish Midland and the Aberdeen companies, it was keen to develop its traffic further. Timetables for March 1858, reveal five daily departures from Dundee for Perth, with most going on to Glasgow, Manchester, Liverpool, Birmingham and London. The fare from Arbroath to London by this route was 37s. third class.

Also at this time, the D&PR recorded that it operated 15 locomotives, the six originals from Kinmond, Hutton and Steel and in addition three Bury types, purchased second-hand from the LNWR and used in place of three Newtyle engines. Three 2-4-0 locomotives were bought from George England and Co. in 1855 and were named *Sprite*, *Spitfire*, and *Scorpion*. There were 57 carriages and 426 wagons on the company books. Passenger trains averaged six carriages and goods trains were composed of an average of 34 wagons.

On 8th August, 1859 the SCR had been authorised to improve the amenities at Perth General, to provide, *inter alia*, a new platform access for the Dundee services adjacent to the rest of the station. The SMJR and AR had meanwhile merged on 29th July, 1856 to form the SNER providing a stronger alliance to the north. So it was, through an Act (26 & 27 Vic. cap. ccxxxiii), on 26th July, 1863 that the SCR, once an opponent, absorbed both the Dundee and Perth and the Dundee and Newtyle lines into its widening net.

Inevitably there were conditions amongst which were the discharging of debts to preference shareholders, and the payment of a 2 per cent dividend to ordinary shareholders up to the year ending 31st July, 1864 and 2½ per cent for

1865 and 3 per cent thereafter. Shareholders of the absorbed companies would also be entitled to a share of any surplus profits from the lines. However, in the heady days of the mid-1860s, the pace of railway expansion was quickening and it was not long before the SCR too fell prey, this time to the Caledonian.

In 1863, the original and rather modest wooden station at Dundee was considered by the new owners, the Scottish Central, to be inadequate for their growing requirements. Plans were submitted for a much more elaborate building, called Dundee West to distinguish it from Dundee East on the Arbroath line. The two storey stone-built structure offered better facilities for both passengers and company servants in a train shed covered by a single span mansard roof of 65 ft by 310 ft long. The central feature of the station was an Italianate building on South Union Street with a pediment midway under a clock turret flanked by a balustrade. The harbour line passed through the right-hand bay of this section.

Roman arches and windows in the adjacent offices and screen wall provided a confusing appearance although the building was to last for 25 years. Additional land was required for this plan and John Arthur Jameson, Secretary of the SCR, signed an order for the new building which was described as being 'a carriage shed opposite the Dundee and Perth locomotive workshops', which was approximately 250 ft long. This was authorised by an Act, (27 & 28 Vic. cap. ccxcii) of 29th July, 1864 which also permitted the extension of Perth General.

As part of the improvements at Dundee station, Yeaman Shore was stopped up and a deviation taken approximately 100 ft to the north. The land acquired for building was described as 'slab' land or mud flats and belonged to the railway company, for the River Tay ran along the southern edge of the railway. The station was the departure point for both Perth and Newtyle trains, the latter no longer using the rails through the streets of Dundee to Ward station, but diverting from the main line at Ninewells Junction. Built by William Paterson, Dundee West was opened in 1864.

As part of the SCR's planned improvements, a new and enlarged goods depot was proposed. This was to sit to the north of the new Dundee West station, with access from Union Street. The stopping up of Yeaman Shore would have had to be permanent had this shed and yard been built. However, only the station was erected with inferior goods facilities incorporated within it, leaving the original goods depot to the west.

So Dundee now had two improved termini for its railway connections with the rest of the country. Traffic for England and the south used Dundee West and for the north, Dundee East. Passengers for Edinburgh and Fife were put to the inconvenience of departing from East station for the brief trip to Broughty Ferry before reversing to the pier branch and the river crossing. A bridge over the Tay was becoming essential for the completion of the railways to Dundee.

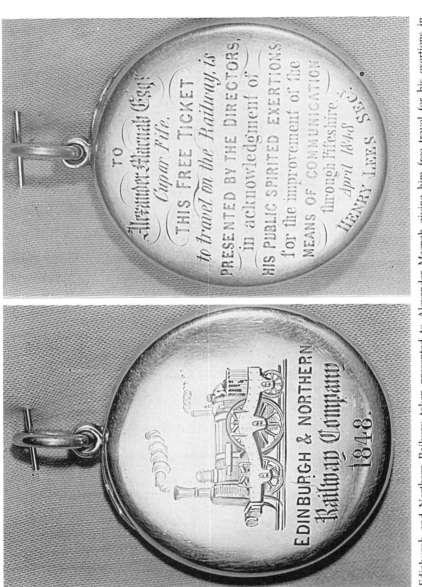

Edinburgh and Northern Railway token presented to Alexander Macnab giving him free travel for his exertions in establishing the railway.

HMRS/Charles Underhill Collection

Chapter Five

The Edinburgh, Perth and Dundee Railway
1845-1862

'The formation of a Railway from the Firth of Forth to the Firth of Tay is measure of National importance'
A meeting of Gentleman, Cupar 1840

Although the Rivers Tay and Forth constituted a substantial barrier to railway promotion from Edinburgh to Dundee, they did not deter the entrepreneurs of the east of Scotland from advancing a number of proposals for a railway through Fife. Unlike the first railways from Dundee, the promotion of a line to the capital did not originate in the town. The earliest railways in the Fife had been created in association with the mining of coal, with Lord Elgin's waggonway from Dunfermline to Charlestown (improved in 1821 by Charles Landale who engineered the Dundee and Newtyle) and the Fordell Railway amongst others which transported coal to the shores of the Forth. The greatest challenge to the construction of a line between Edinburgh and Dundee, however, was that presented by the Firth of Forth and the Firth of Tay. Ferries were the original method of crossing and initially served the railways adequately.

The riches of the Fife coalfield attracted the early railway builders and the many propositions for a railway across Fife become difficult to unravel. As early as 1819, a proposal was put forward by Robert Stevenson and Son, Civil Engineers, for an Edinburgh and Dundee Railway, from the Forth and the West Fife coalfield to the Tay at both Newport and Perth. Stevenson (whose grandson was R.L.Stevenson, the author) was a great believer in railways and had been involved in many schemes including the Stockton and Darlington. Although this first scheme did not progress, the routes he surveyed in the east of Scotland between 1817 to 1827 later became the major lines of the area.

The Earl of Rothes commissioned another plan for a line through Fife from John Geddes in 1835, and Stevenson came forward once more in 1836 with a similar plan to his earlier one. This time he suggested a route from Burntisland, through Kirkcaldy to Cupar and then to Ferryport-on-Craig and Newport for the crossing to Dundee. The 38 mile journey was estimated to take two hours, speeding up the London mails by as much as ten hours. As with many other proposals in the depressed years of the 1830s, subscriptions were not sufficient to permit the project to proceed. Grainger and Miller submitted a further idea in 1836, being almost identical to Stevenson's route.

More serious support for this route came after a 'Meeting of Gentlemen' was held in Cupar on 13th October, 1840. On this occasion, the local landowners expressed their championing of the idea. Even the Town Council of Arbroath were represented, but no-one from either Edinburgh or Dundee attended. A committee was formed to negotiate with landowners likely to be involved along the possible line to facilitate a survey by Grainger and Miller. Grainger's idea also gained the support of both the Duke of Buccleuch and the elderly John

Gladstone (father of W.E. Gladstone), who were active in improving the harbours at Burntisland and across the Forth at Granton. The engineer publicised his scheme in December 1840, when, under a new title of the Edinburgh, Dundee and Northern Railway, it was outlined to a meeting of the Edinburgh Chamber of Commerce.

However, Grainger's route was contested in January 1841 by John Milne, an engineer who believed that his Forth and Tay Railway offered the best route. His line was from Burntisland, through Auchterderran and Loch Leven to Newburgh then crossing the Tay to join a Perth and Dundee railway. Milne contended that Grainger's eastern line would not be likely to carry coals as the people of Kirkcaldy would not buy their coal from the nearby Wemyss coalfield. The Edinburgh, Dundee and Northern Railway Bill was submitted to Parliament in 1842 and again in 1843, failing on both occasions. A further Bill for a Fife and Perth Railway reached the Commons in 1843 but was not successful as the plans were incomplete. John Gladstone pursued the Grainger scheme in 1844 and a prospectus was issued in April of that year with a capital of £800,000. There were also difficulties regarding the railway's rights of passage over the Tay Ferry and the proprietors even gave consideration to a bridge over the Tay. In order to keep the cost of this enormous enterprise, it was proposed to single the track for most of the route. However, insufficient deposits were paid to cover the minimum required by standing orders before a Bill could be submitted to Parliament, due mainly to the local nature of the line, and a new prospectus had to be considered under the name of the Edinburgh and Northern Railway (E&NR).

This was now the beginning of the Railway Mania and, although well supported, the passage of the Bill was not without opposition from several other projects. A new Edinburgh and Perth Railway (E&PR) was put forward in 1845, this time to run from the Edinburgh and Glasgow Railway at Gogar via Queensferry, a much easier ferry crossing than that at Granton. Once across the Forth, the line would run via Cowdenbeath, Loch Leven and Glenfarg to Perth with branches *en route* to Dunfermline and Kirkcaldy. A further branch was added later from Cowdenbeath and Kelty, to the west of Loch Leven, rejoining the original line past Kinross. Here was competition which the E&NR took very seriously, but although the E&PR Bill was not ready in 1845 the latter company strenuously opposed the Northern's line. Its Parliamentary battle was bitter with physical restraint being exerted in the Commons by opponents to prevent its passage.

A Tay Bridge at Newport was opposed by the Admiralty and the promoters abandoned that idea along with the branch from Cupar to the Tay. Despite the struggle, the Bill passed the Commons stage, leaving little time for it to pass the Lords. The E&NR assuaged its enemies by agreeing not to oppose the E&PR Bill for the main line or branch to the E&NR at Thornton, so relinquishing the West Fife coalfield to its rival, but retaining the right of access to the area if the Edinburgh and Perth Bill failed. A second scheme came from the Scottish South Midland Junction Railway running from the Edinburgh and Glasgow Railway, near Falkirk to Kinross and Newburgh, before crossing the Tay to the Dundee and Perth Railway to give access to both towns.

Another prospectus was published, with the support of the Scottish Central Railway, by the Glasgow and Dundee Direct Railway for a line from Dundee, over the Tay by a 'floating bridge' (in effect a caisson which could contain wagons) to Newport, with a link to St Andrews and then to the SCR at Stirling partly by way of the Edinburgh and Perth line.

A more fanciful enterprise was the Scottish Direct Northern Junction Railway which would utilise a ferry from North Berwick to Elie and connect both to an East Fife line and to Dundee via St Andrews. A similar proposal emerged in the Fife Central Junction Railway which sought to leave the Edinburgh and Northern Line at Dairsie and reach the Forth at Elie, then cross to East Lothian and there meet North British line to England. Bills for these and a dozen other lines were deposited during 1845 but none of them was successful.

The victorious enterprise was incorporated as an Act on 31st July, 1845, (8&9 Vic. cap. clviii) under the title of the Edinburgh and Northern Railway, John Learmonth, Chairman of the recently formed North British Railway, being named as Chairman. The Act enabled the construction of a railway, 'commencing at the Low water Pier at Burntisland, and terminating on the one hand, at Perth, and on the other at Cupar, with a short branch to the Harbour of Kirkcaldy.'

The proposed line to Perth was initially abandoned in favour of the often suggested bridge, 'of such an elevation and span as will give ample accommodation to the Vessels navigating the Tay', at Newburgh to join the Dundee and Perth. The opposition of the Admiralty to this idea has already been recorded and the Northern company had to withdraw the idea leaving it without access to Perth.

By 1846, the E&PR had reached agreement with the Edinburgh and Glasgow Railway to build a branch to Queensferry and so submitted a Bill for a line through Fife via Kelty. The plans were not well prepared, failed to pass standing orders and the Bill collapsed, releasing the E&NR to build its branch to Dunfermline. A proposal for a branch from Ladybank to Kinross created to deflect the E&PR was abandoned as soon as the latter was defeated. So too were the branches from Kirkcaldy to Lochgelly and Leslie to Markinch. The E&NR did re-submit a Bill for the abandoned branch from the eastern terminus at Cupar to Newport opposite Dundee. The gentlemen of Cupar had hoped that the line would pass through Guardbridge, which was then the port on the River Eden for Cupar and the hinterland known as the Howe of Fife. This proved too expensive and the line passed about a mile to the west, but with a station at Leuchars. The Admiralty was implacably opposed to a bridge at Newport and the line ended at Ferryport-on-Craig for a ferry borne river crossing to Broughty Ferry on the opposite shore. Its supporters agreed it would 'greatly facilitate the communication between the Southern and Northern parts of Scotland if the said Company were authorized to purchase and acquire the ferry between Ferryport-on-Craig and Broughty on the River Tay'. Together with a working agreement with the Dundee and Arbroath Railway, this arrangement meant there would be a direct route from Edinburgh to Dundee. The need to cross the Tay at Perth was thus obviated. A link to the Fair City was later provided by the little known Strathearn Junction Railway.

This company had already gained approval for a short line from the Scottish Central at Hilton Junction, south of Perth, to join the unsuccessful Glasgow and Dundee Junction Railway at Luthrie near Newburgh. An agreement with its minor associate gave the E&NR a route over the Scottish Central rails into Perth, although its relationship with the SCR (and its successors) was hardly to prove harmonious.

Having spent just over £65,000 to get Parliamentary permission alone, the Directors were no doubt relieved when construction of the line began in the first months of 1846. Initial estimates of the cost of land purchase were, like so many other railways of the time, well below the final price paid. Such was the greed of the landowners along the line, that the eventual outlay for land purchase was three times the original calculation. Learmonth complained that advantage was being taken of the unfortunate promoters of a railway.

Eighteen contracts, some for as little as 1¼ miles of track, were let for the line and given to local concerns who had knowledge of both the area and the men. This also had the advantage that the work could be undertaken concurrently all along the route. The total contract price was just short of £640,000 but, once again, this was exceeded with the total being nearer £784,000. However, there was difficulty at the outset in keeping the additional itinerant navvy labour which work of this nature required. For example, over 800 men were employed on the 2¾ mile section at the summit of the line between Markinch and New Inn which included the Leven Valley viaduct. This structure cost £16,500 to build out of a contract worth £54,000 to the builders Ross and Mitchell. They, like other contractors, faced competition for their labourers from many other railway projects of the time including the Scottish Central who were pushing on with their line to Perth.

The Scottish Central paid higher wages than the Edinburgh and Northern but by the late summer both routes were waiting for the return of navvies from the harvest by which time, it was reported to the Edinburgh and Northern Company's Plans and Works committee, 'a sufficiency of hands will be again on the work.' By September 1846, Grainger was able to report favourably to the Directors on progress. They noted that the line was 'making satisfactory progress and what is of equal importance, the calls are well paid up.' Like many railway projects, when navvies got together after a day's work, drinking was heavy and fighting a common occurrence. The men on the E&NR project were reputed to be better behaved than their contemporaries, but nevertheless the Directors received a request for a 'Subscription to meet the expense of Missionary work amongst the labourers' for which the Board agreed to give £35.

On 7th August, 1847, the Edinburgh, Leith and Granton Railway joined forces with the Edinburgh and Northern, the new company taking the latter's name, under a further Act, (11 Vic. cap. ccxxxix). The Granton line had been authorised in 1836 as the Edinburgh, Leith and Newhaven, but had a chequered early life. A mile long extension to the new harbour at Granton, opened on 19th February, 1846, enabled the name to be amended. The Scotland Street tunnel was opened in May 1847 to a terminus at Canal Street at right angles to Waverley station, terminus of the North British in Edinburgh.

By June 1847, the first stage of the E&NR was nearing completion with nearly 9,000 men employed on the line, of whom more than 5,500 were Scots, over 3,000 were Irish and just 49 English.

However, in early September of that year when the first part of the line was completed, 7,336 men were put out of work, no doubt to seek further employment on one of the other railway schemes then being undertaken.

The line to Lindores and Cupar was passed by the Board of Trade inspector on 3rd September, 1847 and preparations were set in place for opening on Friday 17th September, 1847, with passenger traffic beginning on the following Monday. The various invited parties met at Burntisland, crossing from Edinburgh in ferries and coming by special trains from Cupar and Lindores. On reaching Cupar in the ceremonial trains, the usual collation was served along with 'unlimited champagne'. Newspaper reports of the event noted that the line from Cupar to Dundee was already partly in place leaving around 11 miles to complete, along with about 13 miles on the route to Perth. The intervening distances were covered by horse-drawn coaches.

On the first day of public travel, the connecting coach from Newport to Cupar was crowded with those wishing to sample this new railway through Fife. In normal service, coaches left Dundee at 7.0, 10.0 am, 2.0 and 4.0 pm reaching Cupar in under two hours where they met the train for Burntisland. With stops at Springfield, Ladybank, Kettle, Falkland Road, Markinch, Dysart, Kirkcaldy and Kinghorn the train reached the ferry for Granton in just 2 hrs 12 mins with a further hour allotted for the crossing and trip into Edinburgh. Fares ranged from 7s.6d. (37½p) for the complete journey first class including coach to 3s. 6d. (17½p)for the Parliamentary fare for the same trip, being the statutory penny per mile. Traffic on the partly completed railway was greater than the original estimates envisaged.

Nearly 200,000 passengers used the new service in the first four months of operation which, the Directors suggested, would give an annual figure of 750,000 or nearly twice the assessment of the prospectus. Goods traffic was less successful, perhaps because of the incompleteness of the line, and partly because of the lack of goods facilities.

At the opening on 20th September, 1847, it was announced by the Edinburgh and Northern that the line to Dundee was expected to be in operation by December and that to Perth, early in 1848. However despite the increasing of work to include a night shift, neither line was finished until 17th May, 1848, when the company could announce the completion of the Dundee line to Ferryport-on-Craig (later Tayport), via Leuchars. On the same day, the Strathearn Railway on the Perth line was reached, leaving the link to the SCR and through Hilton tunnel to be completed as the final section and opened on 20th July. Pleasure excursions were run on 29th May and 7th June from Edinburgh to Dundee and a special cheap ticket for a return journey at a single fare of 2s. 6d. (12½p) was issued from Dundee to Edinburgh on 17th June, 1848. By this time, John Balfour of Balbirnie near Markinch was the Chairman, with Thomas Grainger retained as Engineer-in-chief and Henry Lees the company Secretary. The concern was based in offices at 18 St Andrew's Square, Edinburgh.

One of the Directors was William Tullis, the son of Robert Tullis the printer, bookbinder and publisher of Cupar whilst another of his sons, George, was a shareholder. In 1848, Tullis's business published a Guide to the Edinburgh and Northern Railway, written by James Bruce for potential travellers. It boasted that it provided 37 pages 'embracing an account of the various towns and villages on the line with their trade, manufactures &c and descriptions of the natural scenery and antiquities.'

The service was increased to five daily trains each way when the Tayport extension was opened, the last connection departing from Dundee now being 6 pm, although this was reduced again in the winter. On 24th July, 1848, the Edinburgh and Northern Railway offered potential customers the carriage of goods between stations on both the routes with special arrangements for cattle. However, it does not take much imagination to picture the scene at each of the ferry piers when the contents of goods wagons would have to be trans-shipped, only to be reloaded once the crossing was completed, with resultant damage and loss.

Dundee could now claim to have railway services in all four directions from the town, north, south, east and west, but that to the south of course had a major obstacle in the form of the Firth of Tay which had to be crossed, like the Forth, by ferry. The Tay was previously crossed by small boats from Newport and the nearby jetty at Woodhaven to the Craig harbour at Dundee but the two mile journey was so unpleasant that many travellers preferred to take the considerably longer route by Perth, rather than suffer the stormy crossing and the disagreeable ferrymen. The Trustees improved the crossing in 1821 by building the *Union* and *George IV*, twin hulled vessels which entered service to Newport in the following years, the Woodhaven crossing then being withdrawn (*see Chapter Seven*). An Act of 1822 had ensured that the approach roads and buildings at either side of the Tay were brought up to a better standard, thus establishing Newport as the Fife port for the crossing with over 80,000 passengers passing through annually.

In October 1845, the Edinburgh and Northern Railway had bought the rights for the ferry crossing from Ferryport-on-Craig to Broughty Ferry on the northern shore and this was confirmed in the 1846 Act. The railway placed *Express*, a 270 ton steamer, on the passage for passenger traffic, which used fairly spartan accommodation at Broughty Pier since there was the restriction on buildings which might obscure the military garrison at the adjacent Broughty Castle. Goods were taken straight to Dundee from Tayport to avoid the need for trans-shipment at Broughty Ferry. The handicap of interrupting the journey twice would not be easily overcome without some appropriate Victorian inventiveness.

This came in the form of an idea from the railway company's new Engineer, Thomas Bouch, who was appointed on 13th January, 1849 by John Balfour, the company Chairman. His solution was to create a 'Floating Railway' which, in effect, was the first roll-on, roll-off train-ferry in the world. A vessel was designed by Grainger, and built by Napier of Glasgow. *Leviathan*, was a double ended boat with twin paddles which were individually powered by Napier engines, making it very manoeuvrable at both sides of the river. It was initially to have been introduced on the Tay crossing, but the Directors were told that the Forth was more suited to the size of vessel proposed.

As the 'flying bridge', the name Bouch gave to his apparatus for loading trains on to the boat, was not completed on the Tay, an experimental service was tried on the Burntisland to Granton route. On 7th February, 1850 a first class carriage and 20 wagons successfully made that crossing on a ferry without leaving the tracks. Once the associated shore works were complete, crossings began on 1st March, 1850. The boat gave service 'beyond the most sanguine expectations' of the Board, and three further, but smaller, vessels were constructed for both the Tay and Forth Ferries, *Leviathan* being transferred to the Tayport-Broughty Ferry crossing on 28th February, 1851 followed by *Robert Napier* a month later, this coinciding with the inauguration of a new harbour at Tayport, and providing a service to Broughty Ferry pier.

The arrangement on the slipways of these products of engineering ingenuity consisted of a sliding platform which ran on 16 wheels and could be raised or lowered by means of a bascule, powered by stationary steam engine, to suit the tide and the position of the boat. On this platform were placed twin tracks which matched up between those on the shore and those on the ferry. Twenty-one wagons could be carried on the three tracks on the flat ferry deck. Although this working was less than perfect with wagons running away and occasionally blocking the pier, or worse the harbour itself, Bouch's 'Floating Railway' operated successfully until the Tay Bridge was opened. The realigned Broughty branch from the Dundee and Arbroath Railway was opened on 1st May that year. Conventional boats were also employed for passenger and goods traffic.

In April 1849, the Edinburgh and Northern Railway was re-incorporated under an Act (13 Vic. cap. lxxix) and named the Edinburgh, Perth and Dundee Railway (EP&DR). Although this was an Act to restructure the company financially, the change of name more closely reflected the three termini of the line and may even have persuaded its potential passengers that the services were more direct than in reality. £310,000 was raised in £20 shares at this time. Previous subscriptions had provided share capital as follows:

The original 1845 Act	26,000 shares at £25	£650,000
Newport Ext. 1846	29,000 shares at £15	£435,000
1847	Mixed amounts at £15 & £25	£279,000

Criticism of the standard of accommodation was voiced in the autumn of 1850 when the company was accused of saving on oil for the lamps of the third class carriages in order to ensure the dividends for the shareholders.

The Mania had seen an increase in the market value of some of the smaller lines built in Scotland as their greedier neighbours tempted the owners with greater annual returns for a stake in them. This, in turn, made the promotion of minor branches an attractive proposition, for, if they could then be leased to a larger railway, the return was more secure.

On the failure of the Edinburgh and Perth Railway Bill in 1848, a branch was agreed from Thornton through Dunfermline to Queensferry. The first portion was opened to the Dunfermline and Stirling Railway, much to the dismay of the

Scottish Central who wanted access from Stirling to the West Fife coalfield and so through to Edinburgh. However, the promotion of the independent branches to St Andrews in 1851, to Leven in 1854 and to Leslie in 1857 were unopposed. The first two mentioned sought the involvement of Thomas Bouch as Engineer, since he had set up on his own by then, independent of the Edinburgh Perth and Dundee Railway. A St Andrews branch had been proposed as early as April 1845, when the shareholders of the Edinburgh and Northern Railway had favoured the route ahead of Parliamentary approval for their main line. These subsidiary branch lines, indeed, brought further traffic to the railway with connecting coaches from them to the more outlying locations where the tracks were not, and never likely to be, laid.

However, with the Scottish Central now begun in Perth and linking both to Edinburgh and to Glasgow, the ranks were drawn up for a railway conflict which was to be waged between the EP&DR and the SCR and between their successors for generations to come. Passengers from Dundee would have a choice of routes to the two major burghs in central Scotland, and once the Dundee and Perth had been extended from Barnhill to Perth General station, the journeys by this route meant no river crossing!

In February 1851, the SCR scrapped an agreement with the EP&DR to send east coast traffic by the Fife route and promoted their fastest journey between Dundee and Edinburgh at under three hours undercutting the 48½ mile 'direct' route through Fife in both time and cost. The Edinburgh company responded with lower fares, which prompted the Scottish Central to reduce their fares to match the Edinburgh line. In April 1851, the fares had dropped further to 6s., 5s. and 3s. for the three classes on both company's trains.

It seems that the businessmen of Dundee were content to make use of the Dundee and Perth line for their journeys to London but there was no real alternative to the Fife line for trade with Edinburgh, the administrative and legal centre of Scotland. The mails between the two centres had taken as much as 9½ hours in 1822, which combined with a further 49 hours to London put two and a half days between Dundee and the seat of government. Plans had been put forward in December 1822 to speed up this journey. At that time, the coach would leave London at 8 am daily, reaching Dundee at 9.30 pm two days later, reducing the time by nine hours. This improvement was in part due to the larger steam packets which were plying the Tay, providing a much enhanced postal service between Cupar and Dundee.

James Chalmers was a Dundee bookseller who was interested in speeding up the mail and had brought the matter before Town Council in April 1824. In the late 1830s, he suggested the use of cheap postage and the application of slips as proof of posting, unwittingly creating the first adhesive postage stamps before the more famous Rowland Hill, and although never credited with this invention was recognised by the town council in 1846. The opening of the railway through Fife in the late 1840s gave a new impetus to improvements in the postal service. The line to Scotland from London was via Rugby, Derby and Normanton, east of Leeds, and in June 1846 the Provost of Dundee, James Brown, added his support to the idea of a direct line to York.

A contract had been agreed with the Postmaster General, the Earl of

Lonsdale, for the carriage of mails but the railway disputed the method employed by which a mail guard was employed to travel as a normal second class passenger between Edinburgh and Dundee. The guard collected the mail bags in his compartment, depositing or collecting them at each station as required. The Edinburgh and Northern had struck a contract costing £700 per annum to carry the mails, but in 1849 the company wanted to alter the arrangement to allow the interchange of bags at Cupar and Kirkcaldy. This was seen as an attempt to force a regular contract and to raise the payment from the Post Office. Only an interdict and court judgment in 1851 could uphold this system in favour of the Postmaster General. As we shall see, the practice of providing an additional guard on mail trains was later to claim the life of one of them in the fall of the Tay Bridge.

To operate their new passenger service in 1847, Robert Nicholson, the loco-motive superintendent of the Edinburgh and Northern Railway, had ordered ten 0-4-2 locomotives from R. & W. Hawthorn of Newcastle. Hawthorns had provided the first engines for the North British and these were of very similar design, having 5 ft driving wheels and 3 ft 6 in. trailing wheels. The first seven were delivered ahead of the opening in September 1847, followed later that month by the eighth with the remainder arriving in January of the following year. They were numbered 1-8, 19 and 20.

The gaps were filled by two other classes, one for goods and a later express class. The goods engines were 0-6-0s having 4 ft 6 in. coupled wheels, again from Hawthorns and similar to the NBR's coal engines; there were also 10 of these and they were numbered 9-13, 18, 21-24, being delivered from Hawthorns between 1847 and 1848. The express locomotives, numbered 14-17 were, like their stablemates, built by Hawthorns and similar to an NBR type. With a 2-2-2 wheel formation and sandwich frames, they had 6ft driving wheels (although some may have been 5 ft 6 in.) with 3 ft leading and trailing wheels. It is likely that the engines were delivered by sea to Burntisland where the E&NR had set up its locomotive workshop. Later Hawthorn locomotives included Nos. 25 and 26, two 0-4-2s with 5 ft coupled wheels which were delivered in 1849 and Nos. 27-29, three 0-6-0s, also with 5 ft wheels. Other locomotives were built by Hawthorns of Leith for the section of line from Edinburgh to Granton for the ferry across the Forth.

Although in the early years it had great success, being heralded as such by the Scottish railway press, by the turn of the decade the Edinburgh, Perth and Dundee was in a fairly insecure financial position. A shareholders' committee of inquiry had been averted at a meeting on 19th June, 1850 by an admission from the Directors that they were far from blameless in the railway's difficulties, but had tried to resist calling upon the shareholders for more funds. The pressure on finances was attributed to the additional costs of the works then being undertaken. However, in 1852, the idea of an inquiry was revived to investigate the running of the company after it was found that debts were being settled by the issue of securities and a reduction in interest rates had been negotiated.

The competition which had been raging with their neighbours had also proved destructive for the EP&DR, undermining its finances with the cuts in passenger fares and goods rates at a time when traffic was falling. The need to maintain separate depots at both Edinburgh and Perth, particularly the latter where the EP&DR was not particularly welcome, was another heavy cost. Revenue improved after 1852 more than doubling in the next five years. An engine shed was built at Tayport in 1855 and this provided a base for these increased demands on the motive power stock.

By 1854 a temporary peace with the Scottish Central was reached through an informal understanding. An agreement was formalised on 1st February, 1856, but abandoned on 30th April, 1857 when the SCR, which controlled the joint rolling stock, forced the other's hand by insisting on capital for wagons for entirely SCR lines.

Scottish railways were undergoing a period of change and consolidation at this time. The NBR opened its line through from Hawick to Carlisle in 1859 and thus gave the east coast alliance a better chance to compete with the Caledonian and Scottish Central for traffic to the south. At the same time the 'Stirling Agreement' between the Dundee and Perth Railway and the west coast companies was terminated, giving a boost to the conveyance of goods across the Tay to Tayport for the first time in five years. The agreement involved the Scottish Central, the Edinburgh and Glasgow (E&G), the Scottish North Eastern, and both the Dundee and Perth and the Edinburgh, Perth and Dundee, and meant that all goods and mineral trains had been routed to Glasgow and north-west England via Perth, avoiding the Tay crossing at Broughty Ferry.

The increased the use of the ferry crossings put pressure on the existing service and a new boat was ordered to cope with the greater traffic over the Forth, being delivered in October 1860. Stimulated by discontent over the EP&DR service from Dunfermline to Edinburgh via Burntisland, the North British threatened to create a new line over the Forth. The E&G in turn suggested an alternative branch to their route to Glasgow and so forced the EP&DR into secret negotiations with the North British.

This led to a rapid reorganising of the programme of Bills to be presented to Parliament in 1860 and, in September 1861, a formal announcement that the North British and the Edinburgh, Perth and Dundee intented to amalgamate. The advantage of a more certain financial return with the North British was seen as the incentive for the EP&DR's shareholders and through an Act (25 and 26 Vic. cap. clxxxix), on 29th July, 1862, the North British finally absorbed the Edinburgh, Perth and Dundee Railway. In order to keep the cost of merging the two companies to a minimum ingenious ways were found to save money. For example, the new owners saved on a new livery simply by adding a garter marked 'North British Railway Company 1862' round the EP&DR crest on the side of the coaches to transform them to their own.

The Act also unified all the individual companies in Fife and gave the enlarged Edinburgh company a powerful route to Dundee and the north. Now, more than ever before, the logical step from this union was the construction of bridges over the Forth and the Tay to cope with the steadily increasing traffic and to compete with the aspiring Caledonian. The North British were not slow to recognise the value of the slab lands along the river frontage at Dundee. As the Scottish Central Railway, the new owner of the D&PR, was planning to improve its station at Dundee West in 1864, the NBR took the opportunity to purchase two plots of land stretching down from the Nethergate, Dundee to the SCR property. This was the first chance to lay claim to the access the company needed if it was to bridge the Tay.

The original Edinburgh and Northern station on the down side at Cupar in 1971.

Gerald Baxter

An 1878 engraving of the still incomplete first Tay Bridge from the southern end.

Author's Collection

The first Tay bridge from Wormit, showing the foundry and erection of the girders in the mid-1870s.

Dundee District Libraries

Chapter Six

The Tay Bridges
1869-1887

'Beautiful Railway Bridge of the Silv'ry Tay!
Alas! I am very sorry to say
That ninety lives have been taken away.'
William McGonagall, Poet and Tragedian

Since the North British Railway had won the monopoly of railways in Fife, it could now turn its attention to developing traffic from England to the east coast of Scotland. With the Berwick and Waverley routes forming part of the company's domain, it had an opportunity to develop passenger and freight services which had hitherto been the preserve of the Caledonian. Indeed, the North British was under some insistence from its English partners to improve the route to the north. Until the rivers Forth and Tay could be crossed more economically, however, the line through Fife was simply known as the Northern Section and administered separately from the main operations of the company.

The Caledonian, meanwhile, was also set on extending its empire. By absorbing the Scottish Central and the Scottish North Eastern Railways, both in 1865, which in their turn had previously assimilated most of the lesser lines in the north-east, the Caley had succeeded in dominating the very country which the North British had set its sights upon. Even if the NBR could bridge the Firth of Forth and the Firth of Tay, there was nowhere for it to go, except by seeking running powers on the Caledonian or, more expensively, creating a brand new line from Dundee to Aberdeen.

The most effective crossing of the gaps was by bridge, but as bridging rivers the size of the Tay and the Forth had scarcely been contemplated before, let alone attempted, this seemed beyond the reach of reality. James Anderson, an Edinburgh civil engineer had experimented with wood and iron in 1817 to create a 'bridge of chains' over the Forth, but the idea was abandoned. Enter, once again, Thomas Bouch who had provided an earlier solution to crossing the two estuaries with the Floating Railway. Although his invention was a success, Bouch the engineer had aspirations to provide a more satisfactory and permanent solution to the problem of the Firths. He had taken up the position of General Manager of the Edinburgh and Northern Railway shortly before his 27th birthday on 13th January, 1849 with the intention of finding ways to cross the two estuaries. Bouch was an ambitious man who believed that he could design bridges to span each river and told his employers so. As railway management held no appeal for him, he had resigned in April 1851, and set up his own engineering consultancy in St David's Street, Edinburgh, from where he had taken on work ranging from setting out London Tramways to engineering several light railways in Scotland (*see Chapter Five*).

The North British met considerable opposition from a consortium of West Coast companies over the idea of such bridges as well as a great deal of doubt from the public. Despite this, Bouch drew up plans for a gigantic bridge over the Forth, from Blackness on the south shore to Charlestown in Fife, over three miles long and 150 feet high, progressing as far as sinking a pier during the winter of 1864. But the Tay was seen as a far easier river crossing, and on Monday 18th October, 1864, Bouch was invited by Thomas Thornton of Dundee solicitors Patullo and Thornton to outline his plans for a two mile-long bridge over the river to a group of townsmen of Dundee. He had been approached by Thornton a year earlier, but nothing had come of the meeting.

Supported by Baillie Yeaman, a Dundee Town Councillor and James Cox the town's leading millowner, a large and enthusiastic public meeting gathered in the old Town House, better known to Dundonians as *The Pillars*. Included were merchants, spinners and shopkeepers, like Mr Phin of Perth Road, all of whom assembled in the council chambers to hear Bouch outline his grand vision for the impossible - a bridge over the Tay.

The structure was to cross from Newport to Craig Pier at the foot of Union Street on 65 spans and curve westwards into Dundee to a new station in the town. This would have meant that through trains to the north would have had to reverse there. However, the meeting was supportive of Bouch's scheme and at once financial backing was pledged. Notice was given in Parliament on 15th November, 1864 of a Bill to incorporate the new company, and construct the bridge. This was quickly followed on the 8th December by the issue of a prospectus for the Tay Bridge and Dundee Union Railway Undertaking, offering 14,000 shares of £25 to raise the proposed capital of £350,000.

Earlier bridges had been proposed, one as far back as 1842 when a bridge from Craighead, Newport to Craig Harbour, Dundee was suggested, coincidentally, just upstream of the line taken by the present road bridge. In 1864, a slightly longer structure was considered this time between Tayport and Stannergate on the Dundee and Arbroath line. However, the NBR suffered a financial crisis in the mid-1860s culminating in 1866 with a committee of inquiry. The crisis was due to the rising costs of construction for the expansion programme which the company had undertaken, as well as the need to replace decaying rolling stock from the companies which had been taken over. The Directors found themselves unable to make a subscription to the new bridge undertaking.

Subsequently, this led to the abandonment in May 1865 of the scheme to cross the firth, much to the relief of the several railway companies which had joined with Dundee Harbour Trustees and both Dundee and Perth Town Councils to oppose the Tay Bridge project. The railways would have suffered a loss of traffic had either bridge been built. The Scottish Central, which had taken over the Dundee and Perth in 1863, and Scottish North Eastern, which had acquired the Dundee and Arbroath in the same year, were both under threat from the aspiring Caledonian, itself worried by North British intentions. A second scheme was proposed by the NB in November and withdrawn the following year.

In the wake of the 1866 financial debacle John Stirling of Kippendavie had been elected NBR Chairman, despite the fact that he had sold the SNER to the Caledonian under the noses of the North British, being rewarded in turn with a Caledonian Directorship. The deal with the Caley included an assurance that the Glasgow company would not oppose the Tay Bridge and would place the

Dundee and Arbroath under joint ownership with the NBR, once a bridge was open. The SNER capture in 1866, along with that of the SCR in 1865, gave the Caledonian control over all the routes directly into Dundee.

The NBR had to pay £10,000 per annum for the privilege of its trains being 'shunted into Dundee on a Caledonian branch' from Broughty Ferry. This was a significant cost and would be saved if there was an NBR line into Dundee by way of the bridge. On the 7th September, 1869, in more financially secure times for the NBR, Baillie Cox, Thornton and both Dundee Town Council and the Harbour Trustees met Bouch and Stirling at Dundee to resurrect the Tay Bridge proposal. Stirling was enthusiastic about reviving the idea knowing the savings he could make on the ferry tolls alone. As an independent venture, the new undertaking was promised a dividend of 5¼ per cent guaranteed by the NBR.

The idea of an iron structure across the Tay estuary caught the Victorian imagination and support was more enthusiastic than ever. Bouch drew up his estimates and submitted them to the NBR Board on 27th October; Stirling wasted no time in inviting tenders for construction. Two offers arrived the following day! The plans for the bridge were scrutinised by an independent engineer, Thomas Harrison, who declared 'great care has been taken in the design and it is sufficiently strong in all its parts'.

A subscription list was opened and several of the Dundee supporters were among the first to pledge for shares. £350,000 was sought and a memorandum was published confirming the North British would pay 5¼ per cent on any surplus. Of the first subscribers on the list when it opened on 29th November, James Cox, as Chairman of the Undertaking and a Director of the NBR, took 200 shares, George Carmichael, Provost Yeaman and Thomas Buchan amongst many others each took 20. At a special meeting in Edinburgh on 12th December, 1869, the shareholders of the North British gave their approval to the plan for a bridge. It was to be sited west of Dundee to appease the Harbour Trustees who had been asked for £50,000 toward the construction of a structure that would offer substantial competition. The crossing was to be made from Wormit to the 'Binns of Blackness', having a central section high enough for shipping to pass beneath on the way to Perth, a step which would remove the objections from that town.

A Bill was deposited and, despite petty objections from the Caledonian, was passed as the North British Railway (Tay Bridge and Railways) Act on 15th July, 1870 by which time arrangements were well in hand for construction. The Board of Trade gave its permission to reduce the height of the proposed structure by 20 ft to 80 ft. There was a time limit of five years put on the construction of the bridge. The contractors who won the tender were Messrs Butler and Pitts of Leeds with an offer to build the single track bridge for £229,000. Bouch was unhappy that the company had pre-empted the Act, believing that the work could be done for as little as £190,000, had the Board waited for Parliamentary approval. However, the contractor got no further than bringing some equipment to the site before Pitts, the senior and moneyed partner died, and the company asked to be released from its obligations. With a new tender of £217,000, Charles de Bergue of London was next to be appointed, but not until 8th May, 1871, promising the work would be complete in three years.

The foundation stone was laid with modest ceremony on Saturday 22nd July, 1871 by the son of William Paterson, one of Bouch's engineering staff. By October, the foundations of the first pier were being formed but a further development was to delay the construction once again. Charles de Bergue died on 10th April, 1873 with little progress having been made, only a few piers and one or two spans in place at the southern end where the works were situated. The responsibility for the company fell to the widow and daughter of de Bergue who struggled on but were faced with another substantial set back.

The survey which Bouch had sought before construction began maintained that the river bed was solid rock, but, at the fifteenth pier, the contractors found this rock was not continuous across the river. A further survey revealed that a thin layer of consolidated stones and gravel masked the true base which was mud clay and sand of an indefinite depth. The bridge was being built on a line with little or no substance to the sea bed beneath it.

Bouch was not to be beaten, and suggested to the North British Board that the problem could be overcome by lowering the weight of the piers. This would be achieved by abandoning the brickwork and instead making iron columns above the water line, thus reducing the pressure on the base from 4½ to 2¾ tons per square foot. As bridge construction on this scale was unknown, the NBR Board had no option but to accept Bouch's alterations to the plans. Three months after de Bergue's death the construction fell to another contractor, the Middlesbrough business of Hopkins Gilkes & Company who had built bridges for Bouch at Belah and elsewhere. Bouch persuaded Edgar Gilkes to keep the bridge building team which de Bergue had brought together, including Albert Grothe, a Dutchman, who had done much in and around Dundee to publicise the spectacular bridge. He continued as contract manager.

Bouch went on to make savings in the construction of the bridge, reducing the number of central navigable spans by one to an ominous thirteen. The piers were changed from two smaller bases to one large one but not large enough for the eight iron columns which Bouch originally planned. These were reduced to six, but the engineer was convinced that this would not lessen the strength of the structure. Gilkes retained de Bergue's recently created iron foundry near Wormit on the southern shore of the Tay.

The iron columns were cast there using Cleveland iron, amongst the poorest quality which the casters had seen. Scotch iron was normally added to Cleveland iron by Dundee foundries in order to raise the quality of the castings, so the casters on the bridge works were unhappy with using only Cleveland ore for their ironwork. They 'puddled' or stirred the molten metal to bring the impurities to the surface so that it could be skimmed off. However, the more they stirred the iron, the more impurities rose, suggesting that the finished casting was far from being unadulterated.

The wooden mouldings for the columns were set up with a solid core, but when the metal was poured, this core was not always central, leaving a variety of thickness to be found round the circumference. The columns themselves consisted of a series of these cast cylinders bolted together by the flanges; coupled with badly formed lugs for the cross bracing, the columns were not of the highest standard. The men who came from all over the kingdom to employment on the bridge were not skilled in the many trades and were hardly to blame for the quality of their work.

The foundry was one of the worst places on earth in which to work. The mouldings were usually made from sand damped by water, but the supply of fresh water from the pathetic well on site was so poor that they were compelled to use sea water. The resultant fumes when the hot metal met the salt water were so acrid as to drive the men from the casting shop. It was no wonder that many, including the foremen, were frequently drunk. Amongst the more dangerous jobs was the 'powder monkey' who carried the dynamite to blast the river bed for the creation of the foundations for the columns. In the winter, these boys usually carried the explosive in their clothes to keep it from becoming 'jumpy' in the cold.

The girders were assembled on the shore and floated into position before being raised on to the cast columns, each girder taking as long as four weeks to build and erect. The importance of inspection also escaped the contractors, for each completed component received little more than a cursory tap with a hammer to ensure its soundness. Many of the rivet holes were mis-shapen allowing one component to play against the next. Cracks in the crossbracing ironwork were frequent, and castings were repaired with a concoction known as Beaumont egg which was a wax and iron filings putty, indistinguishable from the casting when buffed and painted. There was a sense of competition between the two ends of the bridge, racing to see which could complete first. All this was contributing to the erection of the largest man made structure the world had yet seen.

Progress continued to be slow and with a particularly severe winter in 1875-6, time was repeatedly lost. A further Act was required in 1875 to take account of the delays since the time limit for completion was running out. This new Act acknowledged that the bridge was under construction and it was 'expedient to extend the time'. The North British were anxious to see the bridge complete as they were paying out 5¼ per cent whether the bridge was constructed or not. They offered Grothe an incentive of £2,000 if a local train were to cross the bridge on 1st September, 1877. The works created much interest among the dignitaries of the day. Among the eminent visitors in 1877, the Emperor of Brazil examined the construction, Prince Leopold fourth son of Victoria travelled over the extent of the bridge by wagon, and General Ulysses S. Grant sailed out from Tayport to inspect the bridge from below.

The winter of 1876-77 was less severe than its predecessor and the construction was steady. A pioneering electricity generator was set up by George Lowdon, an associate of James Bowman Lindsay, a Dundee scientist of repute. He installed the first dynamo in Scotland, generating power from the foundry engines and providing lighting for the whole works at Wormit. Considering the scope and novelty of the works, it is no surprise that there were several accidents. Leaky boilers exploded, machinery fell and crushed workmen, and the wind could pick up a man and hurl him into the inhospitable river whenever a storm blew up.

However, 2nd February, 1877 saw the most serious accident to date. The winter was severe that year, foreshadowing worse to come. Just as the steamer *Excelsior* was about to take off the workmen from the High Girders during a storm which had permitted only five days work that month, two recently erected spans were blown from the bridge. It was May before the girders were recovered from the river, but, despite this delay, Gilkes remained confident that the bridge would be finished in September. Hauled by *Lochee*, a four coach Director's special train made a fifteen minute crossing of the completed structure on 26th September, proudly displaying to the world that the North British Railway had succeeded in bridging the River Tay.

There was still the inspection on behalf of the Board of Trade to be carried out and for this purpose the NBR placed six new goods engines weighing a total of 440 tons and exerting 1½ tons per foot on the line. The inspection was completed by Major General Hutchinson after three days on the bridge, on 25th, 26th, and 27th February, 1878. The Major General was satisfied with the 'lateral oscillation', asserting that the masonry was substantial and the ironwork well put together. However, to reduce expansion in the warmer weather, the girders should be painted in white lead. The only other caveat expressed in an otherwise satisfactory report was to see 'the effect of high winds when a train of carriages is running over the bridge', and he limited the speed of trains to 25 mph.

Major Marindin passed the approaches to the bridge on 20th May with the exception of some minor signalling work which was nearly complete. The formal opening by James Cox took place on Friday 31st May, 1878 when over 1,500 travelled through Fife from Burntisland to cross the new bridge by several special trains. Following a ceremony at Tay Bridge station, 600 gentlemen retired to the Albert Institute for a modest lunch and presentation of the freedom of Dundee to Bouch and Stirling. Newspaper reports the following day commented on the 'modest ceremony as befits these adverse times.'

Bouch was responsible also for the supervision of the surveys and plans of the approach lines on both sides of the Firth. To join the bridge to the existing railway system, a direct line had been built from Leuchars Junction through St Fort to the southern end along with a new line into Dundee from the northern end, crossing over the recently extended Esplanade and falling to a new station near Craig Pier. The line continued east from the station in a cut and cover tunnel for 616 yards along the edge of Earl Grey and King William Docks, before emerging adjacent to the Dundee and Arbroath terminus at Camperdown Junction.

A joint committee did their best to ensure the works at the Dundee side were undertaken with all interests considered. They had contracted the works on the Dundee side to John Waddell of Bathgate and Edinburgh on 22nd July, 1871, even before the plans for the new station had been submitted, the proposals eventually being considered on 21st February, 1872. The committee was anxious about the speed of preparatory work necessary as the land was recovered from the river's northern margins. Members insisted on 28th September, 1874 that Waddell should fill in the land taken from the river for the station as the bridge might be completed before the land works! This was followed on 12th November by a reminder to the North British Board of the need to proceed with the filling in.

In fairness to Waddell, there was a substantial amount of land-fill necessary for the new station, to be built to the south of the Dundee and Perth station, behind a new sea wall on the western mudflats adjacent to Craig Pier. In May 1877, Waddell confirmed his intention to 'push the work with the greatest of vigour possible'. He was keen to make use of the bridge in August, as soon as the rails were laid across, for he wished to remove the silt from the river bed and deposit it on the Fife side. This was not looked upon very favourably by Bouch who was anxious that the ties on the bridge should be properly tightened first.

The Dundee Sea Wall, Esplanade and Streets Act had been passed in 1868, to transfer to the town council the Queen's rights to the foreshore. Its passing had simplified the discussions between the town and the railway companies. There had been a dispute between the various railway companies which owned the Perth line and the council over the value of the infilled land at Yeaman Shore and to the west where the railway works were constructed. Expensive litigation in 1864 had remained unresolved, an offer of the intervening land at £500 being fraught with difficult conditions and the sale was abandoned. The NBR and CR contributed equally to the cost of erection of the sea wall and the land behind the wall was given to the companies.

The railway companies had procured rights from the Commissioners of Woods and Forests, independently from the Magistrates of Dundee and in 1867 the Caley had a Bill to acquire 15 acres of foreshore to the south of its station to Craig House, on the site of the land the NB wished for their Tay Bridge station. Provision for this was inserted in the Tay Bridge Railway and Station Act of 1866. The North British reached agreement with the Caledonian on 26th February the following year settling £4,000 for the land including the 15 acres, plus £13,000 contribution to the sea wall to allow the land behind to fall to them.

For the benefit of the expanding population of Dundee, a promenade was built along the sea wall forming a new river frontage between the railway property and the Tay from Craig Pier to Magdalen Point, the bridge landfall. The Esplanade, as it was called, was opened in July 1875 and was described as 'one of the finest marine parades or promenades in the country, part of it being laid out with trees'. The escalating cost of Dock Street tunnel was reported to the Tay Bridge joint committee on 19th May, 1877. The price, initially estimated at £56,000, had risen to £92,812 due to the need for brick to line the tunnel and new rails, instead of the reused ones which had originally been envisaged. The cost had risen even further to £95,774 by the 28th June. The tunnel, being below sea level and immediately adjacent to the town's docks, was continually subject to water seepage, making it wet and the track slippery, doing nothing for adhesion.

The North British built Tay Bridge station as an island with central platforms 476 yards long. Access for the public was either from a staircase leading from South Union Street to the eastern end, or down stairs inside the station building which was 380 feet long and constructed on the island platform, with short links at street level across the up line at platform one to the upper floors. The building was constructed of what was described as 'soft-hued grey stone from Bannockburn'. Finishings were carried out by a variety of local tradesmen, including Mackie the plumber, McRitchie the plasterer and Buttar the slater, the whole described in the newspapers as having 'extensive lavatory accommodation, porter's room, hot water room, three classes of ladies waiting room, gentlemen's waiting rooms, three waiting rooms of different classes, left luggage room, luggage and parcels lifts, station master's room and ticket offices.'

The first revenue earning train was on Saturday 1st June, 1878, a goods train with cattle from Fife for a Dundee slaughterhouse. The regular passenger service began with the 6.25 am and 7.15 am trains to Edinburgh. Almost 850 passengers travelled on the first scheduled service to cross the bridge. The Caledonian noted in its timetable that there were no longer ferries on the Tay crossing, omitting to indicate that they had been superseded by the bridge!

The North British complied with the inspector's request to limit the speed of trains, by issuing a notice to all drivers restricting passenger trains to 25 mph, goods trains to 20 mph and ballast trains to 15 mph. Sadly, for the bridge's condition, this was regularly disregarded. With signal boxes at either end, the single line bridge was a self contained single line block section, operated by Tyer's Block Telegraph and train staff and ticket. No more than one train was allowed on to the bridge at any one time. Prior to opening, control was exercised through a pilotman. Some goods were still taken by the Tayport to Broughty Ferry route, a passenger service also being retained until the beginning of 1879.

Local services to St Andrews were started, linking Dundee to the university town. The Newport Railway, incorporated by an Act of 1866 (and extended in 1867, 1870, and 1873) began services along the Fife coast from Wormit to Tayport from 1st May, 1879. The route left the bridge on a sharp eastern curve, with three stations at Wormit, West, and East Newport and joining up with the original line at Tayport station. Newport expanded as a suburb of Dundee as a result of the new line and the North British provided a regular commuter service over the river. There was even a pipe to carry fresh water from the reservoirs in Angus to the growing community in Fife.

The last train to cross the Tay Bridge on Sunday 28th December, 1879 was the 5.50 pm local from Newport. There had been a storm blowing down the Tay estuary for several hours but by evening, the wind had become violent, gusting to over 60 mph. At 4.15 pm, passengers had boarded the Dundee train in Edinburgh and just over an hour later had crossed the tempestuous Forth by the ferry *John Stirling* and re-joined the train of five coaches and brakevan at Burntisland pier for the run to Dundee. The locomotive was No. 224, a 4-4-0 Wheatley design which had been pressed into service due to the usual engine needing repair.

When the Newport train arrived in Dundee at 6.10 pm, the crew and passengers told of their concern as they crossed the bridge, taking the full force of the gale and causing their wheels to create sparks as they were forced against the guard rails of the single track through the high girders or central spans. By 7 o'clock, No. 224 and the Edinburgh train had left Leuchars, and set off for St Fort, which served as a ticket platform before arrival in Dundee.

Bouch's bridge was taking a pounding by this time. The poorly cast columns and the hundreds of subsequent inadequate repairs were put under the greatest pressure they were ever likely to suffer. Bolts were being loosened, joints were being strained from the vibrations set up by the wind. In addition the piers

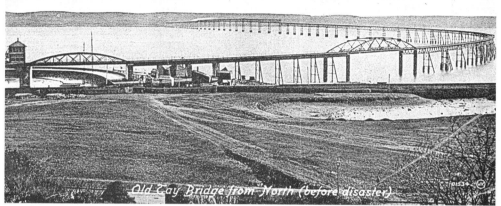

The original Bridge from Esplanade station in 1878.   *Author's Collection*

The original Tay Bridge from the Wormit side in 1880, after the fall of the High Girders.
Author's Collection

Old Tay Bridge Disaster,
Last standing Pier at North End.

The northern end of the gap left by the fall of the High Girders in 1880 on the original Tay Bridge.

Author's Collection

were taking a battering from the turbulent river. What happened at 7.20 pm, when the Edinburgh train moved on to the stressed and shaking structure, will for ever be a matter of conjecture, perhaps best saved for elsewhere. Whether the trembling girders finally shook their last, a coach was blown off the track and collided with the high girders or was derailed, or even a combination of those and other unknown factors may forever remain a riddle.

Whatever did occur, the Edinburgh train fell at the height of the storm as it crossed through the high girders, with the loss of 75 lives, both passengers and company servants and a relief Post Office guard, travelling with the mails. Initially, over 300 were feared to have perished as many people might normally have travelled on the Sunday train. This was revised to one hundred, with some onlookers, hopeful of compensation, claiming to have relatives on board, giving rise to McGonagall's poetic claim that 'ninety lives' had been taken away.

A thorough investigation into the design, construction, maintenance and use of the bridge was undertaken immediately. The Court of Inquiry opened on Saturday 3rd January, 1880 at the Dundee Courthouse and a relief fund was established. The NBR Directors subscribed £500 from the company and £60 each privately. Bouch gave £250 and by 19th January £4,725 had been raised reaching £5,600 a month later. The inquiry resumed in Dundee in late February and transferred to London on 19th April, during which time the story of the slipshod workmanship, poor supervision and inadequate repairs began to unfold.

On 5th July, the inquiry report was published having been presented to both Houses of Parliament at the end of June. It placed the blame for the loss of the bridge on poor standards in all of these aspects, but a minority report was issued by H.C. Rothery, Commissioner for Wrecks and a member of the tribunal. He went further than his two colleagues, Barlow and Yolland and condemned Bouch for lack of care throughout the project. This was enough to destroy the engineer who had received a knighthood for his bridge the previous summer.

Work on the Forth Bridge, to which Bouch had turned his attention since the opening of his Tay Bridge, was stopped directly and Bouch lost his position as consultant to the North British. The company wanted to have no more connection with the man who had helped them to cross the Tay and beat the Caledonian. Bouch was a broken man and, retiring to Moffat, he died in October having failed to recover from a cold. Ironically, No.224 was salvaged on 8th April, 1880 and found to have suffered very little damage. She was rebuilt and put back to work on regular duties crossing the very bridge which had been her downfall. She spent her last days either around Dundee when employed on the North Fife line or in the Borders, although she was known from then on, in the way railwaymen nickname their locomotives, as 'The Diver'.

In order to re-establish confidence with its passengers, John Stirling took an early step on the 9th January for the NBR to promote the reconstruction of the bridge. The Board approved a scheme which was prepared by Sir James Brunlees the prominent Scottish engineer. He petitioned Parliament to dispense with Standing Orders and allow the Bill to be included in the present session. It was presented by coincidence on Friday 2nd July, 1880, only three days before the report of the inquiry was made public. The Bill had its opponents at the second reading, who felt that the NBR should not be allowed to rush a new Bill through for a 'patching up' of Bouch's 'miserable old structure'. The member for Perth tried to delay the proceedings and generate concern by maintaining that Bouch had signed the specifications for the new bridge, but the President of the Board of Trade vehemently denied this assertion.

The opponents succeeded in remitting the Bill for further consideration by a committee of seven members as to whether the bridge should 'be rebuilt in its present position or whether there is any situation more suitable'. The seven advised that the scheme should not be authorised but that the location at least was the most suitable. They believed the bridge would be safer if it was erected on new foundations and lowered in height. To lend weight to any future plans, the committee wished them to be shown to two or three independent engineers.

William H. Barlow, a member of the Board of Trade Inquiry and by then the President of the Institution of Civil Engineers, had been invited by the North British to advise the company on the replacement bridge. He was an Engineer of repute having participated in the building of the Clifton Suspension bridge at Bristol, sufficient reputation to appoint him engineer to the new bridge. Barlow set about examining the original structure, applying load tests on the piers and considering the effect of the tidal and fast flowing river on the brickwork. Even on the weakest part of the river bed, the settlement of the sand did not fluctuate after the initial stresses had been applied.

Of the several options which Barlow considered, including widening the original bridge or linking a new structure alongside, he suggested a completely new and independent bridge. By building it adjacent to the original but 60 feet upstream, several of the sound girders could be reused in the new bridge and there would be easy access via the first bridge for both men and materials. A Bill for a bridge of Barlow's design was deposited in time for the 1881 session of Parliament.

The citizens of Dundee were generally in favour of the bridge being rebuilt lower than its predecessor but not so the people of Perth, concerned more for access for their shipping. The disagreement between the two towns grew more acrimonious, so much so that in February 1881, Joseph Chamberlain, President of the Board of Trade, had to arbitrate. He listened to two deputations, one from each town, on the merits of their respective cases. That from Dundee was by all accounts better organised with several members of both Houses of Parliament in support of the lower bridge, while the Perth delegation could barely muster assistance from their own MPs for the higher structure. Chamberlain's only promise was that the Tay would be bridged once more.

The North British wanted the Commons to waive Standing Orders once more to enable their plans for the lower bridge to be considered, but the House was not to be persuaded so easily a second time. Delay was the last thing that the NBR wanted and therefore the Barlow plan was left to go ahead. A victory for Perth despite the poor representation of their case. The Select Committee reported favourably on the Barlow plan with several *caveats* about the design and safety of its construction, thus clearing the way for the North British Railway (New Tay Bridge Viaduct) Bill to become law in July 1881. This was to be a point of discord at the outset, for a condition of the Act was that the old structure should be completely removed to the satisfaction of the Board of Trade. Any remnant of that symbol of failed Victorian engineering would not be left to form a blot on future projects.

However, Barlow intended to use parts of the old bridge so the structure could not be removed first. The ensuing argument gave rise to the very delay that the North British wanted to avoid although it was eventually settled by 22nd June, 1882. William Arrol & Company of Glasgow, whose tender had been previously accepted in October 1881, were able to begin work on the preparatory stages almost immediately. The foundations were commenced on 6th July, 1883 and so the four year construction of the new bridge was underway. The whole subject of the demolition of the first bridge remained a matter of contention with the Board of Trade until the NBR gave an undertaking to Parliament in 1885 that they would remove every part of the original, except for the piers which could be retained as cutwaters against the incoming tide. Five of the piers had to be removed to fifteen feet below low water level.

Barlow's double-track design was substantial, but was primarily determined by the spacing which Bouch had determined for the first bridge since the navigable channels had to be kept clear for shipping to Newburgh and Perth. The plans were entrusted to Barlow's son, Crawford, who had assisted his father on previous railways in England. Barlow senior drew up a robust design, unimaginative in appearance, but sufficient to convince the concerned Victorians that the second Tay Bridge would not suffer the same fate as its predecessor. This was reinforced by a further condition in the Act which required that pier foundations be tested to at least 33 per cent more than the maximum pressure they would ever be likely to experience. Whatever else, the Victorians were not going to permit their pride to be dented a second time by a defective bridge over the Tay. The comparative details of both bridges are:

	Bouch's Bridge	*Barlow's Bridge*
Length	10,395 feet	10,711 feet
No. of piers	85	85
Southern approach	piers 1 to 29	piers 1 to 28
High Girders	piers 29 to 41	piers 28 to 41
Northern approach	piers 41 to 85	piers 41 to 85
Southern gradient	Down, then up 1:490	Down 1:762
High Girders	Level	Level
Northern approach	Down 1:130, then 1:74	Down 1:113.5
Height at navigable channel	88 feet	77 feet
Cost	£350,000	£670,000

The need to build a strong bridge left Barlow with little scope for imagination and the new structure has a solid rather than graceful appearance. Ingenuity, however was to be found in some of the methods of construction, for William Arrol devised several improvements to existing techniques including the transporting and raising of the new spans over the navigation channels.

One hundred and eighteen of the original, sound, girders were used in pairs as part of the construction of the new bridge, forming part of the additional

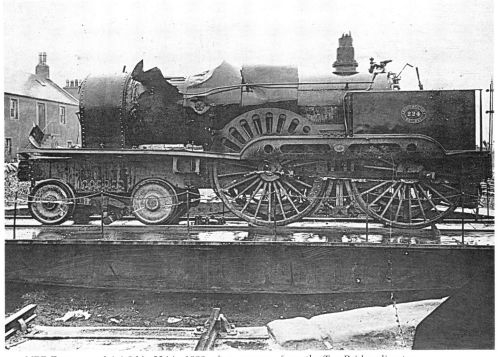

NBR Drummond 4-4-0 No 224 in 1880, after recovery from the Tay Bridge disaster.

Dundee District Libraries

The girders from the first bridge are transferred to the second, while the new High Girders are constructed at Wormit in the mid-1880s.

Dundee District Libraries

strengthening. A uniquely designed pontoon was employed, using the incoming tide to raise the old girders off the old bridge one at a time and float them across the sixty foot gap to the new. The pontoon had telescopic legs to raise the girder the remaining distance to its new position in the centre of each span. Thus in place, the new girders could be transported by trolleys along the old to their location on the outside of the span.

The piers were built as two columns of brickwork round a concrete centre, all created within an iron caisson floated out by means of another of Arrol's inventions, a pontoon with adjustable legs. As the Act required, each pier was load tested by applying half ton iron blocks to produce almost 2,500 tons of pressure per pier. Life was hectic for Arrol in the 1880s for he was involved in the construction of both the Forth Bridge and Tower Bridge at the same time. His timetable took him to the Forth two days, the Tay for one and with a day at his Glasgow works this left the weekend to travel to the Thames in order to oversee the work at each site!

Once the bridge was far enough progressed, the contractor employed a small 0-4-0ST outside cylinder locomotive to service the various works along the line. Built by Andrew Barclay in 1882, this locomotive was first owned by the builder of the Paisley Canal line and brought to the Tay by Arrol around 1885. On the completion of the bridge, it was transferred to the Forth Bridge work.

At a total cost of one million pounds, the bridge and its improved approaches were ready for traffic in the summer of 1887, the first 'official' train being a special for the Directors of the company. The special ran on Friday 10th June from Queensferry, where an inspection of the construction of the new Forth bridge was made. The following Monday, some goods trains began to make use of the crossing, and all before the bridge had passed inspection from the Board of Trade.

The completed bridge was inspected on 16th, 17th and 18th June, 1887 by the Board of Trade's inspectors including Colonel Rich and Major-General Hutchinson, the same inspectors as had inspected the first bridge. Although they were concerned at the five piers below water level, they believed it was undesirable to remove them. (Eventually, in 1888, the company was relieved by Parliament of the responsibility of removing all the remaining vestiges of the five sunken piers of the old bridge.) A full load test of 16 six-coupled goods locomotives was undertaken, eight on each track run at slow speed to examine the effect on both piers and girders. The deflection on the imposing ironwork was virtually nil and following this examination, the Board of Trade inspectors pronounced themselves satisfied. The resultant tragedy if the bridge had not been adequate for the weight of 16 locomotives does not bear contemplation!

Later in the day, after the formal approval had been given verbally, a party of Dundee Town Councillors and 200 prominent citizens took another special to Newport. The first revenue-earning passenger train crossed on Monday 20th June, 1887, the fiftieth anniversary of the Queen's accession to the throne. Once again passengers and freight could cross the Tay by rail and when the Forth bridge, the final piece in the picture, was completed in 1890, the North British Railway was restored to its pre-eminent position with a complete and commanding line from Edinburgh to the north.

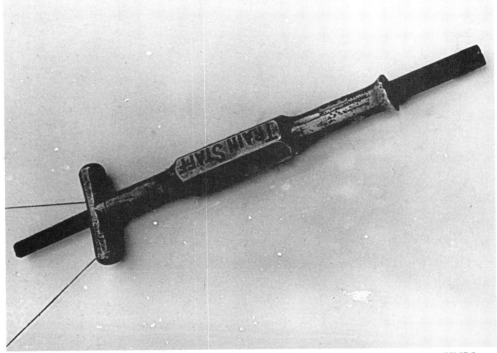

The train staff used on the single line over the original Tay Bridge. *HMRS*

Esplanade station with a NB stopping train departing for Fife. Note the coal trader's wagons in the NB coach sidings. *Author's Collection*

TAY BRIDGE,
DUNDEE

An aerial view of the Tay Bridge with the railway owned recovered land along the river edge.

Author's Collection

Wormit station, at the southern end of the Tay Bridge. *Author's Collection*

Chapter Seven

The Dundee Locomotive Building Industry
Its Men and Machines
1829-1852

'We already have a rising trade in locomotives - there are six in course of being constructed in Dundee at present and there may be more.'
Dundee Courier 1838

As Dundee has been a significant textile town from its early days, it was natural for there to be a progression in the development of power for the mill machinery from water to steam. The first application of this new resource was in 1815, and by 1822 there were seven mills in the town with steam assistance, although the most powerful engine was only 25 hp. By 1830, 13 establishments, including a flour mill, a bone grinder, and two foundries had steam engines in use. The two foundries were J. & C. Carmichael and the Dundee Foundry Company, both of which soon turned their hand to producing engines for themselves.

Carmichael's had been established in 1810 when James and his brother Charles, who was eight years younger, joined forces at West Ward Foundry, Guthrie Street, in the rapidly expanding textile manufacturing area at the bottom of the Scouring Burn to the north-west of the town. James was a dour but inventive man and among his ideas devised universally accepted tables for the specification of cog wheels. As well as the foundry, the brothers owned a forge and a shipyard at Seabraes, Dundee which gave them opportunities to expand their work.

Since both brothers were millwrights, they had concentrated on work for the flax spinning mills, but the construction of steam driven engines was soon undertaken. The first steamboat built on the Tay was launched in 1814 and fitted with a Carmichael engine. It was followed in 1821 by *George IV* (*see Chapter Five*) the first of two steam driven ferries across the Tay, *Union* following in 1822. These were unusual craft with twin hulls placed eight feet apart and a central paddle wheel. Horizontal beams were placed over the two divisions and covered by decking, beneath which cattle and carriages could be carried. They cost between £4,000 and £5,000 each, and were built at Perth, the Carmichael engines having castings from the Dundee Foundry. James made a significant improvement to them when he invented a valve gear that allowed reverse running. His invention was adapted in later years for the *Hibernia*, built by Sharp, Roberts in 1834, one of the locomotives of the Dublin and Kingstown Railway and for other locomotives in France and the USA.

Thomas Grainger, the engineer, was invited by the coal lords of Midlothian to plan a railway from the Dalkeith area south of Edinburgh to the coast, and in October 1831, two months before the Dundee and Newtyle, the Edinburgh and Dalkeith Railway was opened to the same 'Scotch' gauge of 4 ft 6 in. with steep inclines and horse-drawn wagons also reminiscent of the D&NR. The Carmichael brothers were asked in 1829 to build an engine for the inclined plane at the St Leonard's end of the line. This was the precursor of the engines for the three inclined planes on the Dundee and Newtyle. The company was contracted by the D&NR to build the three stationary engines installed for haulage up the inclines created on that railway (*see Chapter Two*).

James Carmichael is known to have had his own copy of the authoritative work of the 1820s, Nicholas Wood's *Treatise on Railroads* and this, coupled with experience in building steam engines, could well have led to the order for the first two steam locomotives on the Dundee and Newtyle. These were to an unusual design with bell crank levers and the first trailing bogies on any locomotive up to that time. The first was an 0-2-4, No. 1 *Earl of Airlie*, delivered in September 1833 followed by its sister 0-2-4, No. 2 *Lord Wharncliffe* later that month.

Richard Roberts used a similar design in his locomotive, *Experiment*, for the Liverpool and Manchester Railway. This engine incorporated the vertical cylinder and bell crank principle and was built by Sharp, Roberts in 1833. James's son-in-law, Peter is believed to have visited the Liverpool and Manchester Railway to see the locomotive. Sadly, the brothers were not good businessmen and the company was in financial difficulties by the end of the 1830s. These problems had put paid to their episode of locomotive building and they expanded the marine engine and shipbuilding work. However, this stretched the resources of the Carmichael brothers and work was then concentrated on the foundry business.

A second foundry company in Dundee was formed by a partnership between John Stirling, who was originally a farmer from Methven in Perthshire, and William Stratton, a Dundee iron founder. It was from Stratton that the castings were bought by J. & C. Carmichael for the steam engines which they installed in the ferries *Union* and *George IV*. However it was John's son, James Stirling, who made the company well known at the time for the construction of steam locomotives. James was born in 1800 and originally was destined for a life in the church but changed his studies to mechanical engineering. He completed his apprenticeship in Glasgow before moving back to become manager of his father's foundry. James invented a patent air engine in which steam was replaced by air and in 1827 one of these machines was installed at the Dundee Foundry premises between Seagate and Dock Street.

Once again the shipbuilding industry proved to be the starting point for steam engine manufacturing in the town, when the Dundee Perth and London Shipping Company placed an order worth £1,200 with the Dundee Foundry for engines for its new ship *William Wallace*. The first steam locomotive to be built there was the *Trotter*. It was to James Carmichael's design and was delivered in March 1834 as No. 3 to the Dundee & Newtyle Railway. Subsequently, James Stirling was a shareholder in both this latter and the Dundee & Arbroath Railway. The foundry built five locomotives in 1839 for the Arbroath and Forfar Railway, but none for its sister enterprise, the D&AR. The first three were 2-2-2s with No. 1 *Victoria* delivered to the line early in 1839 on 3rd January; although originally it was to be named *Robert Bruce*, the Board believed that this would not be appropriate and renamed it after the monarch.

Victoria was involved in an accident shortly after the opening of the line which was blamed on the manufacturer and as a result Stirlin'gs reduced the account

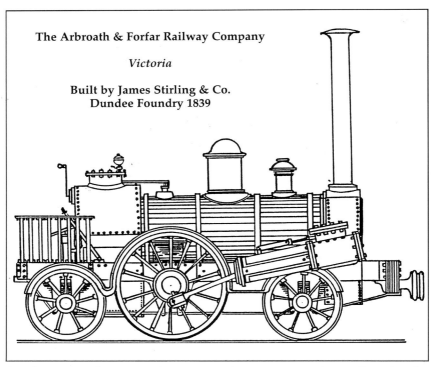

The Arbroath & Forfar Railway Company

Victoria

**Built by James Stirling & Co.
Dundee Foundry 1839**

for the Arbroath and Forfar Railway by £10 3s. 11¼d. to allow for the 'derangement' of the locomotive. *Caledonian* was delivered on 8th February, 1839 and *Britannia* on 14th May. By the end of May, the locomotives were giving trouble again and James Gow, locomotive superintendent, requested the wheels of No. 1 be turned and supplied with iron tyres. The last three of the locomotives, including two 0-4-2s delivered in 1840 and 1841, were not retained by the A&FR when the line was regauged but were sold by auction for £607 on 21st December, 1848. The first two were not very reliable and up to £1,800 was spent on their repair.

The Stirling family went on to distinguish itself in the next generation through Patrick Stirling who was James' nephew. Born in 1820 at Kilmarnock, the son of Reverend Robert S. Stirling, Patrick was apprenticed to his uncle at the Dundee Foundry in 1837 and assisted in the building of the five Arbroath and Forfar locomotives. He left Dundee in 1843 to work on marine engines at the Vulcan Foundry before becoming shop foreman at Neilson and Co. and works manager at Hawthorn's of Newcastle. Patrick was later locomotive superintendent of the Caledonian and Dumbarton Joint Railway and the Glasgow & South Western Railway. He was succeeded in 1866 in this last position by James Stirling (his younger brother), when he moved to be locomotive superintendent of the Great Northern Railway. His famous eight foot singles produced a celebrated performance in the Railway Races of 1895 (*see Chapter Nine*).

There were, however, other famous engineering names connected with the Stirlings. For a year before Patrick Stirling's arrival at the Dundee Foundry, an 18 year old Daniel Gooch was employed there. From January 1835 until January 1836, he worked with James Stirling as a draughtsman before moving on to Newcastle where he was employed by Robert Stephenson & Co. for a few months before moving again, this time to the Gateshead works of Robert Hawks. After a disagreement and a period without work, Gooch eventually found himself working for Isambard Kingdom Brunel at the Great Western Railway in 1837, as the first locomotive superintendent there.

Another notable name who served with Stirling was Archibald Sturrock who worked alongside Gooch at the Dundee Foundry. He was born in Angus on 30th September, 1816 and was apprenticed to James Stirling in 1832. During his time there, he is believed to have assisted with the despatch of *Trotter* for the Dundee and Newtyle Railway in 1834. Sturrock left Stirling in 1839 and joined his former colleague, Gooch, on the GWR in 1840 as assistant locomotive superintendent. One of his early claims is to have driven home the first bolt in the framework of the new Swindon Works in 1843. At the recommendation of Gooch, he successfully applied (as one of 41 candidates) to become the locomotive superintendent for the GNR at Boston, succeeding Bury who relinquished responsibility on 27th March, 1850, before eventually taking up the same position at Doncaster in 1852 and retiring in 1866. Archibald Sturrock lived until New Year's Day, 1909 when he died in his 93rd year.

The Dundee Foundry changed hands in 1845 when James Stirling dissolved it in February of that year, leaving Gresholm Gourlay as manager in charge. After a troublesome year, the Dundee Foundry was under the control of Gourlay and the former engineer there, David Mudie. In December 1846, the Aberdeen Railway Company considered and rejected a tender from Gourlay, Mudie and Company for two locomotives. The newly formed Dundee, Perth and Aberdeen Railway did, however, place an order with Gourlay's in 1847/8 for two 0-4-0s, and, in 1849, the Dundee and Arbroath received two more engines. When they altered the gauge from 5 ft 6 in. to 4 ft 8½ in., the Arbroath and Forfar found that only Gourlay's was prepared to offer to alter and repair the two engines built in 1839 by Stirling at the Dundee Foundry. The company also ordered two new turntables from Gourlay's.

Another foundry, that of Kinmond, Hutton and Steel, came later to the locomotive construction industry in Dundee. William Kinmond was a partner in a flax spinners in Upper Pleasance, Lochee while James Steel and William Hutton were neighbours in Cotton Street. The company was established by 1837 at the Wallace Foundry in the north east of Dundee. Just as J. & C. Carmichael served the mills in the Scouring Burn area, so must the Wallace Foundry have served mills along the length of the Dens Burn.

On 8th December, 1837, Kinmond, Hutton and Steel offered what turned out to be the lowest tender for locomotives for the Arbroath and Forfar Railway. However, the Dundee Foundry won the contract, as it was believed that Kinmond, Hutton and Steel were too busy with an order for the six initial Dundee and Arbroath Railway locomotives to be able to complete their requirements in the requisite time. The Directors of the A&FR had some foresight for there was a severe fire at the Wallace Foundry on 22nd June, 1838 when the first D&AR locomotive was being erected. However, most of the engine was saved and work continued in other foundries throughout the town until the foundry could be rebuilt. The remaining five locomotives for the Dundee and Arbroath were duly completed and delivered by 1840.

Following these engines, Kinmond, Hutton and Steel built four in 1840/41 for the Glasgow, Paisley, Kilmarnock and Ayr Railway (GPK&AR), being 2-2-2s like the D&AR locomotives. The general design was that of John Miller (of Miller & Grainger), the company Engineer, but the builder was able to add his own touches to those he built. The locomotives were shipped in parts by sea from Dundee to Ayr where they were assembled on the line. One of them, No. 6 *Bruce*, hauled the first train from Glasgow to Ayr on 11th August, 1840 .

In 1843, Peter and William Kinmond, two nephews of the original William Kinmond became partners in the foundry, giving rise to the revised name of Kinmond's, Hutton and Steel. The company constructed two more locomotives for the GPK&AR, in 1843 and 1845, once again having a 2-2-2 wheel arrangement, and similar in design to the 1840 order. Four additional engines were built for the Dundee and Arbroath in 1846/7, by which time an order from the Dundee and Perth Railway for a further four was in hand.

These were boom years for the locomotive building industry in Dundee, for although only one major foundry was manufacturing at this time, orders were coming in from the many new railway companies springing up during the railway mania in Scotland. On 15th September, 1847 an order was placed by the Glasgow, Dumfries and Carlisle Railway for nine new locomotives. Work had just begun on the construction of this new line and the GPK&AR undertook to place orders for the rolling stock, which included another 31 engines from Hawthorn and from Bury. In 1846, Kinmond, Hutton and Steel delivered two 0-4-2 locomotives to the Aberdeen Railway Company.

By July 1847, however, William Hutton and James Steel had sold their shareholding to Peter Kinmond whereupon he and William the younger reformed the business as Messrs Kinmond and Company. The new partners remained at Wallace Foundry until 1852 and continued to make steam engines there. The nine locomotives were completed and delivered under the new ownership, the new works for the Glasgow, Dumfries and Carlisle Railway being far from complete. The line was joined to the GPK&AR by the end of 1850 at which time the two railways amalgamated to form the Glasgow and South Western Railway.

Also at this time, the Scottish North Eastern Railway Company ordered a small 0-4-0 engine from Kinmond's, although it was rebuilt as a pannier tank in 1855. During the early 1840s, the Edinburgh and Glasgow Railway had placed work with the Wallace Foundry, including an invitation to bid a price to construct a tender, and the purchase of a turning lathe. The Edinburgh, Perth and Dundee Railway Company paid £2,150 for an engine which was handed over by Kinmond's in December 1848. An offer of two more locomotives was rejected by the Aberdeen Railway as was a tender for 60 wagons.

Three speculative locomotives were offered for sale in August 1849 when the railway mania was coming to an end. Patrick Stirling attended a sale in February 1850 and was keen to complete his purchase but it is not known whether he did or not. There were three steam engines built at the Wallace Foundry in 1847 for export to Canada and, in 1852, William Kinmond left for that country where he set up a locomotive building works in Montreal when his brother joined him in 1853.

The Tay Foundry became known in 1834 when its owner, Peter Borrie, provided the machinery for a new steam ship on the Dundee to Perth route. Borrie was a member of that small group of working men who rose to become employers. After increasing his engineering reputation with further marine orders, he was elected in 1835 as a Director of the Watt Institution of Dundee. This august body was founded in 1824 as a recognition of the memory of James Watt, as inventor of the improved steam engine. John Stirling and William Stratton were founding Directors and James Carmichael was also elected vice president. James Steel became a Director in 1830 and William Kinmond was subsequently elected as a trustee of the Institution's new hall and library in Bank Street, Dundee.

Peter Borrie turned his attention to locomotives in 1837, when in December of that year he unsuccessfully tendered for the provision of motive power on the Arbroath and Forfar Railway, of which he was a member of the committee of management. This lack of success was repeated in February 1841 when his offer failed a second time. A further offer to the Edinburgh and Glasgow Railway was made in March 1841. This was for five locomotives at a reduced price. Only one was bought by the E&GR, a 2-2-2 named *Euclid*. Payment for this engine was not made promptly, but in instalments over the next few years. This may have contributed to the financial difficulties which the Tay Foundry Company faced around the middle of the 1840s for, in 1846, Borrie had to sell up. It has been speculated that it was at this time that Cubitt visited the Tay Foundry at Dundee and bought a locomotive named *Croydon* for the South Eastern Railway at a price of £210.

The departure of James Steel from Kinmond, Hutton and Steel in July 1847 did not see the end of his involvement with the construction of rolling stock. The owner of the Lilybank Foundry was killed in a railway accident at Wolverhampton in June 1847 and the foundry was sold to James Steel in 1848. He set up in partnership with his sons James and John and, as well as the products associated with the textile industry, continued to make wheels for locomotives, carriages and wagons

Although many towns across the country took advantage of the emerging railways to provide locomotives, it was a particular advantage for the foundries in Dundee that they already had an expanding marine and textile trade to permit the number of engines to be built. As the railway companies grew in size, many of them constructed workshops for the building and repair of their own motive power. Locally, the Dundee and Perth had its own workshops at Seabraes and, when the Scottish Central widened its sphere of operation, Alexander Allan was persuaded to come back north from Crewe and many of the company's engines were built at the workshops in Perth.

Dundee also had a coach building industry, although not of any substance.

Cuthbert and Sons built enclosed four-wheelers to the order of the Glasgow, Paisley, Kilmarnock and Ayr Railway in 1838. These were employed at the opening of the line and a contemporary engraving shows them to have three compartments, similar to horse-drawn carriages. In 1838, Cuthbert and Sons also built coaches for the opening of the Dundee and Arbroath Railway.

There were other famous names in the annals of Scottish railways which had an early association with the district round Dundee. Although not associated with the locomotive building industry, David Deuchars was for many years the North British Company's representative in Dundee. He began his railway career at the age of 15 in 1861 in the goods manager's office on the D&AR in his home town of Arbroath. He found himself in Dundee in 1867 as assistant to the goods manager, taking the job himself in 1875. He looked after the NBR's interests north of the Forth, seeking every opportunity to direct goods by his company through Fife rather than the Caley's competing route to the west.

It was he who arranged the return of traffic to the Broughty Ferry crossing when the first Tay Bridge fell, remaining true to the NBR in the area until he was transferred to Edinburgh in 1891. The Town Council of Dundee gave him a farewell dinner when he was given several gifts in recognition of his efforts on behalf of the railway and the town. Deuchars went on to become superintendent of the line in 1893, although it was some time before the Board recognised his talents and his dedication to the success of the North British Company.

One of the greatest names in the Caledonian Railway, John Farquharson McIntosh, also began his railway career as a lad at Arbroath, this time at the workshops of the SNER in 1860. He was moved to Montrose in 1867, before a series of appointments took him to Glasgow where he became locomotive superintendent in 1895.

Appendix 1 contains fuller details (where known) of the locomotives built in Dundee in the early 19th century.

Caledonian Railway tickets.   *Bob Drummond*

Chapter Eight

The Caledonian and North British Years 1864-1914

'Lay down your rails, ye nations, near and far,'
Charles Mackay, Illustrated London News, 1846

Dundee and Arbroath Joint Line

After the Tay Bridge disaster, the Dundee and Arbroath Railway was soon restored to its previous significance as part of the East Coast route, when the ferry across the Tay was hurriedly brought back into use. North British trains for the south had to resort to departures from the eastern end of Tay Bridge station, opposite to the happier days when their ribbon-like bridge was the wonder of the whole world. These trains passed through Dock Street tunnel before reaching the D&AR rails *en route* for Broughty Ferry, where once again they reversed and entered the branch to the pier for the river crossing.

Prior to the disaster, the NBR had applied to Parliament for a common interest with the Caledonian in the D&AR to ensure its passage toward Aberdeen. Joint ownership was authorised by the North British Railway (Dundee and Arbroath Joint Line) Act of 21st July, 1879, and a new improved service from Arbroath with connections to both Glasgow and Edinburgh was initiated from 1st August, 1879. However the bridge fell before the Act came into force on 1st February, 1880. The Broughty Ferry branch came back into use that same day to enable NBR services to reach Fife, and remained open until the second bridge was opened, the final train running to the pier on Sunday 19th June, 1887, the day before the public service started over the new bridge. The redundant tracks were then used as carriage sidings.

To ensure the day to day running of the joint line went smoothly, a Joint Line committee was formed under section eight of the same 1879 Act. This committee comprised three members each from the Caledonian and North British with the Chairman being appointed annually from each company in alternate years. To ensure fairness, he was not allowed a casting vote.

The Carmyllie branch, the Harbour branch at Arbroath and the line to St Vigeans were included in the 1880 joint arrangement, which cost £171,566 in compensation to the Caledonian for the loss of their half share, plus £28,000 in accrued interest. On 13th July, 1871 the North British had been authorised to build a line from St Vigeans to Montrose and Kinnaber Junction where it joined the Caledonian. This railway was opened between October 1880 and 1883. Thus the NBR now had an element of control over the east coast line in Angus and running powers over the remainder of the route to Aberdeen.

The citizens of Montrose were more than happy to have the NB line completed, feeling that they had been treated in a 'cavalier manner' since the CR had absorbed the SNER. Trains had been run from Montrose to Dundee via Friokheim, fast trains running on Tuesdays and Fridays, others on the remaining days taking 2½ hours and going by Guthrie. At that time, Montrose

The Royal Arch built for Queen Victoria's visit dominates the Harbour branch with Dundee East station in the distance.

Author's Collection

Broughty Ferry Pier station before 1890.

Author's Collection

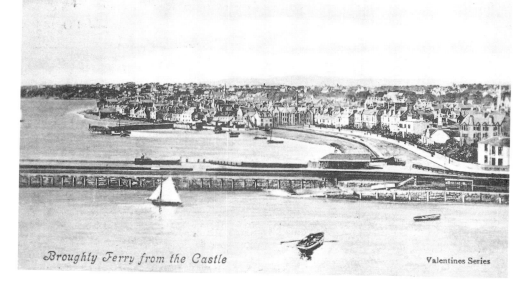

dealers complained that they had to pay £200 per month to transport dead meat by this longer route through Dundee to the London markets.

The Carmyllie branch was a mineral line, running north from the Dundee and Arbroath to the quarries of Lord Panmure beyond Carmyllie village. The D&AR reported on 30th April, 1854 that they had agreed to construct a junction for the Carmyllie railway at Elliot west of Arbroath. Built as a private line and opened in January 1855, the line was worked by the SNER on 1st February, 1864 under an agreement of 2nd and 12th March, 1864. It was sold under the SNER (Purchase of Carmyllie Railway) Act of 1865 and then to the Caledonian in 1866. Initially the Carmyllie railway did not provide a passenger service but one was authorised through Scotland's first Light Railway Order passed on 6th August, 1898, services beginning on 1st February, 1900, lasting until 30th November, 1929.

Even before the joint ownership of the Dundee and Arbroath, the Caledonian and North British had various agreements for the operating of the East station at Dundee, a Joint Station committee negotiating the details. There were regular disputes about access for the NBR to the station and goods facilities, especially if their presence meant more competition for the Caley.

To encourage more through booking to English destinations, a request was made to the committee early in January 1870 by the NBR, seeking premises for the Midland Railway carting agent, having the effect of strengthening their joint share of the traffic. The horses employed by the committee to shunt passenger carriages are recorded as costing (during the period up to 16th May, 1870) 4s. 6d. per horse or £300 per quarter.

At the end of July 1871, the NBR complained to the Joint committee about access to the sidings at Dundee East, and once again in February 1872, this time making a suggestion about setting out new sidings to the north of Dock Street. There was an attempt to settle the disagreement between the NBR and the Caley by allocating the number of wagons in each of the sidings at Dundee East mineral yard as follows:

Siding No.	NBR wagons	CR wagons
1	35	
2	39	
3		34
3a	to be used for shunting by both companies	
4	12	
5	13	14
6	22	5
7		30
8		36
Total	121	119

For the privilege of having rails crossing Dock Street, a payment had to be made to the Dundee Police Commissioners. The Joint committee minutes reveal that, on 4th October, 1872, the charge had been increased from £10 per annum to £100 with effect from the previous Whitsunday.

Discipline amongst the company's employees was not much better than on other railways and the minutes of 1873 meetings divulge an ongoing problem with some of the men, and record the reprimanding of Peter Grant, a harbour guard, for 'recklessly shunting wagons'. The cost of wages for the staff was evenly shared between the two companies, as shown by returns for the period from 1st November, 1873 to 31st January, 1874, during which the North British contributed £578 10s. 11d., and the Caledonian £578 17s. 8d. The wages of men working in the Dundee East Mineral Yard were also shared and, in 1879, these were:

2 yardsmen at 26s. 6d.	per week
1 yardsman at 20s.	per week
2 nightwatchmen at 19s. 10d.	per week of seven nights

There were also difficulties with the functioning of the hydraulic crane at the dock side reported in that year.

Since Dundee now had goods yards at three locations in the town centre, there had to be operational agreements over the transfer of traffic between them. Arrangements were instituted for traffic from the eastern mineral yard to both Dundee West and Dundee Tay Bridge. It was agreed on 21st August, 1879 that this would always be through Dock Street tunnel, all traffic being labelled 'Dundee East Mineral Yard'. Traffic from both the NBR and CR to Camperdown and Victoria Docks also had to pass through the tunnel (rather than use the former Harbour Branch line) and be left at the Harbour sidings, to the south of the main line near Camperdown Junction, to be lifted either by horses or the engine working the harbour traffic.

Goods trains for Earl Grey or King William IV Docks often provided bunkering for the ships which berthed there. They supplied them with coal from Fife or Lanarkshire, and so had to use the Harbour branch being hauled by either horse or locomotive traction. The North British was instructed to deposit its wagons in the siding on the north side of the NBR goods shed, and the Caledonian, too, deposited its trains for transfer on the Shore road inside the passenger station.

Services on the Dundee and Arbroath line were operated in alternate years by the two owning companies, those to Broughty Ferry remaining particularly busy during the affluent 1880s and, as a consequence, a series of season tickets were issued. A two month ticket was 25s. for first class, 21s. 6d. for second and 16s. 6d. for third. A lady's ticket was available at one third rate if a gentleman held a full ticket.

Examples of other fares in 1881 were:

From/to	Dundee	Single		Return	
Aberdeen	1st class	2s.	8d.	4s.	
	2nd class	2s.	2d.	3s.	3d.
	Parliamentary	1s.	4½d.	2s.	1d.
Broughty Ferry	1st class		6d.		9d.
	2nd class		4½d.		7d.
	Parliamentary		3½d.		5½d.

The Dundee and Arbroath Joint Railway Board agreed to undertake further improvements to the station at Dundee East. On 13th May, 1882 the platforms were extended and the concourse at the west end was widened by 30 feet. The intention was expressed to extend the southern or arrival platform to the signal cabin at the station throat although this was not fully achieved . In October 1883, the platforms were considered to be too low and the Joint Board recorded that 'the defect had been remedied' by raising them one foot in height. As Dundee East was an open station, tickets were inspected and collected at West Ferry where trains stood and locomotives could take water if required.

As Dundee prospered and expanded, houses were built on the eastern edges towards Broughty Ferry, and there was deemed a need for improvements on the line. A meeting of the Board on 27th March, 1899 recommended that two additional tracks be constructed eastward from Dundee East. The proposal was confirmed at the 7th July meeting when the members agreed that the widening would be on Harbour Trust land and a new junction would be formed at Carolina Port signal box, which could then be closed if a new box was erected at the harbour connection. There was a report three days later that the Board had also discussed the possibility of a new 'east end station' but Dundee East was never replaced.

The Joint Board meeting on 20th October, 1899 considered the new plans for improvements at Dundee East and around the harbour. The East station subsequently had gas lighting installed in 1901. Amongst other improvements were plans for a new hydraulic coaling station to replace the troublesome crane, a fish dock at the east end, and a new station at Stannergate. A site was chosen close to the original Craigie station, at Stannergate.

Local builders, D.P. How and Son, were contracted to build the station which opened in February 1901, the two station signal boxes coming into action on 27th January, 1901. As part of the proposed scheme to widen the line between Dundee East at a location known as No.2 Gates level crossing and the new Stannergate station, additional tracks were laid either side of the up and down lines at the site of the new station and the platforms constructed facing them, joined by a footbridge.

The 8th March meeting that year proposed that the Stannergate station should include a ticket platform, to replace that at West Ferry station. Stannergate was also planned to include a 'large marshalling depot for Dundee East traffic and East End Harbour traffic', including a linking line south-west from the goods depot which was formed in the land south of the passenger station towards the river. The line, which was never completed, was intended to join up with the harbour lines but was truncated in two tracks at the Tay Oilcake Works, a long established company at the eastmost end of the harbour.

The harbour authorities were not happy with this potential threat to their trade by the railway company's proposal, despite assurances in October 1902 that bunkering would be necessary for increasing number of jute steamers thereby ensuring coal traffic. Agreement was still not reached by 3rd November, 1902, when the *Evening Telegraph* reported that there was deadlock between the two parties. This impasse was borne out four days later when it was confirmed that the Harbour Board was concerned with losing its revenue

Reproduced from the 25", 1902 Ordnance Survey Map

Broughty Ferry showing station, Pier station, goods depot and Forfar branch.

from handling rail traffic to the new Stannergate yard.

The widened lines were therefore not built and the goods yard did not reach its projected levels of use. Neither was the passenger station at Stannergate a great revenue earner, and it had a short operational life, closing on 1st May, 1916. The ownership of that part of the Dundee and Arbroath line which lay within the bounds of Dundee Harbour remained with the Dundee Harbour Trust until a new agreement dated 20th November, 1906 between the harbour authority and the Caledonian and the North British Railways, acting for the D&AR. The arrangement confirmed that the line, the Trades Lane and Carolina Port Railway, would become part of the Dundee and Arbroath Joint Railway from 15th May, 1904.

Operating arrangements came under scrutiny once more in 1911 when the two parent companies reached agreement on new managing arrangements. The line was worked from then by the two companies themselves rather than as a separate company, the management being vested in the chief officers of both the Caley and the NBR. This meant changes at the Dundee office including the loss of certain jobs such as the separate manager and a his staff of clerks. The same principle was applied to the Dumbarton and Balloch Joint Railway near Glasgow which was also controlled by the Caledonian and the North British. A joint line audit office was set up in Glasgow to deal with the accounts of both joint lines.

The Dundee and Perth Line

The opening of the Tay Bridge in 1878, put the Caledonian on its mettle as the traffic on the Dundee and Perth line was at risk from the new and more direct route to England. In order to encourage more business in the town for the west coast, a joint CR and LNWR booking office was opened in the Clydesdale Bank at 94 High Street, Dundee on 6th November of that year. However, the affluent 1880s saw an increase in traffic on the Perth line as it did on all the routes from the town, putting subsequent pressure upon the operation of the railway and its infrastructure.

It was not long before there was a need to improve Dundee West station, and on 27th March, 1883, the *Dundee Advertiser* announced that the Caledonian Railway had submitted plans for a new passenger and goods station costing £130,000. The passenger station would be built 'partly on the present passenger shed and partly on the present goods shed' with the goods depot on the ground between the goods shed and the NBR 'underground' station, namely Tay Bridge. Two new streets were to be created by these plans. Tay Street was to have a continuation leading up to the new booking hall and Magdalen Yard Road was to be extended at the eastern end to form a new road 27 ft wide alongside the railway to the new 'depot'. These schemes were completed only in part, and although the roads were never built, construction of the new amenities was soon underway.

In November 1884, the *Dundee Advertiser* reported that the new goods station was nearing completion. It was of brick construction, 425 ft long and 134 ft

A train shunts at the River Tay at Perth. The ancient Brittain engine is in charge of mixed stock.
HMRS

The Inchture 'Dandy' sets out from the village for the station around the turn of the century.
HMRS

Opposite page, top: The second Dundee West station with the third taking shape behind in 1890.
Opposite page, bottom: The Harbour branch is still in evidence in front of the magnificent Dundee West. The railway horse bus awaits travellers for East station on 8th August, 1904.
Both Dundee District Libraries

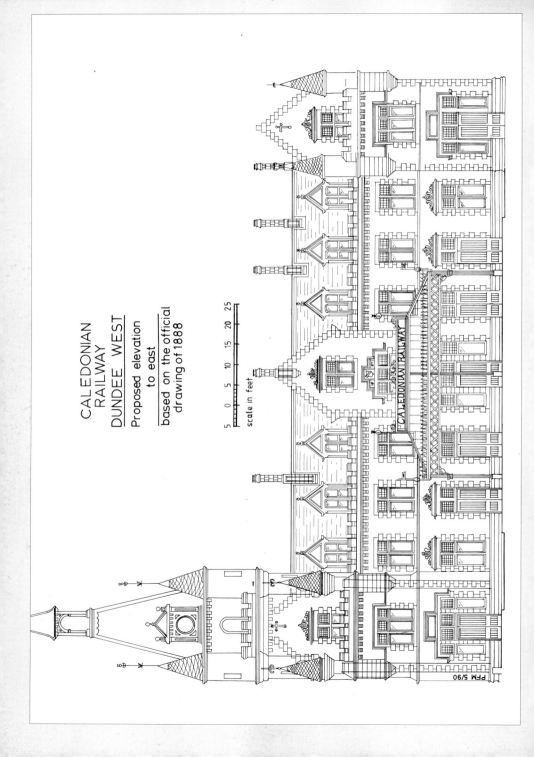

CALEDONIAN
RAILWAY
DUNDEE WEST
Proposed elevation
to east
based on the official
drawing of 1888

scale in feet
5 0 5 10 15 20 25

CALEDONIAN RAILWAY

PFM 5/90

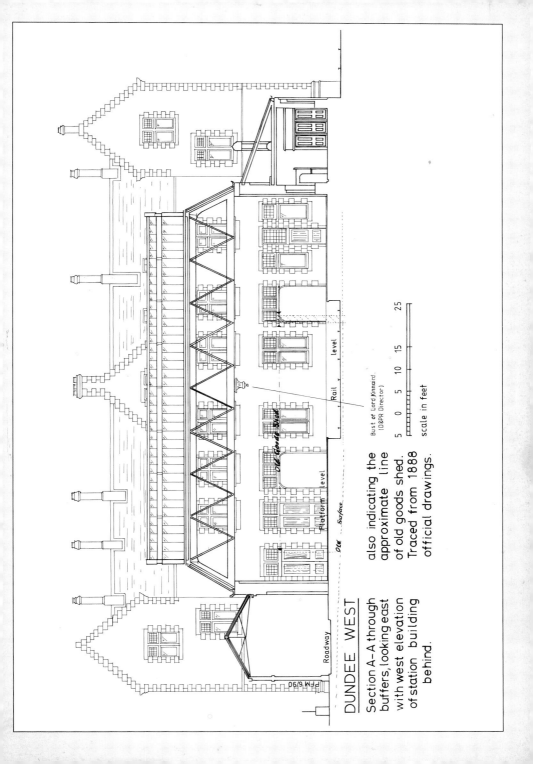

DUNDEE WEST

Section A-A through
buffers, looking east
with west elevation
of station building
behind.

also indicating the
approximate line
of old goods shed.
Traced from 1888
official drawings.

Bust of Lord Kinnaird.
(D&PR Director)

5 0 5 10 15 25

scale in feet

Old Surface

Platform level

Rail level

Roadway

PFM 6/90

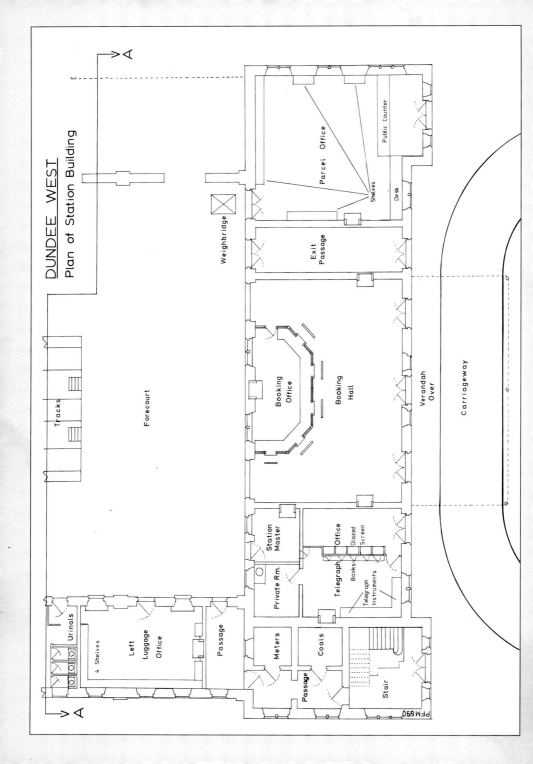

The Caledonian Railway carting office at the entrance to the Goods depot in Dundee overshadowed by the West station on 4th October, 1901. *Dundee District Libraries*

Goods depot and offices at Dundee West on 4th October, 1901. *Dundee District Libraries*

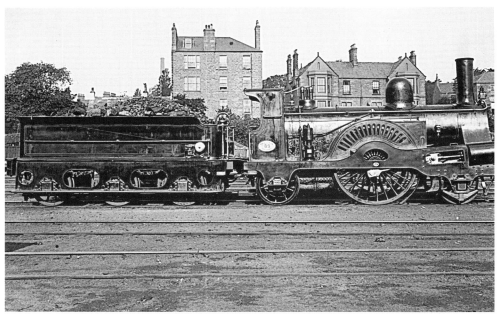

Caledonian Railway '88' class 2-2-2 No. 89, a Conner 8 ft single outside Dundee West shed in the 1880s. *HMRS/Vintage Collection*

Caledonian Railway '1' class 2-4-0 No. 59 (formerly No. 1) a Conner locomotive at Dundee West in the late 1880s. *HMRS/Vintage Collection*

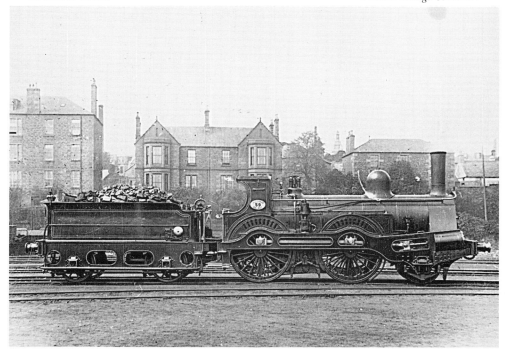

wide with a warehouse above. At the front, there was a two storey brick office building. Inside the shed were two platforms stretching the entire length with three sets of rails between them, plus another outside to the south of the building. Wagons were transferred within the shed by means of traversers and hydraulic capstans. Access to the storage above was by hydraulic cranes which raised goods into the 132 ft x 128 ft warehouse. Squeezed in between the goods shed and the northern retaining wall of the NBR station was a 500 ft long loading bank, with rails either side. There was also a bothy to the west. These greatly enlarged goods facilities were opened on 6th April, 1885.

Also in 1885, a new locomotive shed opened at Dundee West, being constructed on former mudflats near Buckingham Point some distance to the west of the original Dundee and Perth shed. Repairs had been transferred to Perth locomotive works from the Seagate shed at Dundee when the SCR took over, but Dugald Drummond, the Caledonian's recently appointed locomotive superintendent, had complained in 1883 about the lack of facilities at Dundee. The new brick-built shed was certainly an improvement on the early D&PR establishment, with eight through roads, having access from the eastern end and storage at the rear, although the configuration was reached from a spur approached from the west.

In 1889, Thomas Barr, the Caledonian Chief Engineer, designed a grand new passenger station building to enhance the railway and replace the second Dundee West, which was also too small for the traffic which it handled. This at last was a building in which the citizens of Dundee could take pride. Blyth and Cunningham were the engineers of the red sandstone-built terminal which was of substantial proportions, being three storeys high with a clock tower at the southern end. Often described as being in the Scottish Baronial style, the building did indeed look like a Scots castle, and was arguably one of the most striking in the town. It was erected behind the previous building and so used the land resulting from the demolition of the older structures to form an apron and taxi road, with a canopy at the entrances to the booking hall.

Inside the spacious interior, there was a semi-circular wooden booking office with access to the four platforms on either side. To the left as you entered were the telegraph and station master's offices. On the right was an exit passage to avoid conflicting movement with incoming passengers. This separated the parcels office from the booking hall. The left luggage office was to be found beyond the station building proper, as part of the external wall. The offices were generous enough to accommodate all the employees of the railway for the Dundee district. Down the southern flank wall, were the offices of the stations daily activities, while the northern wall was open to permit access for parcel collection.

The train shed was about 700 ft long and 112 ft wide with a ridge and furrow roof and a squared end screen at the western end. There were four platforms in two islands with numbers one and four outside the roof. The harbour branch line ran between the southern wall and the goods depot beyond. The architects planned to incorporate a bust of Lord Kinnaird in a niche on the western elevation of the station building within the train shed, but more recent employees remember this as a representation of George Kinloch.

Plan of Dundee showing the main line stations around the mid-1880s.

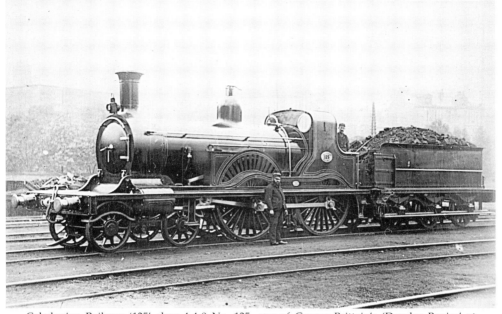

Caledonian Railway '125' class 4-4-0 No. 125, one of George Brittain's 'Dundee Bogies' at Dundee West around the turn of the century. *HMRS/Vintage Collection*

Caledonian Railway '294' class 0-6-0 No. 353 on the turntable at Dundee West.
HMRS/Vintage Collection

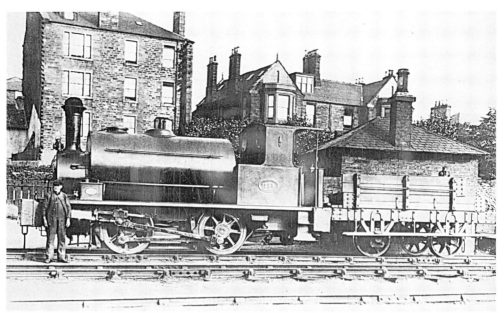

Caledonian Railway saddle tank No. 1265 outside West shed.   *HMRS*

Dundee Gas Works around 1904 with the newest Andrew Barclay 0-4-0ST No. 4 and one of the four Kerr, Stuart 0-4-0WT working on the 2 ft gauge internal system.   *Dundee District Libraries*

An amusing reflection of railway work on the Dundee and Perth line was reported in 1898 in the *Weekly News*. The paper recounted that, at that time, coke was expensive but gave good heat and was much desired by railway companies to burn in locomotives. To keep running costs down, premiums were offered to crews using the smallest quantities, bringing competition between railwaymen. The driver and fireman of a Dundee and Perth train had tried to save so much that their train came to a complete standstill in the Carse of Gowrie, the crew anxious not to let the guard (who did not benefit from the premium) and passengers know the reason. Thus the driver went down on to the track and began to strike the engine with a hammer until the fireman had built up steam and the train could once again move on.

Industrial Branches

The Fairmuir mineral branch on the Newtyle line was completed in 1885 to serve the north of the town which was rapidly growing both as a residential and an industrial area. In 1884 the Caledonian had submitted plans for a triangular junction near Fairmuir, about a mile from Lochee station to provide access from both the north and the south to a new branch and mineral yard, planned for construction there. The south to east curve left the line passing transfer sidings and a bakery, with the north to east curve intended to run along the original D&NR trackbed. Although the second link was never constructed, the completed line did cross over the old tracks of the first Dundee and Newtyle line just north of Crossroads station before fanning out into the sidings with further exchange and release lines. At Fairmuir, several coal merchants had their depots, including Dundee Eastern Co-operative Society.

The branch was extended some years later by a further mile from Fairmuir depot to Maryfield where a smaller goods depot was established, Francis East & Company, furniture makers, having their siding here. The final stretch was all in a cutting and the spoil removed during construction was transferred back down the Newtyle line to Dundee, where a siding was created between Ninewells and Buckingham Junctions. Here the returning wagons were discharged into the River Tay to help in the formation of the Esplanade, (known today as Riverside Drive), which is land recovered from the river by disposal of refuse and rubble from the town. Traffic for the branch was virtually all with the main lines at Dundee and included coal from Fife as well as timber and building materials for the continuing expansion of the town.

An extension of the Esplanade in early January 1888 was agreed by the Dundee Works committee. The intention was to take it as far as Windsor Street, which leads south from Perth Road, and to build a road from there west to Wills Braes. The road would be 40 ft wide and be met by an extension of Windsor Street over the railway. A cost of £15,000 was estimated and tenders were invited. Although the road was eventually constructed as Riverside Drive, the road bridge over the line at Windsor Street was not, only a foot bridge being erected at Magdalen Green station.

The two Dundee Gas Light Companies were extended at the end of the 19th century under the Dundee Gas Street Improvement and Tramway Act of 1899. The Act extended the area of land for the production of gas to 13 acres and allowed for the creation of an internal railway system which was formed adjacent to the Dundee East Mineral Yard, crossing Dock Street from the D&AR main line. There was a total of 3,168 yards of standard gauge track round the plant for the storage and shunting of coal and coke wagons. Two Andrew Barclay 0-4-0ST locomotives were employed in 1900 with a third arriving in 1929, replaced in the 1950s by two diesel shunters. There were 500 yards of 2 ft gauge line also built to take four smaller Kerr, Stuart 0-4-0 well tanks and hoppers beneath the gas making plant carrying coke and returning ashes and refuse. Incoming wagons were raised by hydraulic ram and emptied into these hoppers for transfer.

A standard gauge railway was laid out in 1908 by Dundee Corporation Electricity Supply Department, at the Carolina Port power station, with overhead wires operating at 420 volts DC. A four-wheeled locomotive built by United Car Company of Preston was supplied by British Thomson Houston. It was of open construction with twin collectors at one end and the cab at the other and was used for moving coal wagons from the Harbour line. Unusually, there were no junctions in the overhead wires, the collectors being lowered at each set of points. From 1930, battery powered locomotives worked the mile-long network until it closed in 1963. Apart from the more than three miles of internal railway track owned by the Harbour Trust, there was also a second short branch into the oil refinery of William Briggs and Co. Crude oil was consigned to the port and the refined product, mainly for road-laying, was sent out by rail in the company's black tank wagons.

The Dundee and Newtyle Line

The final route of the Newtyle branch was not the most tempting for commuters wanting to reach central Dundee from the northern outlying districts. As mentioned above the line left the Dundee and Perth line at Ninewells Junction, about 2½ miles from Dundee and formed a circuitous route to the north of the town. There was a signal box here, opened with the original deviation in 1863 and rebuilt on 8th March, 1893. The box was closed on 9th January, 1968.

The first station from Ninewells on the branch was a single platform at Liff, two miles from Ninewells and remote from the village it purported to serve. Later, the Dundee Floorcloth and Linoleum Company works was served by a short branch at the station. The next station was a mile to the east and was another modest affair of wooden construction, also with a single platform and siding, primarily used for handling timber for Brand's Sawmill. It enjoyed a variety of names, initially known as Victoria, then Camperdown from 1st May, 1862 and finally Lochee West from 1st February, 1896. The station closed to passengers on New Year's Day, 1917. Half a mile on, the most important station on the line was to be found.

Lochee had developed and prospered through the growth of the jute industry, the suburb being dominated by the 250 ft decorated chimney of the giant Camperdown Jute Works which was owned by Cox Brothers, employers of around 6,000 people. The station here was provided with two platforms having an attractive red rubble sandstone building by James Gowans on the up platform. The line went from a cutting to an embankment at this point and the station sat between a road to the south and a lane to the north with a flight of stone steps at the western end. These were next to the booking office, and on the opposite side from the centre of Lochee, so wooden steps were erected at the eastern end of the station nearer the main Lochee to Dundee road to assist arriving passengers on their way home. It seems odd now to consider why the station building, with waiting rooms and other facilities, was on the up platform, which was where passengers from Dundee would arrive, and the departure platform had scant shelter for the waiting commuter. No wonder the trams were more attractive! Fortunately the building remains, substantially unaltered to this day, although the modern extension does not blend well with the 1860s original.

A tall signal box was found on the down side platform, providing a clear view over the bridge to the west and round the curve to the east and the north. The box was opened on the same day as that at Ninewells and closed with the rest of the line on 12th December, 1967, a month before its contemporary on the main line. Passengers crossed the line at Lochee by a typical Caledonian wooden footbridge. Goods facilities were provided from the down line across the Lochee Road overbridge to the east and behind a retaining wall to the north of Loons Road. In keeping with this important suburb, there were both mineral and goods sides to the Lochee yard although both were severely cramped in space. Also at Lochee, a branch was built for the jute trade transferring raw bales from the harbour and returning finished goods. The line into Camperdown Works described a west to north curve immediately beyond Lochee station, with exchange sidings adjacent, and then it formed an elaborate configuration of turntables and sidings to serve the various sheds and buildings within the jute mill complex. The company did not operate its own locomotives but did have several private trader wagons and at least one tank wagon. A public siding lay beyond at Balmuir.

Baldovan and Downfield station was north of the Fairmuir branch and served the bleachfields around the settlement there. Baldovan grew up on the back of textiles although it was absorbed into the burgh as the town expanded. Trams later served the area and, as with Lochee, provided a shorter journey into town than the train. Further on lay Baldragon which was reputed to have the longest wooden platform in Scotland, followed by a branch into two quarries, Leoch and Balbeuchley at Rosemill. Next came Dronley and Auchterhouse stations both built on the line avoiding the incline at Balbeuchley. Shortly after, the line swept away again from the original route to reach a new station at Newtyle to the north of the village. The old route was then rejoined before Alyth Junction was reached.

Manure, as a regular source of income to Victorian railways, cannot be underestimated. When horse-drawn traffic was the only means of transport in towns, the residual manure had to be frequently removed and transferred to the country, where it could be used beneficially on the land. The significance of manure trade from the towns to the country is reflected in a series of letters between the estate of Strathmore and the Caledonian Railway.

The commissioner for the trustees of the estate, C.M. Barstow, wrote to the Secretary of the Caledonian on the 11th December, 1877, offering to permit the company to make use of land at Rosemill for sidings if they would examine the difficulty experienced by the tenants who wished to have manure delivered there. Loads were regularly consigned to Rosemill but the wagons were dropped off at Baldragon station, one stop down the line. The tenant at Rosemill protested at the additional £30 per year in tolls to bring the manure to his farm. He accused the railway agent there of being in the pay of the owner of the manure works at Rosemill who did not wish manure to be brought from the town.

The CR replied promptly but passed the responsibility for resolving the dispute to none other than James Smithells, the General Manager. By March, there was no response from the company and further loads had been diverted to Baldragon. Barstow was furious at the disregard to his letters and in April sent a bill for £7 4s. for the cost of transferring two wagon loads to Rosemill. The Caledonian continued to treat the correspondence with disdain, delaying their reply by referring the problem to back Smithells who was away in London.

Barstow extended the argument by pointing out that the railway, as common carriers, were obliged to deliver the manure to the sidings at Rosemill and that they were in contravention of their own Act of Parliament by refusing to do so. Eventually the matter was put before the Board of the company in May 1878, but sadly the correspondence does not record the outcome.

The Dundee and Forfar Direct Line

The Newtyle branch provided services to Blairgowrie via Alyth Junction, where passengers could change for Forfar, the county town of Angus. Passengers had an alternative way to reach Forfar by rail from Dundee by Arbroath and then over the former Arbroath and Forfar line, both these two options being lengthy and far from direct. As early as 1845 a proposal had been put to the D&AR Board to consider a branch to Forfar. Despite a plea from Lord Kinnaird at their meeting of 11th September, 1845 that a direct line was of great importance, the Directors rejected the idea on the grounds that it was 'inexpedient to undertake'. The committee set up to examine the possibility heard P.H. Thoms comment on the expense to build the line. It was estimated to cost £150,000 with a likely return of 6 per cent. Mr Hastie, a local MP, expressed his belief that the 'Fife Railway' would cross at Ferryport rather than Dundee as the river is narrower there and that the company should not become involved with branches at that time.

However, it was not until 1864 that a Bill was put to Parliament by the Scottish North Eastern Railway, which briefly was the owner of the D&AR, to construct a 17¼ mile route from Dundee East to Forfar providing passengers with a more straightforward journey. The resulting Act (27 & 28 Vic. cap.

clxxiii) was passed on 14th July, 1864, enabling the SNER to raise £125,000 in preference shares, in one fifth calls, and giving borrowing powers of £40,000 once half the shares were paid up. Amongst the usual conditions was a clause that most goods should be charged at one penny per mile and passengers at two pence per mile plus a penny surcharge. As with most other railway contracts, the line was divided into several sections. Wood and Lynch won one eight mile section south from Forfar while William Leslie was the contractor for a further section.

The Dundee and Forfar Direct Railway was opened for freight on 12th August, 1871 but did not open for passengers until 14th November, however, by which time it was firmly in the domain of the Caledonian Railway which had made some minor amendments to the course of the line. Of the many proposals which were intended to originate from the Dundee to Arbroath line, this was the only one to diverge from the south side before crossing over the line. Rather than leave the main line near Dundee, the route branched off east of Broughty Ferry, rising on a sharp incline before swinging north across the D&AR line and heading over Monifieth Road.

The first station on the branch was Barnhill, a select and desirable suburb of Broughty Ferry about half-way between there and Monifieth. The single track line then took a twisting course through the undulating land on the eastern edge of the Sidlaws, with stations for several villages in the vicinity before Forfar was reached from the east. However, as was often the case, the stations were some distance from the settlements they were intended to serve - Kingennie, Monikie, Kirkbuddo and Kingsmuir. In 1911, what was then considered a long felt want was satisfied by the Caledonian with the introduction of Residential expresses in each direction on the route from Kirriemuir to Forfar and Dundee.

The Newburgh and North Fife Railway Company

The North British were concerned that the Caledonian had the monopoly of services between Dundee and Perth, particularly as they themselves had services to both towns but not from one to the other. The company, therefore, supported a request to create a new line for which the Newburgh and North Fife Railway Company sought consent from Parliament. The N&NFR was a local enterprise which had been incorporated on 6th August, 1897 to construct a line from Glenburnie Junction, east of Newburgh on the original Ladybank to Perth route, to the main line to the Tay Bridge near St Fort.

William Beattie and Sons constructed the new line, known simply as the North Fife line. It was 13¼ miles long, begun in June 1906 and opened after almost three years on Friday 22nd January, 1909 for goods traffic, three days later for passengers. The line was laid inland but roughly parallel to the southern shore of the River Tay with many short steep inclines greater than 1 in 100. Despite the fact that there were few settlements of any size on the line, stations were opened at Lindores (which was the summit), Luthrie and Kilmany to serve these villages. However, goods traffic levels were good, if seasonal,

Smith, Hood & Co's coalyard at Dundee Tay Bridge in the early 1890s. This view, looking east shows the third West station and is on the land to be taken for the new turntable in 1912.

Charles Underhill

An advertisement for Smith, Hood, & Co.

Jim Page

depending upon agricultural produce and materials for revenue.

The NBR introduced two stopping passenger services over this new connection. One was by way of the Tay Bridge from Dundee to Perth, in direct but slower competition with the Caley, and the other was a new service from St Andrews to Perth using the southern side of the triangular junction at St Fort to reach the branch line from Leuchars. Later these trains travelled from Perth as one and split at St Fort station, where the St Andrews portion reversed instead of using the triangular junction. The North Fife line was single track throughout with double track passing places at Kilmany and Luthrie stations. There was a great deal of optimism evident when the line was planned, as it was built with overbridges wide enough to cross double tracks and platforms long enough to handle excursion trains.

The North British, despite its agreement to operate the line, began to divert traffic from the line to others of its own and, three years after opening, the Newburgh company sought arbitration from the railway commisioners. It was suggested in evidence that the NBR was anxious not to put its other arrangements with the Caley at risk, but the NBR showed that its receipts were too small to make the line profitable. During the early years of World War I passenger services on the line were withdrawn due to a shortage of staff, but restarted on 10th July, 1916.

Developments at Dundee

As well as a larger locomotive shed at Dundee West, better facilities were soon required at Tay Bridge and the NBR set about enlarging their shed facilities. In 1891, plans were put forward for the removal of the engine shed and turntable at Esplanade, south of the main line. A new shed was proposed for a location adjacent to the junction with the CR, and included a new 'signal tower', loading bank and water column. Fewer than 20 years later, the turntable was considered too small to accommodate the new and heavy 'Atlantic' locomotives which W.P. Reid had introduced on the NBR.

The most suitable space for a replacement turntable appeared to be on land at the rear of the Tay Bridge shed, which was occupied by Smith, Hood and Company, well known Dundee coal merchants. Their yard lay to the north, behind the retaining wall of the cutting of the western approach to Tay Bridge station from the bridge and to the east of the shed. In July 1910, W. Kettles traffic superintendent at Dundee wrote to William P. Reid, himself a previous holder of the position, but who was by then the NBR locomotive superintendent, informing him of the negotiations with the coal merchants. He advised his masters on 17th August, 1910 that the parties had met at the site to consider replacing the old turntable. By 5th September, a 65 ft turntable was recommended, to be installed to the east of the existing 50 ft one on the land leased by Smith, Hood. This was confirmed nine days later when an estimate of £1,660 was put forward for the replacement turntable. In October, a delay was announced, due to the reluctance of Smith, Hood to agree to lose part of their land. On 29th October, 1910, the original turntable was earmarked for the

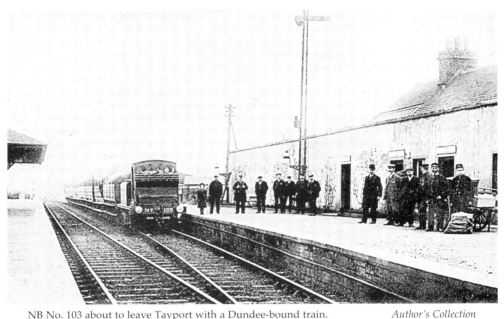

NB No. 103 about to leave Tayport with a Dundee-bound train.   *Author's Collection*

Inside Dundee West shed in 1904 with CR No. 496 and No. 1180.   *Author's Collection*

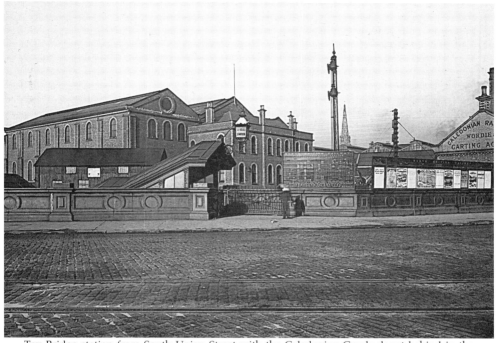

Tay Bridge station from South Union Street with the Caledonian Goods depot behind in the early years of the century. Note the NBR signal over the bridge adjacent to the entrance steps.
Dundee District Libraries

Tay Bridge station from the road with the passenger and parcels entrances over the tracks below shortly after the turn of the century.
Dundee District Libraries

TAY BRIDGE STATION, DUNDEE. 1710. J.V.

British Railways Board

Tay Bridge station looking west. An NB train for the south waits in platform 1 with a variety of NB coaches.

new shed being constructed at the time at Dunfermline Upper.

Progress was slow, and on the 7th July, 1912 the old turntable at Dundee was declared unsafe. A fortnight later it was decided to extend it to 56ft as it was unbalanced. Smith, Hood twice succeeded in delaying the replacement of the turntable to enable their winter stockpiles to be retained. In negotiation, they asked the NBR for another siding, three wagon lengths shorter than the others, to act as a storage. Meanwhile engines were turned on the old table using ropes attached to another locomotive on an adjacent road. It took until September 1913 for the situation to be resolved and the new turntable to be installed.

At the western end of the Caledonian yard at Dundee was Buckingham Junction, where the Tay Bridge and Perth lines converged. The first signal box there had 20 levers and was erected in 1878 when the junction was created with the opening of the bridge, having been authorised by the original Tay Bridge Act. The more familiar structure was built to replace this and was opened by the Caley on 22nd August, 1886 at a cost to the North British of £669 13s. 2d. The box was staffed by Caledonian signalmen, but their wages were paid by the NBR. The base was brick and narrower than the timber first floor, which housed back to back twin frames of 54 levers each.

This arrangement was unpopular with the signalmen and was prone to faulty locking making it particularly difficult to learn as it needed a great deal of walking about. The box was equipped with original Tyer's block instruments which remained in the cabin long after they had been superseded by more modern apparatus. It controlled the main line from Magdalen Green station to Dundee West station, the mineral sidings and the locomotive shed, turntable and engine sidings, as well as the junction with the North British main line and carriage sidings.

These had been constructed near Esplanade station in the lee of the bridge incline and on the land that had once served as an open-air swimming pool near Magdalen Point. There was more than one proposed design for Esplanade station, one of which was to be called Magdalen Green like the D&PR line station. The eventual station was a red brick structure with wooden platforms, built on the arches of the viaduct at the landfall of the bridge.

This may have been in an attempt to encourage promenading passengers to take advantage of the brisk walks becoming possible along the Esplanade, the tree lined thoroughfare adjacent to the river, between Tay Bridge station and the bridge itself. Esplanade station was also close to houses in the west end of the town but, unlike the adjacent Magdalen Green station which was to the west on the Caledonian main line, it was not near to the large and affluent west end villas. There was little traffic from this new NBR station and services were soon curtailed. The only advantage in using Esplanade station was to avoid a journey into Tay Bridge station before setting out on a journey to the south.

Reproduced from the 6", 1923 Ordnance Survey Map

Dundee Esplanade, Tay Bridge and West stations.

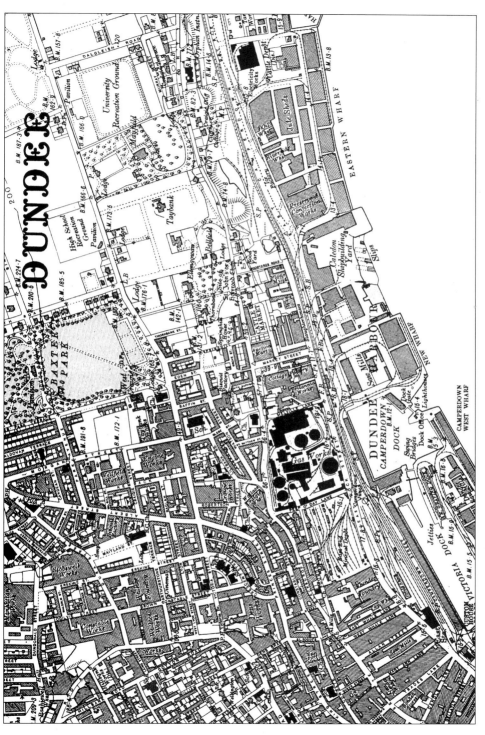

Dundee East station.

Reproduced from the 6", 1923 Ordnance Survey Map

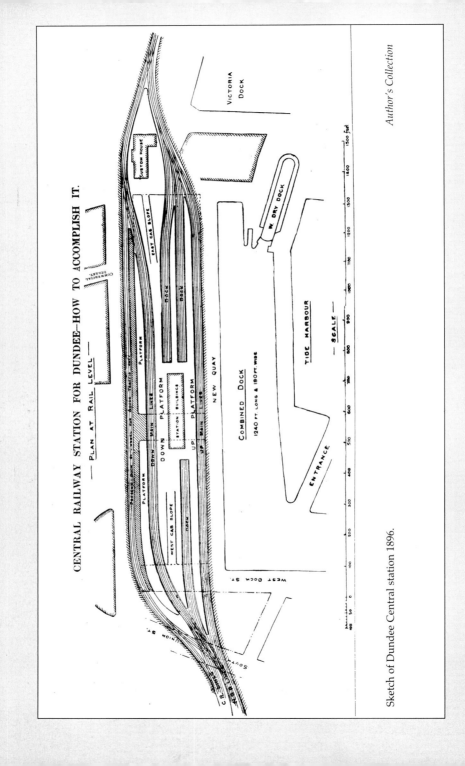

CENTRAL RAILWAY STATION FOR DUNDEE—HOW TO ACCOMPLISH IT.

— PLAN AT RAIL LEVEL —

Sketch of Dundee Central station 1896.

Author's Collection

Chapter Nine

Proposals Unfulfilled
1845-1902

'The best laid schemes o' mice an' men, Gang aft a-gley'
Robert Burns, 1785

With the establishment by the beginning of the 1840s of railway connections from Dundee both to Newtyle and to Arbroath, and the prospect of a connection to Perth and another to Edinburgh in the foreseeable future, the townsmen of Dundee considered it essential that there be a line built direct from Dundee to Forfar, the county town of Angus. This was first considered, in 1845, when the Dundee and Forfar Junction Railway was proposed. Gresholm Cumming who described himself as a civil engineer asked James Leslie, also an engineer from Dundee, to produce a plan of this suggested line giving a much more direct route than that achieved by the D&NR. The line was never built and it was not until 1864 that an Act was passed to give a direct route to Forfar.

In Cumming and Leslie's plan, an incline branching off from the D&AR to the east of Trades Lane station would carry their proposed line up onto the higher land to the east of the town. The course then to be followed was north, past Claypotts castle and then eastwards to Murroes before turning north-east towards Monikie. From there, a swing to the north-west was to be taken up bringing the suggested line as far as the villages of Whig Street, Kinnettles and Douglastown, the latter it will be remembered being an original destination of the D&NR. Having skirted the high ground to the south of Forfar, the line was to swing north-east again before entering the county town. Although the original plan of this line still survives, there is no clear evidence of the fate of its promotion.

Later in the century, once there had been an establishment of the railways in Dundee, further schemes for expanding rail travel were proposed. Like the early days of the railway promoters, many of these ideas were put forward by the community which was to benefit from them, often land owners or merchants and tradesmen. Sadly, the support of the general public for an idea was seldom translated into hard financial support, and therefore usually resulted in the ideas having a short life and very little chance of coming to fruition.

The proximity of the three terminii in the centre of Dundee gave the traveller a confusing choice. Departures for the south could be made from either Dundee West or Tay Bridge stations, while a journey to the north could start from West station going via Perth or Newtyle and from Tay Bridge or East stations if the route was to be via Arbroath. Add to this the fact that harbour goods traffic could use either the surface route along Dock Street from both Dundee West and Tay Bridge or the NBR tunnel beneath the road and the variety becomes difficult to comprehend.

A point in favour of a joint route was the lack of a straightforward link between the Perth line and the Arbroath line. This could no longer be achieved by way of the original Harbour branch since there were restrictions on both type of traffic and its destination. The usual route was over the west end link with the NBR at Buckingham Junction to Tay Bridge station and then through the tunnel, to join the rails to the north. The independent spirit of the Caledonian found this hard to accept and ways of circumventing this dependence on the NBR were likely to be considered.

Schemes had been proposed before the completion of the Tay Bridge to join the Perth and Arbroath routes, as we saw earlier in Chapter Three. There were several similar ideas put forward in the 1870s. On 17th October, 1871, one notion was considered to link the two railways by a new line running via Sea Wynd, Reform Street and Panmure Street which Lord Kinnaird was believed to favour. That debate prompted four more proposals which were discussed on 26th October, 1871, and which, like the previous idea, involved the line passing round the north of the town centre with a new station being created at a mid point, in the vicinity of New Inn Entry near Meadowside and reaching along the line of the present day Murraygate.

Proposal one would leave the Dundee and Perth line at a point known as Gray Bank and tunnel via Sea Wynd under Nethergate to a station at Panmure Street, before turning south east to rejoin the Dundee and Arbroath line at Roodyards. This was said to cost £255,307. Number two proposal was similar to the first but, instead of returning at Roodyards, the line would turn south at Blackscroft and rejoin the main line at Dock Street, much nearer town. The cost of this scheme was to be £259,422.

A cheaper option (at £233,697) was number three which followed the number one route to Reform Street, but then kept to the south along Murraygate and then via Seagate and Trades Lane rejoining the line at Dundee East station. The final idea was to keep the line much closer to the harbour by traversing Greenmarket, on the quayside at Earl Grey Dock, and joining the D&AR at East station. The estimated cost if this was built on pillars would be £278,647, but if an embankment was considered then the cost would have been the cheapest of all at £201,172. How the look and access to the town centre would have altered if any one of these lines had been built.

As the centre of Dundee was improved and rebuilt, it became more difficult to conceive a connecting line driven through the centre of the town which would not disrupt the commercial life of the burgh. A proposal in 1876-7 was to build a station on the site opposite the present Caird Hall. In 1896, public consideration was given to a more serious proposal, published in the Dundee press, to create a central railway station within the northern periphery of the harbour and utilising both Earl Grey and King William Docks. The report gave an excellent description of the manner in which the docks could be turned to good use as a central station for Dundee and declared that:

> . . . the question of providing a Central Station came recently before a conference held in the Town House, at which Lord Provost Low presided. Mr R.M. Short (of Short and Smith, Whitehall Street) approached Sir James Low, and submitted the plans to his lordship, who considered them so well adapted to meet all the requirements of the case that he advised Mr Short to make them public and mention that the scheme had Sir

James Low's warm approval.

The plan permits of a portion of the docks being retained. By the removal of the KIng William Dock Lockway and the southern portion of the Mid Quay the quay space remaining is actually improved. The King William Dock would be increased in depth to correspond with the Earl Grey Dock. The station occupies the northern half of the two docks, and is bounded on the north by Dock Street, and on the south by a new quay, 1,240 feet long and 50 feet wide, which would then form the north quay of the combined docks.

The plan shows the actual space occupied very clearly. Dock Street is preserved intact, and its width is undiminished, while the Royal Arch is actually turned to use, and becomes the main portal of the central entrance to the station and new quay. The station is, of course, low level (the same as Tay Bridge station), and sloped carriage entrances are provided at the west end of Earl Grey Dock and the east end of King William Dock. One large island platform and several docks are so disposed as to give the required accommodation. It may be mentioned that the rails and platform under cover provide accommodation far in excess of all the stations in Dundee combined.

Upon this island platform are all the requisite offices, including left luggage, waiting and refreshment rooms, etc., are provided (sic), and in arranging these, Messrs Short & Smith have taken the opinion of a railway expert, who has expressed his entire approval of the scheme. No pillars or other obstructions are allowed on the platforms, and every arrangement has been planned to secure a station worthy of the city. The present Dock Street tunnel will be utilised for passing all goods trains through the city clear of the station, which will be used solely for passenger traffic.

The railway approaches to the station at the east and west call for very little alteration. The NB connections are already made; but owing to the Custom-House, which cannot be ruthlesly sacrificed, a cutting to the south will supplement the eastern approach. To the west of the station the Caledonian lines are brought in alongside the NB Railway, and to carry these down to the low level a cutting and tunnel would have to be constructed, beginning about half a mile to the west of the West station.

All this would provide one central location in place of the existing three stations, and so thorough was the concept that there were suggestions for the new use to which each of the existing stations could be put. The report explained that Tay Bridge station could be cleared to form a marshalling yard for making up trains and Dundee East could be made into a goods station, with very little alteration. The Caledonian station, it was proposed, would become a station hotel under the control of the railway companies.

There was one aspect to which the proposer had not given obvious consideration. In view of the continual seepage of water into Dock Street tunnel ever since it was built, the idea of a complete station built below sea level opened up the risk of continual pumping and possible difficulties with drainage. Despite these dangers, the central station plans were submitted to the town council on 28th January, 1896, but were not taken any further and the city was left without its co-ordinated terminus. It does, however, conjure up a most imaginative scheme which could have strengthened the town's railway communication for years to come.

A High Level Circular Railway was put forward in 1872 to link with the new Tay Bridge when it was completed, such lines being known in the press as 'circumbendibus'. On 26th December of that year, a line was projected from the bridge to Perth Road, past Invergowrie House, taking the line of the Lochee

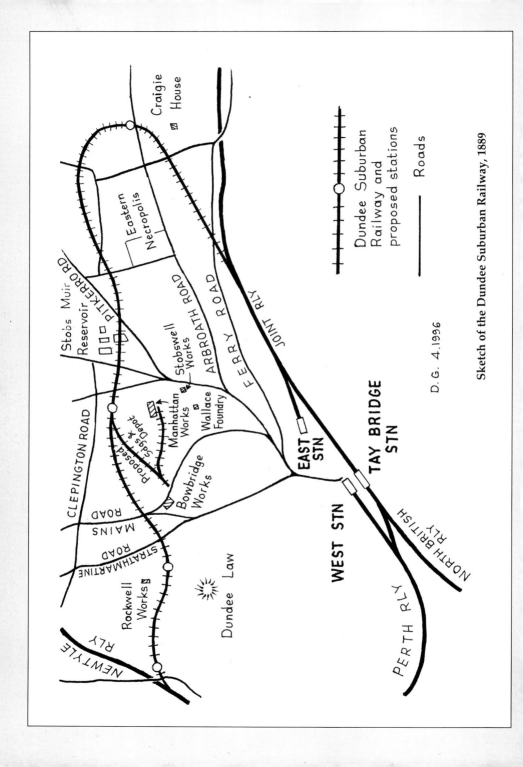

Sketch of the Dundee Suburban Railway, 1889

D. G. 4.1996

Dundee Suburban Railway and proposed stations

Roads

Craigie House

Eastern Necropolis

Stobs Muir Reservoir

PITKERRO RD

Stobswell Works

ARBROATH ROAD

FERRY ROAD

CLEPINGTON ROAD

Manhattan Works

Wallace Foundry

Proposed Sdgs & Depot

Bowbridge Works

MAINS ROAD

STRATHMARTINE ROAD

Rockwell Works

Dundee Law

NEWTYLE RLY

JOINT RLY

EAST STN

WEST STN

TAY BRIDGE STN

NORTH BRITISH RLY

PERTH RLY

deviation of the Newtyle line, then to Coldside and on to Clepington Road and Stobsmuir ponds, then to the Dundee and Arbroath line near the Orphanage. The nine mile, double track, route was costed at £200,000 with five stations at Ninewells, Lochee, Coldside, Maryfield and Craigie.

An almost identical line, called the Dundee High Level Railway was announced in 1885 leaving the Tay Bridge at the Esplanade station and taking the same route as the 1872 scheme to the Dundee and Arbroath Railway. Plans for a Dundee Suburban Railway were published in November 1883 and again in 1887. Earlier, on 7th May, 1896, a Bill was submitted for a railway round a similar route to the east and north of Dundee, the last part of town not yet served by rail. Since the building of the Lochee deviation of the Newtyle line from Ward station and the Law tunnel to Ninewells Junction and the north-west of Dundee, it must have seemed a natural continuation to build a line round the north and east to meet the Arbroath line. This would have given access for the expanding jute mills to the railway system and provided passenger services for the increasing workforce.

This latter scheme would have left the Newtyle line north of Lochee with a station constructed at Kings Cross Road and another near Coldside, to the east of where the original Newtyle line emerged from Law tunnel. The line was then intended to swing slightly north to a third station near Maryfield, preceded by a branch to Bowbridge and Manhattan jute works. The new railway was taken through Stobsmuir ponds and crossed Pitkerro Road, before eventually describing a full semi-circle and dropping down to the Dundee and Arbroath line near the Orphanage at Roodyards. A fourth station was intended for Craigie where the line crossed the Arbroath Road.

The earlier plan, dated 20th November, 1883, gave details of a similar railway and indicated the steep nature of the proposed line, with gradients from the Arbroath line to Lochee. This required an ascent of 1 in 52 from the Arbroath line opposite the Orphanage easing after 2½ miles to 1 in 265 for only a quarter of a mile, then 1 in 136 for a further three-quarters of a mile, before resuming 1 in 265. The incline continued with a 1 in 75 to the summit of the line, where level ground was reached for one furlong, followed by a drop of 1 in 73 to the Newtyle line.

For whatever the reason, be it a lack of financial support from the city or a lack of sponsorship from the two main players, the Caley and the NB, neither the Dundee Suburban Railway nor its antecedents was ever constructed. Thus, as well as losing a much needed central station, Dundee forfeited the opportunity to have a complete suburban railway system which might have stood a better chance of competing with the forthcoming public tramways.

A rather unusual proposal emerged in 1881, when the Highland Railway Directors announced their opposition on 29th April to a new line from their northern territory to Dundee. This would have provided the harbour with the possibility of a direct line to new markets in the north of Scotland and reduced the cost of importing raw materials and finished goods to the inland regions. However, not until 29th August was the scheme brought before the Directors of the Caledonian. When they had discussed the idea, they decided that it had merit and they should take it further. The Board met on 24th

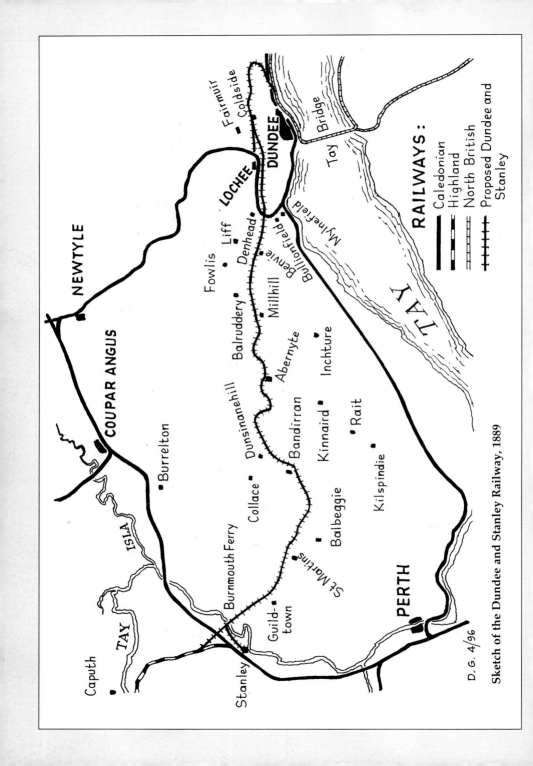

RAILWAYS :

Caledonian
Highland
North British
Proposed Dundee and
Stanley

Sketch of the Dundee and Stanley Railway, 1889

D.G. 4/96

NEWTYLE

COUPAR ANGUS

Caputh

Burrelton

Collace

Dunsinanehill

Balruddery

Fowlis

Liff

Denhead

Benvie

Millhill

Abernyte

Bullionfield

Mylnefield

Fairmuir
Coldside

DUNDEE

LOCHEE

Tay
Bridge

Burnmouth Ferry

Bandirran

Inchture

Kinnaird

Rait

Kilspindie

Balbeggie

St Martins

Guild-
town

Stanley

PERTH

TAY

ISLA

TAY

September, 1881 with proprietors and tenants on the line of a possible railway from Dundee to Stanley Junction, where the Highland line left the Caledonian's Strathmore route.

Nothing more came of the idea at that time and the Dundee and Stanley Railway was considered again in 1887 when the local press published a drawing showing a route from the proposed Dundee Suburban Railway westwards, passing south of Lochee and on to Benvie and Abernyte, then by way of Dunsinane Hill towards Balbeggie before turning northwards and crossing over the Tay at Barmouth Ferry to the Highland line north of Stanley.

The notion did not catch on at that occasion either, but persistence brought it before the citizens of Dundee in 1902, when a public meeting was held in the city to consider the proposal once again, the latest survey having been completed the previous year. This time Dundee West was the starting point, with the route following a similar 15 mile course through the Sidlaw Hills to Balbeggie and Stanley.

The Highland Railway Directors attended the meeting but were still lukewarm about the idea, perhaps because the company was going through a period of financial difficulty, although they did agree to work the line if it was ever built. A great deal of popular interest existed in the new line but there was little financial support for any formal proposal, and like all the other propositions it did not progress any further. A further proposal for a line to the north from Dundee was considered by the Highland's competitor. As part of its attempt to gain a share of the route south from Aberdeen, the Great North of Scotland Railway proposed a Dundee and Ballater line but this was yet another scheme which was to remain no more than a suggestion.

In 1898, an idea was advanced to build a light railway from the centre of Dundee through Broughty Ferry to Barnhill. Proposed by a Leeds concern, Greenwood and Batley, the line was to be operated by electric traction, as a half way house between the increasingly popular trams and the now familiar trains. Although the Dundee Town Council did not give approval for the section of track within the city boundary, that part beyond, via Broughty Ferry and Barnhill, was given an Order under the Light Railways Act.

The Dundee and Arbroath Joint Railway Company naturally expressed its strong opposition to the proposal and the Board of Trade withheld its approval of the Order, accepting the evidence that the main line would be severely affected if the light railway was to be constructed. The tramways, which in due course were built instead of the electric railway, did provide stiff competition to the D&AR and local train services were considerably curtailed in future years. Despite these many unfulfilled proposals, rail traffic grew in the boom years of the end of the 19th century and some more expansion was yet to come in the new century.

An LNWR publicity picture showing the West Coast Corridor Express, a service which did not run from Dundee. CR No. 49 and the local officers in front of a train of Caledonian stock.

Author's Collection

Former Caledonian racer No. 123, as No. 14010 in LMS days' passes Magdalen Green with a local of Caley stock for Perth on 29th May, 1930.   *Author's Collection*

Chapter Ten

Travel Near and Far
1895-1960

'Rumble under, thunder over, train and tram alternate go.'
John Betjeman

The Railway Races of 1895

The completion of the Forth Bridge in 1890 gave a new opportunity to the North British through long distance services. Barlow's Tay Bridge had been open since 1887 but direct access from Edinburgh to the east coast of Scotland put the Caledonian and its west coast allies under threat once more. Ever since the Midland-Waverley route was opened, there were in effect three lines available from London to central Scotland. The 1888 races had scarcely receded in the travelling public's mind than the competition to reach Aberdeen first began.

The closeness of the distances involved give a hint of the challenge ahead:

London to	via East Coast	via West Coast
Perth	441	450
Dundee	452	471
Aberdeen	523	540

Initially, Perth or Dundee were seen as the prize, the former having the additional spice of sharing the Caledonian rails from Hilton Junction, about two miles south of Perth. Because the North British route through Fife was so tortuous, a contest to Dundee, even with the potential of a race finishing with a sprint from the Tay Bridge where both routes ran parallel to each other, was not seen as an attractive option.

The Perth line from the Forth Bridge, opened on 2nd June, 1890, was less serpentine, but had very severe gradients. A race to Aberdeen would still leave the NBR at a disadvantage because of the comparatively poor route north of the Tay. The exit from Dundee by way of the steep (and wet) incline from Dock Street tunnel was followed by a comparatively flat straight track along the Angus coast, but north of Arbroath the similarity to the Caley's Strathmore line does not bear much scrutiny. All these handicaps reduced the Edinburgh company's possible advantage of distance to very little in time.

Another factor which hampered the ability of the NBR to challenge the Caley successfully was the chaotic conditions which prevailed at Waverley station. Since the opening of the Forth Bridge, the cramped station was unable to cope with the increase in traffic and delays of several hours were common on some services. Regardless of these handicaps, observers were keen to see a resurgence of the rivalries of the last decade. Not long after the opening of both the Tay and Forth bridges, the 8.00 pm night services between King's Cross and Aberdeen were speeded up to reach their destination in just 12 hours 15 minutes. The West Coast companies replied with a reduction in their time to

Week-Days.

Station	a.m.	a.m.	a.m.	a.m.	a.m	a.m	a.m	a.m.	a.m.	a.m.	a.m.	a.m.	a.m.	a.m.	a.m.	a.m.	a.m.
Aberdeen .. leave																	
Dundee (Tay Bridge) .. leave	5 50	6 40			7 10	8 10	8 15	6 20	9 3		9 32	7 40	9 50	10 0	9 55	12·15 12·25	10·20
Esplanade	5 53				7 13				9 13		9 35		9 53				
St Fort			6 56		7 23		8 32		9 20				10 3	10 10		12 32 12 42	
Leuchars Junction .. arrive					7 30								10 10	10 17			
Wormit .. leave	5 59										9 41				9 55		
West Newport	6 1	6 7									9 45				10 21	12 10 12 10	
East Newport	6 4	6 7									9 49				10 25		
Tayport	6 12				7 10		8 10		9 0		9 54				10 32	12 33 12 43	
Leuchars Old Station	6 22								9 21		10 6				10 39 10 44		
Leuchars Junction .. arrive	6 24	6 10					8 33		9 28						10 50	12 43 12 53	
St Andrews	6 10	6 10							9 35								
Leuchars Junction .. leave	6 26	7 31		7 32		8 18	8 59		9 40			11 35	10 21	10 25	10 32		1 16
Dairsie	6 33					8 24			9 46								1 23
Cupar ..	6 40 7 10		7 44				10 6		9 48			11 35	10 33	10 39	10 50		1 30
Springfield	6 45						10 26		9 52								
Ladybank Junction .. arrive	6 51		7 53		8 16		10 40		9 59			11 45	10 42	10 50	11 3		
Perth .. arrive				8 50	8 55				10 7						10 56		
Kinross Junction .. arrive	6 55	6 55			8 57							11 13			11 35		
Kingskettle	6 59	6 59		8 1					10 15			11 19	11 45		11 13		
Falkland Road	7 1	7 14		8 8			10 6		10 59			11 40	11 45		11 45		1 40
Markinch Junction .. arrive	8 5	7 14		8 16			10 26		11 24			11 45			B		
Leslie .. arrive	8 5						10 40		10 58								
Markinch Junction .. leave	7 24 7 31		8 32	8 18	9 0		9 25		10 16			11 4			1 55		1 47 2 28
Leven .. arrive	8 16			8 39	9 22		10 16		10 22			11 14					2 42
Elie ..	8 55			8 45	9 43		10 34		10 26								
Anstruther .. arrive	8 5			8 57					10 31			11 14					1 15
Methil .. arrive	8 32	7 31							10 37			11 48					1 25
Dunfermline (Upper) arrive		7 34 7 48	9 0	9 0		8 31			10 43			11 55				1 35	1 55
Alloa .. arrive	7 57 3 15	9 0 9 22	9 43			8 39			10 50			12 3					2 2
Stirling ..	7 57 3 15	9 0 9 22			9 0 9 43				10 59			12 17					2 10
Thornton Junction .. leave	7 34	7 42			9 0		9 9		10 16			11 4			1 44		2 20
Dysart		7 49			9 17				10 22			11 23					2 28
Sinclairtown		7 54	8 39		9 23				10 26			11 31					2 35
Kirkcaldy	7 43 8 0	8 0 8 45	8 57		9 30		9 25 10 16		10 31	11 14		11 41	11 23				
Kinghorn	7 49 8 7				9 37		10 34		10 41			11 48	11 31				
Burntisland	7 57 8 13	8 15			9 44				10 48			11 55	11 35				
Aberdour	8 0	8 23							10 50			12 3	11 41				
Inverkeithing .. leave	8 35				9 49				10 59			12 17	11 48				
North Queensferry	8 40				8 9 9 32		10 22		11 11				11 55				2 28
Dalmeny (for South Queensferry) ..	8 23 8 49	9 11			9 38 9 36		11 5			11 44		12 3	12 3				2 35
Grahamston .. arrive	9 11				9 38					12 40			12 17				
Grangemouth ..	9 30						10 43			1 11			1 11			3 0	
Glasgow (Queen St.) .. arrive	9 30									12 50			12 50				
Corstorphine .. leave	9 4	9 32			9 54				11 24	11 58			11 58			1 52	2 51
Haymarket ..	9 8	9 36			9 58				11 28	12 2			12 2			1 56	2 55
Edinburgh (Waverley) .. arrive																	

Legend / footnotes:
- Tuesdays only
- Tuesdays only (p.m.)
- **M** Connection to Elie and Anstruther on Mondays only.
- ‡ Does not convey bulky or heavy luggage to or from Intermediate Stations between Aberdeen and Edinburgh.
- **W** Calls at Markinch on Wednesdays only at 10·54 a.m.
- **B** Connection to Elie on Thursdays only.
- **F** Connection to Leslie on Mondays.
- **C** Calls at Guyar on Wednesdays only at 8·41 a.m. only to pick up passengers.
- § Arrives at Dunfermline (Lower)
- Runs via Dunfermline (Lower)

Extracts from NBR timetable. 1st June, 1897.

via the Tay Bridge, Fifeshire, and the Forth Bridge.

	Sundays.							Week-Days.											
	a.m	p.m 3 30	p.m 3 30		S 7 45	p.m 9 35	p.m	p.m 5 30	5 30 / 7 35	p.m	p.m 6 30	p.m 3 30		p.m	p.m 1 25	3 40	p.m		
leave **Aberdeen**		3 30			7 45	9 35														
leave **Dundee** (Tay Bridge)	7 15 / 7 19	05 30 / 3													1 25 / 3 40				
" Esplanade															3 35 / 3 52				
" St Fort								7 30 / 7 46	7 30 / 7 46	6 30 / 6 34		5 28 / 5 44						
arrive Leuchars Junction	7 26	9						7 51	7 51	6 40									
leave Wormit	7 31	4 13								6 45									
" West Newport	7 34	4 17								6 49									
" East Newport	7 41	4 22								6 54									
" Tayport	7 51	4 33								7 5									
" Leuchars Old Station										7 14									
arrive Leuchars Junction								7 25	7 25	7 21		5 30			3 30		1 10		
leave St Andrews	8 1	1 44								7 28					3 30 / 3 53		1 15 / 1 19		
leave Leuchars Junction	8 4	4 51			8 40			7 59	7 59	7 34		5 45			4 / 4		1 25		
" Dairsie	8 8	4 56			8 45					8 30							1 36		
arrive **Cupar**	8 15	5 2			8 51					8 8		5 57			4 10	4 34	1 38		
" Springfield																			
arrive Ladybank Junction								8 13	8 13	9 10							1 40 / 1 48		
" Perth	8 25	4 8						10	10								1 55		
arrive Kinross Junction	8 26	5 15																	
leave Ladybank Junction	8 35	5 23						8 14	8 14								2 11		
" Kingskettle	8 41																2 14		
" Falkland Road																	2 21		
arrive Markinch Junction								8 20	8 20								2 29		
arrive Leslie																			
leave Markinch Junction	8 43	5 25						9 25	9 25								2 31		
arrive Thornton Junction	8 48	5 33						10 29	10 29			6 27			4 34		2 39		
arrive Leven																	2 47		
" Elie																	2 57		
" Anstruther																	3 11		
arrive Methil																	3 19		
arrive **Dunfermline** (Upper)	8 49	9 7						9 7	9 7	8 7							3 29		
" Alloa	8 56	9 56						9 56	9 56								3 36		
" Stirling	9 5	10 20						10 20	10 20								3 46		
leave Thornton Junction	8 55	5 48						8 32	8 32	8 17					4 36	5 14			
" Dysart	9 12	5 55													4 45				
" Sinclairtown	9 26	6 2													4 45				
" **Kirkcaldy**	9 28	6 12													4 55				
" Kinghorn	9 39	6 21													5				
" Burntisland	9 46	6 33																	
" Aberdour	9 53	6 37																	
leave Inverkeithing		6 47						9 12	9 12			6 42				5 14			
" North Queensferry								9 16	9 16			6 49				5 18			
" Dalmeny (for So. Queensferry)												6 53							
arrive Grahamston																			
" Grangemouth																			
" **Glasgow** (Queen St.)	11 0	8 10				10 58									6 25				
leave Corstorphine	10 4																		
" Haymarket	10 10	7 12																	
arrive **Edinburgh** (Waverley)	10 14	7 16				11											4 3 / 4 7		

S — Saturdays only.

S — Does not convey bulky or heavy luggage to and from Intermediate Stations between Aberdeen and Edinburgh except for English Stations.

§ — This train may leave Stations earlier than shewn, thus (§) six minutes earlier than shewn.

M — Calls at Ladybank on Mondays, Tuesdays, & Fridays, and connection to Perth on those days.

† — This train may leave Dundee at 3-35 p.m.

‡ — On Tuesdays does not arrive till 3-37 p.m.

* — Connection to Leslie on Mondays, Thursdays, and Saturdays.

F — Connection to Perth on Mondays and Fridays only.

Extracts from NBR timetable, 1st June, 1897.

arrive 10 minutes before the East Coast train, which could seldom keep to time due to the congested conditions at Waverley.

In 1891, and again in 1893, the East Coast shaved minutes off their timetables, trains now arriving in 11 hours 35 minutes with the Euston train arriving in 11 hours 50 minutes. The North British was determined to beat the Caledonian and gave instructions to ensure that its trains made a smart departure from both Waverley and Dundee stations. By 1st July, 1895 rivalries were hotting up and the NBR had to shave a further 15 minutes off its schedules for it to arrive safely ahead of the Caley at 7.20 am. A fortnight later the Caley train was scheduled to arrive at 7.00 am, the following day actually arriving at 6.47 am.

Over the next few days, the battle increased in intensity so that by the end of the month the NBR and its allies operated a schedule giving a 6.25 am arrival, even although the slowest intermediate journey times from King's Cross to Aberdeen were to be found between Edinburgh and Dundee and between Dundee and Arbroath. With average speeds between 45 and 50 mph, the timings either side of Dundee were still good even when compared with those of the 20th century. The night that the new fast service was introduced, the train left Edinburgh late, behind two new Holmes 4-4-0s but reached the stop at Dundee ahead of time, arriving in Aberdeen two minutes early, only to be beaten by the West Coast. Indeed, it was not until 18th August that the NBR arrived ahead of the Caley at 6.17 am, six minutes before its rival.

The East Coast side gained new confidence from its success and a revised target of 5.40 am was set from the 19th August, 1895. An arrival at Tay Bridge station, Dundee of 4.08 am, departing two minutes later resulted, and as the train was not to carry passengers for stations south of Dundee, a prompt departure was confidently expected at any stops *en route*. That night another Holmes 4-4-0, No.293, was attached to the train which had arrived early at Waverley but was held by signals and set off for the two bridges and Dundee with just two minutes in hand. A record breaking run to Tay Bridge station resulted, where it arrived 6¾ mins ahead of time. As the water column at Dundee was notoriously slow, taking on water would have slowed the train and it left only 2½ mins early, having a brisk run to Aberdeen only to find the Caley had been there for more than 15 minutes.

The next day another revised schedule was published with a 5.13 am arrival at Aberdeen, leaving Dundee at 3.50 am after a two minute stop. That night, 20th/21st August, the train made time throughout the journey and left Dundee early once again, but disappointing work by the NBR driver from there allowed the Caley train, driven by the renowned John Soutar, to reach the key junction of Kinnaber first and thus beat the East Coast by just over a minute. A superb run of 59 minutes from Edinburgh to Dundee was made the following night, once again with Holmes 4-4-0 No.293 which handed over to its sister No.262 at Dundee. This ensured the train reached Kinnaber first, beating driver John Soutar and the Caley by nearly 15 minutes. The NBR inspector was concerned about the racing since it was being carried out with a blatant disregard for speed restrictions through junctions and over the Tay Bridge. Having travelled on the previous two nights, he was able to report that the crossing of the Tay Bridge had taken one minute and forty seconds.

The Directors of the East Coast companies were all consulted as to the wisdom of continuing the race and the conclusion was that they must consider safety as of paramount importance. The West Coast ran against the clock on the night of the 22nd and the Caley arrived in less time than the NBR had the previous night. Their even speedier response brought on a temporary resurgence of racing fervour from the North British but common sense prevailed that night and the racing was over. Both companies felt that they could truthfully claim to be victors.

The following year, the Tsar of Russia was carried from Leith Docks to Ballater by the NBR on a special train. Special notices for this 'Imperial Train' showed that it was to depart at 2.30 pm on Tuesday 22nd September, 1896 and arrive at Dundee at 3.53 pm, where an engine change was scheduled to take three minutes. Originally scheduled for the previous day, the royal party was taken forward to Aberdeen and it is interesting to note that 18 trains were affected on the D&AR section of the line alone by the passage of the special.

Public Transport

The first public street transport in Dundee ran in the 1870s, when the Dundee and District Tramway was formed. The first route ran from the Head Post Office, in Euclid Crescent in the town centre to Dalhousie Terrace, Perth Road, the horse-drawn bus service beginning on 30th August, 1877. On 1st February, 1878 the company took over horse-drawn services to Lochee, Maryfield, Hilltown and Blackness Road, and tram lines were laid on these routes, beginning in 1879 to Lochee and Blackness.

Steam haulage was experimented with in April 1880 on the East End lines. An experimental combined car was delivered to Dundee West by Caledonian Railway from the makers, Dickinson & Co. of Birkenhead, having been out of gauge for some of the tunnels on the way. It was towed up Sea Wynd but stuck on the way and it took two days to release and place it on the tracks at the Nethergate. Six horses then moved the vehicle to Lochee depot for trials and was returned to its makers in December 1880. Loading gauge problems also delayed the delivery of cars from Preston in 1900

Broughty Ferry and Monifieth were also reached by public tramway, when the Dundee Tramways Act was passed in 1872 and track was laid along Cowgate and Seagate to Broughty Ferry Road and then a new thoroughfare into Broughty Ferry at Queen Street. Routes eventually reached as far as Baldovan, Lochee, and Maryfield stations as well as Craig Pier adjacent to both Tay Bridge and West stations.

Winter Alarms . . .

Accidents, of course, will happen and the railways around Dundee were no exception to this maxim. The most notable, perhaps of all time, was the Tay Bridge disaster in the depths of a winter storm but this does not totally eclipse

A class 'J37' 0-6-0 struggles through the snow at Kirkbuddo in February, 1961.   *Michael Smith*

another disaster which happened as a result of winter weather. The year 1906 had already seen serious accidents occur at Grantham and Salisbury, when winter had fallen early in December and, by Christmas, the country was in the grip of a blanket of snow and ice, whipped up by strong winds.

On 28th December, 1906, 27 years to the day of the Tay Bridge collapse, the dreadful weather throughout the east coast of Scotland was influencing train services and, at Arbroath, the situation had been further affected by the breakdown of a goods train which had divided into three on the up line at Easthaven. The driver attempted to reconnect his train and promptly derailed the wagons in the drifting snow, resulting in the imposition of single line working between Easthaven and Elliot Junction, although this was not notified to Arbroath until the afternoon due to damage to the telegraph lines. An express from Edinburgh to Aberdeen had been delayed by these events, reaching Arbroath at 10.41 am. The lines to the north were completely blocked by snow, with several trains already stuck. The express was crossed over to the up platform and held while a following train arrived around one o'clock, thus limiting access to the St Vigeans line and the turntable there.

At 3.10 pm, a local train to Dundee East, operated by the Caledonian, set off in the poor conditions, and the express followed some time later, returning its passengers to Edinburgh. As the locomotive, class '317' 4-4-0 No. 324, had not been turned the driver, Gourlay, was exposed to the full force of the storm. The train emerged from the cutting, constructed to accommodate the Joint Line with the Arbroath and Forfar, into the face of the storm. The local, not surprisingly, had been held up at Elliot Junction waiting for the single line pilotman when the returning express struck the stationary train at an estimated 30 mph. Twenty-one passengers were killed as well as the fireman of the express. Gourlay was charged with 'Culpably and recklessly driving his train while under the influence of drink.' It was alleged that he had spent the time at Arbroath in the nearby Victoria Bar. Driver Gourlay was found guilty of failing to obey instructions to go carefully but not of being drunk.

Winter weather often had an effect on train working throughout the north-east of Scotland and there were many occasions when trains were held up. Snow had been the cause of a delay at Kirkbuddo on the Forfar direct line, when a Dundee to Forfar train was stuck in a snowdrift. The *Weekly News* reported in 1898 that:

> . . . passengers were famishing with hunger and shivering with the cold. Some young men bethought in desperation of the guards van and rummaging about amongst the baskets and boxes, they found about a dozen loaves of bread which had been sent by a Dundee baker to one of the country houses in the district. Hunger and cold combined was too much to be borne and the bread was annexed and divided among the starving passengers.

Farther afield, a more distant accident involving a Dundee train happened again in the winter, this time at Castlecary on Friday 10th December, 1937. Snow was again falling, when 'D29' class 4-4-0 No. 3896, *Dandie Dinmont*, was struck in the rear by an Edinburgh train, resulting 35 deaths.

LONDON AND NORTH EASTERN RAILWAY

DAY EXCURSIONS

FROM

DUNDEE (TAY BRIDGE and ESPLANADE)

On MONDAY, 9th APRIL 1923

TO	Time of Departure — From Dundee (Tay Bdg.)	From Esplanade	Time of Return	Return Fare, Third Class — From Dundee (Tay Bdg.)	From Esplanade
	a.m.	a.m.	p.m.	s. d.	s. d.
Aberdeen ...	7 50	...	7 40	7 6	...
Abernethy (via Lindores)	9 3	9 6	6 57	2 6	2 6
Alloa (via Dunfermline)	7 15	...	6 9	5 6	...
Anstruther (via St Andrews)	7 56	7 59	7 32	3 0	3 0
Bervie ...	9 31	...	5 53	4 6	...
Berwick ...	7 15	...	2 23	9 6	...
Burntisland ...	8 25	8 44	8 15	4 6	4 0
gCoatbridge (Sunnyside)	8 25	...	5 45	7 6	...
Cowdenbeath (New)	7 15	...	5 45	4 0	...
Crail (via St Andrews)	7 56	7 59	7 41	2 6	2 6
Cupar ...	8 25	8 44	8 24	2 0	2 2
Dalmeny ...	9 50	...	5 25	5 0	...
Dollar ...	7 15	...	3 32	5 0	...
Dumbarton ...	7 34	...	5 56	8 0	...
Dunbar ...	7 15	...	4 35	4 6	...
Dunfermline (Lower)	7 15	...	5 30	4 0	...
Edinburgh (Waverley)	8 25	...	7 30	6 0	...
Elie (via St Andrews)	7 56	7 59	7 12	3 6	3 6
Falkirk (High)	7 34	...	7 33	6 6	...
Glasgow (Queen Street)	7 34	...	7 0	8 0	...

TO	Time of Departure — From Dundee (Tay Bdg.)	From Esplanade	Time of Return	Return Fare, Third Class — From Dundee (Tay Bdg.)	From Esplanade
	a.m.	a.m.	p.m.	s. d.	s. d.
Galashiels ...	7 15	...	6 18	8 6	...
Gullane ...	7 15	...	4 51	7 6	...
Helensburgh ...	7 34	...	5 35	8 6	...
Kinross Junction ...	7 15	...	5 43	3 6	3 6
Kirkcaldy ...	8 25	8 44	8 25	3 6	3 6
Leven (via Thornton)	8 40	8 44	5 57	3 6	3 6
Lindores ...	9 3	9 6	7 10	2 5	2 5
Largo (via Crail)	7 56	7 59	6 56	4 0	4 0
Leuchars Junction	8 40	8 44	7 20	1 3	1 3
Melrose ...	7 15	...	6 8	8 6	...
Montrose ...	9 5	...	7 30	3 0	...
Newburgh (via Lindores)	9 3	9 6	7 3	2 6	2 6
North Berwick ...	7 15	...	5 10	8 0	...
Peebles ...	7 15	...	5 17	8 0	...
Perth (via Lindores)	9 3	9 6	6 40	2 6	2 6
Pinkhill (for Zoological Park)	9 25	...	6 38	6 0	...
Rumbling Bridge	7 15	...	3 50	4 6	...
St Andrews ...	10 30	10 33	7 5	1 11	1 11
Stonehaven ...	10 50	...	8 5	5 6	...

g ... Edinburgh

* Pinkhill passengers ... 10.20 p.m. ... train from Edinburgh.

Extract from LNER publication *Programme of Excursions to Stations in Scotland*, 1923.

. . . and Summer Excursions

Dundee, having its situation near the Angus and Fife coasts and within easy reach of the Highlands and the other major centres in Scotland, meant that the working man and his family could take advantage of excursion trips organised by the railway companies whenever a holiday fell. Bank holidays in Scotland follow a different pattern for each town and surrounding area.

A series of holiday excursion programmes were published by both the LNER and LMS in the 1920s and 1930s. An extensive programme of excursions was published by the newly established LNER for the Spring holiday on Monday 9th April, 1923. (The Caledonian did not join the Grouping until July 1923.) Special cheap third class return tickets were issued throughout the weekend from Dundee Tay Bridge to all stations in Scotland with a minimum fare of 5s. 0d. but for the day of issue only. Ten excursions were laid on, trains departing from Dundee for all points of the compass at 7.15, 7.34, 7.50, 7.56, 8.25, 8.40, 9.03, 9.31, 9.50, and 10.30 am, all utilising former NBR routes. Four of the southbound departures called at Esplanade station as well.

Day excursions were also run *from* Carnoustie, Monifieth and Broughty Ferry to destinations as far apart as Melrose and Glasgow, Queen Street, the latter routed via Kinross. The excursion for Glasgow left Carnoustie at 6.12, Monifieth at 6.21 and Broughty Ferry at 6.27 am, presumably fast through Dundee and then via the Tay Bridge. Fares ranged from 1s. 3d. to Leuchars Junction to 8s. 6d. to Helensburgh. Further departures were run from Tayport, Newport and Wormit to Dundee Tay Bridge to meet specials to Aberdeen, Montrose and Edinburgh. There was, however, one departure in the opposite direction from Wormit at 9.35 am to Cupar and St Andrews.

An autumn holiday for Dundee was held on Monday 26th September, 1932, and the LMS ran several trains that weekend. On Saturday 24th, a 2.45 pm departure was run from Dundee West for Glasgow, Buchanan Street and, on Sunday, a 10.00 am train was run to Glasgow Central. However, the main excursions were worked on Monday when additional services left West station at 7.50, 10.35 and 11.35 am, and from East station at 12.07 pm. The LMS had the advantage of both the Newtyle branch and Forfar direct line to operate trains to stations within the county of Angus, allowing a greater variety of destination than the LNER. A concession to west end passengers was that they could travel by local train from Magdalen Green via Dundee West in both directions if their excursion train did not stop there.

In 1935 the Spring holiday for the city fell on Monday 8th April and the LNER and LMS had by then combined their efforts and issued joint details of fares from Dundee and district to holiday destinations. Cheap return tickets were available from Dundee West by any train all day, examples of third class return fares being:

Aberfeldy	5s. 6d.	Callander	6s. 0d.
Largs (by train and ferry) 11s. 3d. cabin, 10s. 9d.steerage.			
Peebles	9s. 6d.	Perth	2s. 6d.

There were special trains running that Monday, including one departure at 7.50am to Glasgow, Buchanan Street, but there were several return options at

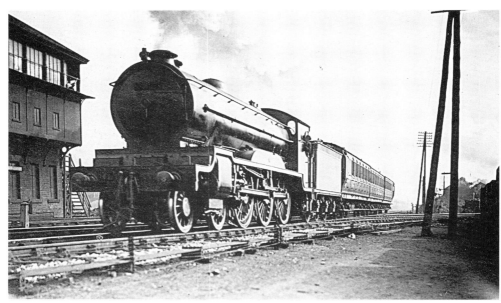

Pickersgill '956' class 4-6-0 passes Buckingham Junction signal box with a local train for Perth.
Author 's Collection

A view of Magdalen Green station during the Highland Show in the 1930s. *Author's Collection*

ROYAL HIGHLAND SHOW, DUNDEE. 1949.

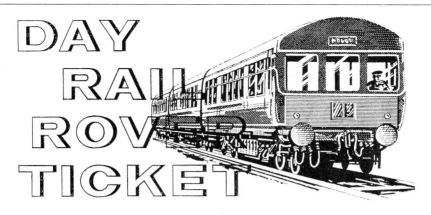

DAY RAIL ROVER TICKET

all day — any day

Day Rail Rover tickets, Price 22/- second class (33/- first class) give unlimited travel throughout the area shown on the map.   Issued daily 1st May to 31st October, 1963.

BRITISH RAILWAYS

B.R. 35001/1—EK—B. 35292—January, 1963   Printed by Hugh Paton & Sons Ltd. Edinburgh

Day Rover poster, 1963.   *Author's Collection*

7.15, 7.40, 7.55 and 10.50 pm. The last train would allow day trippers the chance of a return boat trip from Glasgow down the River Clyde or 'Doon the watter' to any one of the many seaside resorts. Later in the summer, on Saturday 23rd June, 1935, the LMS ran six special excursions from Dundee West to St Fillans, on the shore of Loch Earn, followed the next weekend by two more to Oban, a trip which was repeated three weeks later on 14th July.

Road Transport

Although Dundee could be considered to be well served with goods depots both at the three main stations and on the Newtyle line serving the northern side of town, the jute industry was not blessed with a railhead at any but the Camperdown works of Cox Brothers in Lochee. The hilly nature of the town necessitated an intense delivery and collection service from the centre of town to the jute mills spread along the two streams (or burns) which served as their original source of power.

One of the early companies to undertake deliveries for the railways in the area was Wordie and Co. The first record of an office is in 1853, and it is known that they undertook to deliver for both the SCR and SNER, the North British having an arrangement with the Dundee company of Mutter Howey. This left the field clear for the Caledonian to contract Wordie to act as their carting agent in Dundee, paying them more than £500 per month by 1880.

The office for the railway business was at the new goods depot of the Caledonian Railway adjacent to Dundee West station on South Union Street. In the early years of this century, Wordie had established their main base in Dock Street, Dundee where 224 horses were kept in three large stables. Most of the jute carts (known as lorries) were two horse affairs with brakes applied to the rear wheels, in view of the steepness of the hills.

A handful of horses were also employed in the 3½ miles of harbour railways to shunt wagons and vans to ships on the quayside. Other services which Wordie and Co. provided for the railways included delivering oil from William Briggs refinery, and transporting prize animals to the Highland Show in the years when it was held on Riverside Park.

Of course, as road transport became more reliable and more popular, the railway companies provided their own delivery and collection service, calling at stations along the main routes. From Dundee Tay Bridge for example, the services provided by the LNER included 'road vans' to Anstruther via both Thornton and St Andrews, Dunfermline and Lindores as well as Perth via Ladybank. Arbroath was served by vehicles from both Tay Bridge and East stations. The LMS had a similar series of 'road wagons' delivering from the West station. These vehicles operated to a strict timetable in order to be marshalled into certain daily trains and were met at the stations by lorries to make the local deliveries.

The new companies which took ownership of the old enemies at the Grouping clearly were maintaining the traditions of the North British and the Caledonian railways around Dundee.

Chapter Eleven

From Grouping to ScotRail
1923-1995

'The railways are still the mainstay of the inland transport system'
Lord Leathers, one-time HM Government Minister

New Companies, Old Rivalries

Rapidly rising costs after World War I, increased the operating difficulties experienced by both the Caledonian and the North British. Throughout the country, they had served the war effort well but their revenues had been protected by the subsidies received during hostilities. Although the Railway Executive Committee had exercised control over the companies from the outbreak of war until 15th August, 1921, the years immediately after the war revealed that both the infrastructure and rolling stock had suffered from heavy use and neglect during the previous four years. Reorganisation was essential.

The Railway Act of 1921 provided compensation, amounting to £60 million to all companies, for arrears of maintenance and replacement of stores consumed during the war years. More significantly, however, the Act set about forging the many individual railway companies of Great Britain into four large concerns covering the country geographically. Initially it had been suggested that there should be seven groups, with all of the Scottish companies formed into one unified body, but this was opposed on economic grounds. With privatisation dominating railway organisation in the 1990s, it may seem ironical that one of the earliest franchises which the new legislation sought to create was for the whole of Scotland! The Grouping Act eventually maintained the west and east coast distinctions by the creation of the LMS and LNER which absorbed the Caley and NBR repectively. Thus the two companies which had served Dundee since the mid-1860s were destined to remain in competition for another 25 years, if under different names.

Passenger and Freight Services

By the time of the Grouping on 1st January, 1923, the NBR and CR had established a regular pattern of train services which the new owners generally maintained. The NBR provided around a dozen daily passenger services over the Tay Bridge to Edinburgh Waverley via Cupar, including Anglo-Scottish trains to and from both Kings Cross and St Pancras. There was also a service via the Fife coast to both Edinburgh and Glasgow, Queen Street. About 20 local trains from Tay Bridge station to Fife were destined for Tayport, some travelling through to Leuchars Junction and one each day went onwards to St Andrews.

Other St Andrews trains were routed via St Fort. The Perth trains through Newburgh still numbered four per day, one of these starting back at Arbroath. Through trains ran between Edinburgh and Aberdeen and the NBR also had its

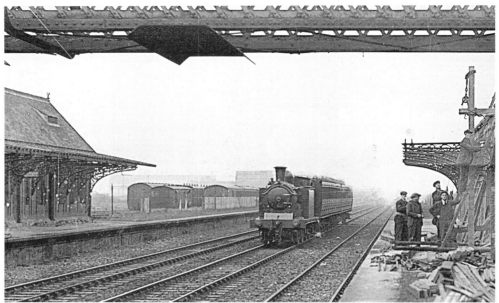

Stannergate station in the 1930s with a Forfar train on the through tracks as the down side buildings are demolished. *Michael Smith Collection*

Invergowrie station in LMS days, looking to Dundee, round the curve of Invergowrie Bay. *HMRS*

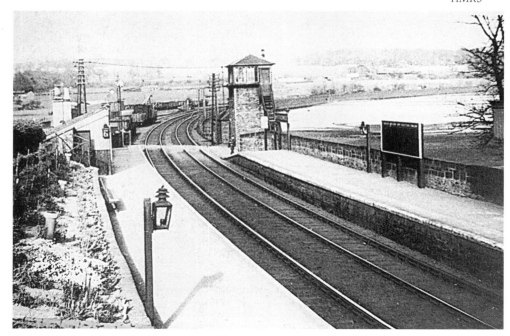

McIntosh '439' class 0-4-4T, No. 15180, on the Dundee West turntable. *Author's Collection*

Neilson '502' class 0-4-0ST, No. 16003, with an adapted wooden tender, both with dumb buffers. *RAS Marketing*

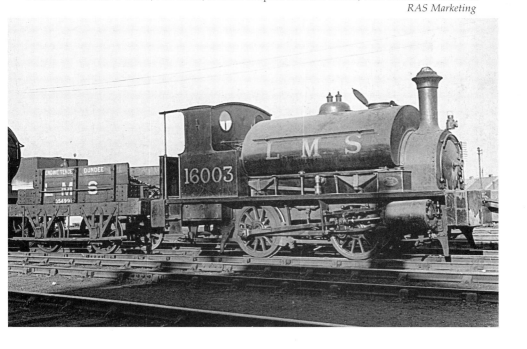

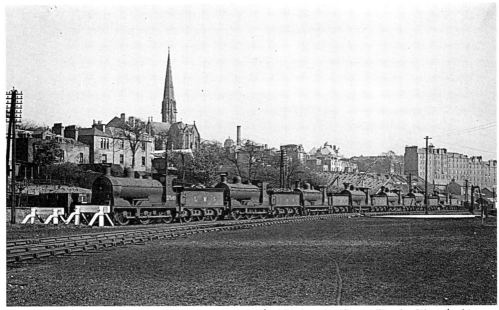

A row of seven ex-CR and ex-HR locomotives on the 'dead engine' line at Dundee West shed in May 1936. *Author's Collection*

Dundee East in its original form with a fan shaped end screen. Also visible in this 1930s view is the entrance to Dock Street tunnel (*right*), and the mineral yard and gas works (*left*) as well as the eastern end of the Harbour branch (*right foreground*). *Dundee Courier*

share of local trains to Arbroath. Although most main line services called at Arbroath, neither the NBR nor the LNER as its successor offered local passengers the choice of travelling to Dundee by these fast trains, relegating them to the stopping trains from East station.

The Caley did not join the new LMS until 1st July, 1923, although its share in the D&AR was transferred to the west coast company from 1st January, at the same time as the NBR's share passed to the LNER. Caledonian services which were passed on to the LMS remained focused on West station still running to Perth, Edinburgh, Princes Street through Stirling, and both Glasgow, Buchanan Street and Central. Other services from Dundee West went via Ninewells Junction to Newtyle (one fast daily service stopping only at Lochee) and then on to either Blairgowrie or Alyth. By the time of the grouping, however, trains no longer called at Lochee West.

From East station, trains still departed for Forfar, either semi-fast or all stations with some additional peak services terminating at Barnhill. There was also a Saturdays only afternoon train to Kingennie to permit the rural communities to spend the afternoon in Dundee. During the 1920s and 1930s, the regular commuter service from Arbroath to East station was maintained.

Goods services were from the same four directions as their passenger counterparts. General merchandise came from the south often by way of Carlisle and a nightly train served Dundee in each direction from the border town. A regular goods service also ran nightly between both College and Sighthill, Glasgow and Dundee over the NBR lines. This was as well as a similar service from Edinburgh via the Forth and Tay Bridges, leaving the capital nightly except Monday with a matching return. During 1932, the LNER introduced the 'agreed flat rate' and Keillers, the marmalade manufacturers, were amongst the first to take advantage of it to send their products all round the country.

Of course, coal continued to arrive in the city from West Fife and Lanarkshire coalfields giving the LNER and LMS regular traffic from both these regions. The destination could be any of the mineral yards serving the area: Dundee West, Tay Bridge or East as well as Broughty Ferry, Fairmuir, Maryfield, Lochee and Baldovan where coal merchants were to be found. Many of these merchants had their own traders' wagons which had been registered with either the Caley or the North British. However the increasing tendency for common user to reduce the cost of returning wagons empty spread these interesting wagons around a much wider network.

Local pick-up goods travelled to Perth, Newtyle and the stations on the south bank of the Tay, and Fife coast to collect both vans and wagons which had been left on a previous visit and to drop off further vehicles or small consignments. The fish expresses from Aberdeen were the premier overnight service through Dundee, operating to express timings from the north in order to reach the London markets by the following morning.

The railways brought different traffic to the town when agricultural or entertainment events were held. In 1933, the Highland Show was held in Dundee, this annual show being staged at Riverside Park now extended to the area to the south of the Perth line. The Esplanade station was used by many

Workmen raise the platform on Magdalen Green station in the early 1950s. The station was closed on 11th June, 1956. A very dirty ex-LMS Fowler/Hughes class '5' 'Crab' 2-6-0 eases a short freight through the station. *Dundee Courier*

An ex-NBR 'J37' class No. 64547 draws a train of mineral wagons back to Camperdown Junction along the harbour branch network. *Michael Smith Collection*

more passengers than usual when the show was on as it was the nearest LNER station to the showground. The waiting rooms were fitted out as cloakrooms in case of inclement weather, but were little used. Magdalen Green station was much closer to the showground and served the LMS line. When the annual circus came to Dundee, often it too arrived by train and latterly set up its tents on Riverside Park. In order to generate the most publicity on the Sunday before the week's entertainment began, a parade of animals, entertainers and circus vehicles was held along the Esplanade from either Tay Bridge or West station, much to the delight of many a child and adult. Esplanade station closed to passengers from Monday 2nd October, 1939, although it is still in use by civil engineers. In common with other towns and cities, football specials ran whenever a fixture demanded it, probably the most significant being when Dundee FC played in the Scottish Cup final at Hampden Park in Glasgow in 1951.

British Railways, Scottish Region

On 1st January, 1948, the four main companies were absorbed into the nationalised British Railways, a part of the monolithic new British Transport Commission which was set up by the post-war Labour government to run a nationally co-ordinated transport system. The Dundee and Arbroath finally lost its independence under the Act, which brought the major railways of Scotland under one management. One hundred and ten years after it first began to operate as an independent company between the two towns on the Angus coast, the D&AR was reduced to just another line in the national railway system.

There were economies to be obtained by having the whole network under one management. One example of this was demonstrated when the role of the station master at Tay Bridge and West stations combined into a single post in 1951. In the same year, Dundee West shed was closed to steam, having had a minimal allocation since nationalisation. Thereafter it handled the overspill from its considerably busier and cramped ex-North British neighbour. Formerly identified as 29C under the LMS method of coding locomotive sheds, Dundee West was reduced to a sub-shed of Tay Bridge (62B, its BR identity). As the ageing NB and Caledonian classes were withdrawn from service, Dundee West turned into a graveyard for redundant locomotives.

Metropolitan-Cammell built diesel multiple units were stabled at Dundee West from their introduction to the area in July 1958, initially on stopping services from Tay Bridge station to Edinburgh Waverley, Glasgow, Queen Street and Thornton Junction, and to Glasgow, Buchanan Street from West station. These were later increased in January 1959 to include services from Tayport to Arbroath and Perth to Arbroath via Tay Bridge station. The twin units were augmented by three-car units in May of that year. The following spring, a further diesel multiple unit service was introduced, this time from Edinburgh by the Fife coast route, trains beginning on Monday 4th April, 1960. Dundee West shed was converted for diesel multiple unit servicing and for

Ex-LNER class 'B1' No. 61172 at Dundee East in December 1958 with a local train for Arbroath.

Michael Smith

Dundee West station in its final form.

Dundee Courier

'A3' class 4-6-2 No. 60052 *Prince Palatine,* inside Tay Bridge shed.   *Author's Collection*

The west end of Tay Bridge shed during roof repairs. Ex-LNER 'V2' class 2-6-2 No. 60892, and ex-NBR 'J37' class 0-6-0 No. 64531 are amongst the locomotives on shed.   *Dundee Courier*

Ex-NBR 'J35' 0-6-0 No. 64492 on the turntable at Dundee Tay Bridge shed with ex-LNER 'V2' class 2-6-2 No. 60834 and ex-CR '439' class No. 55267 alongside. *RAS Marketing*

Kingsmuir station on the Dundee and Forfar line in 1959, looking towards Dundee.

Michael Smith

handling diesel shunters and main line locomotives. It was demolished in 1985 after lying unused for years while Dundee Tay Bridge shed lost its steam allocation and closed from Monday 1st May, 1967.

The importance of Tay Bridge shed up to its closure is reflected in the complement of men in September 1965, 150 drivers, 52 passed firemen, 44 firemen, 24 passed cleaners, and 89 maintenance staff. There were 25 steam engines, 40 dmus and 15 diesel shunters on shed.

In 1955, the second of two returning Sunday school outings ended in tragedy for one of the crew and two of the passengers. Class '5' 4-6-0 No. 45458 was returning to Dundee tender first on Saturday 28th May when it was derailed at speed as it reached the curve at Wormit station. With a ruling speed limit of 20 mph through the station reducing to 10 mph for the tablet exchange, the train was reckoned to be travelling at 50 mph or more as it entered the tunnel near the south end of the Tay Bridge. The tender left the track first, inside Wormit tunnel, followed by the locomotive as they emerged at the station. Both overturned on to the platform, dragging the first four coaches including some of NBR ancestry with it. None of the 500 picnickers in the coaches was seriously injured but, sadly, the fireman and two unauthorised footplate observers, an adult and child, lost their lives.

Contraction and Closure

Contraction of the less well used lines came quickly in the 1950s. Commuter traffic by rail was suffering from wider car ownership and the improvements to the trunk roads. Additionally, the bus services provided by Walter Alexander and Sons from Angus towns to Dundee became more popular as people became more dependent on the employment which the city provided. Despite an inconvenient depot in North Lindsay Street, bus services brought passengers from all round the county, improving on the services previously offered by rail. Within Dundee, the Corporation Transport department were expanding their bus services to the new housing estates on the outskirts of the city while replacing the ageing tram services which had earlier been the downfall of local rail passenger services.

Only the half-hour river crossing by the Tay Ferries restricted bus services from Fife and extended the life of the train service to Tayport. However the passenger services beyond Tayport had ceased on Saturday 7th January, 1956 as had through freight traffic. A local mill was served just beyond Tayport, although there was a passenger service between Leuchars and Tayport for a short time. Equally the end of passenger traffic on the north Fife line on 10th February, 1951 left only the more populated area around Newport supporting a passenger service. Goods traffic ended on the north Fife line as late as October 1964.

The direct line to Forfar from East station, which was by then reduced to a Monday to Friday only service, was closed to passengers on Saturday 8th January, 1955. This removed the only direct passenger link between the county's major centre of population and the county town. The year 1955 also

Dundee West yard from a southbound train on the incline to Espanade station and the Tay Bridge. *Michael Smith*

The 1930s coaling tower at Tay Bridge shed dominates the mineral and goods yards in the late 1950s. *Dundee Courier*

An ex-LNER class 'V2' 2-6-2 heads clear of Camperdown junction and past the gas works with an Edinburgh to Aberdeen express. The branch into the East mineral yard is on the right, and the Harbour branch is to the left. *Author's Collection*

William Briggs bitumen tanks sit on the Harbour branch in the distance as an 'A2' class Pacific heads for Aberdeen. The banking in the foreground would have formed the start of the Dundee Suburban Railway, had it been built. *Author's Collection*

Ex-LNER 'D49' class 4-4-0 No. 62706 *Forfarshire* at Dundee West on 17th July, 1950 with a stopping train for Perth. Stanier class '5' 4-6-0 No. 45473 backs on to a Glasgow train on the right. *George Robin*

BR Standard class '4MT' 2-6-4T No. 80123 climbs up from Tay Bridge station to Esplanade station with a local train for Tayport, 16th May, 1957. *George Robin*

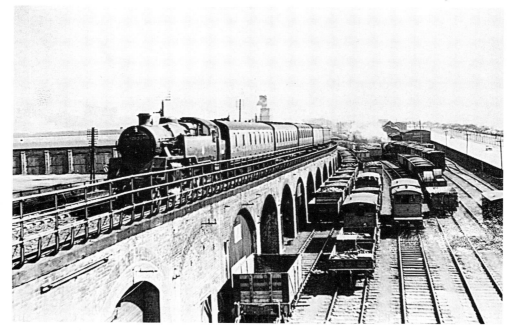

Ex-Caley 'Single' 4-2-2 No. 123 on exhibition at Dundee West in 1958.   *Michael Smith*

Ex-Caley 'Single' No. 123 with two ex-Caley coaches at Broughty Ferry bay platform in June 1961 with a Stephenson Locomotive Society railtour.   *Michael Smith*

Baldovan station in BR days, looking north.

Dundee Courier

Lochee station in the 1960s showing the imposing signal box and James Gowan's station building.

Dundee Courier

saw the cessation of passenger trains on the Newtyle line, a service which had divided there, to go on to either Blairgowrie or Alyth. Passenger trains ceased on Saturday 1st October, 1955, but goods continued for another 12 years, closure being a piecemeal contraction from Newtyle. Latterly, passenger services too had diminished in number, in this instance to only three up and two down trains each weekday (but five each way on Saturdays). The withdrawal of goods services began on 5th May, 1958 with their removal from the Newtyle to Auchterhouse section.

There were moves in the late 1950s to close West station and concentrate all passenger traffic on Tay Bridge but this was rejected on the grounds of capacity at the latter, being both cramped and below ground level. However, all Sunday services had been routed there from West station since 7th October, 1951, and through trains from Perth had used the Dock Street tunnel for some time. Tay Bridge was always the busiest of the three termini, handling over half the city's services. Thirty-six passenger trains started and terminated there daily in the late 1950s with around seven through trains in either direction. West station handled the Glasgow, Buchanan Street trains, 16 daily in each direction, whilst the modest East station before closure still handled the local traffic to Carnoustie and Arbroath, totalling about a dozen each way.

Through coaches on trains from Dundee West to Edinburgh, Princes Street were a remnant from the Caledonian days when an alternative route from Dundee was part of that company's competition with the NBR. Absent from the timetables for some time before 1957, two daily up through coaches appeared from 4th May, 1957, at 7.45 am and 12.00 noon, but without a down return working. The two were reduced to one in 1964, but a supplementary timetable revealed that this connection was not run from 15th June. Diesel powered haulage was introduced to the Edinburgh to Aberdeen services through Tay Bridge station in 1959, and followed by the Glasgow trains to West station in 1960.

The dominance of traffic at Tay Bridge station demanded improved facilities for passengers. For most of the station's existence, the booking office was in the upper storey of the building with access by a walkway over the tracks from the service road between the passenger and goods stations. Although there was a staircase to the entrance at South Union Street, this arrangement was inconvenient. In the late 1950s, a new booking office was constructed adjacent to the West Goods station linked to the South Union Street staircase. The creation of a taxi stance in front of this rather utilitarian building, echoed the much grander apron which graced the approach to West station. As the services from East station fell off and the Arbroath trains were run through Tay Bridge station to Perth, the former terminus of the Dundee and Arbroath Railway was allowed to deteriorate and decline. The station was closed from 5th January, 1959.

BR Standard class '5' 4-6-0 No. 73145, a regular on the route, heads the last train from Dundee West to Glasgow, Buchanan Street in May 1965.

Dundee Courier

The Beeching Years

The publication of *The Reshaping of British Railways* was made in March 1963, and the resulting axe of its author, Dr Richard Beeching, fell heavily in Scotland during the next few years. At Dundee, the Tay Bridge Goods shed, which had been built at the time of the opening of the bridge and lay just south of the station, was closed and all workings were transferred to Dundee West. In addition, the coal merchants yards of Smith Hood, Thomas Muir, Son and Paton, and many others which had been a feature of the railway landscape since the earliest days, were swept away and superseded by concentration depots.

All of this meant a re-arrangement of workings for freight trains at Dundee. Included in the contraction was the final section of the Newtyle line. However, before closure began there had previously been an expansion, albeit of a minor nature. With the post war expansion of housing in the north of the city came Kingsway industrial estate, located off Kings Cross Road to the west of the Newtyle line and near to Fairmuir Junction. A trailing branch line was constructed here to give access to several new factories. Trains reversed into the branch, crossing Kings Cross Road and running alongside two service roads, Dunsinane Avenue and Carlunie Road, between the modern factories of Veedor Root and others.

As the line contracted, the coal merchants who had established bases for themselves on the northern edges of Dundee transferred their businesses to town relying on motorised deliveries rather than the horse. The Baldovan yard disappeared with the closure of the line from Auchterhouse to Fairmuir Junction from 25th January, 1965, followed by Fairmuir and Maryfield mineral

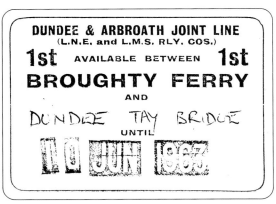

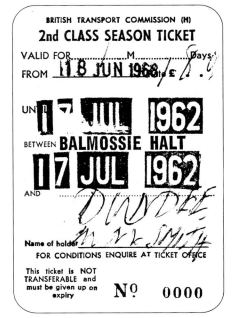

Above: A season ticket issued for the Dundee & Arbroath Joint Line. Note that although the ticket was issued in 1963, the ticket still refers to the LNER and LMS companies.

Right: The first season ticket to be issued from Balmossie Halt, No. 0000. Note the incorrect validity date.

An ex-LMS Stanier class '5' crossing Monifieth Road bridge at Barnhill with a freight for Forfar.
Michael Smith

A Carnoustie to Dundee dmu passes an Edinburgh to Aberdeen fast at Monifieth station.
Michael Smith

The interior of Dundee East in the 1950s, with its more recent end screen, clearly showing the arched nature of the roof. *Dundee Courier*

The inside of Dundee West shows the ravages of the demolition gangs in April 1966, less than a year after the last train. *Dundee Courier*

Leading porter Willie Ogilvie at West Ferry station.

Michael Smith

Ivatt 4-6-0 No. 46464 causes some anxiety amongst BR staff as they contemplate moving it during preservation.

Dundee Courier

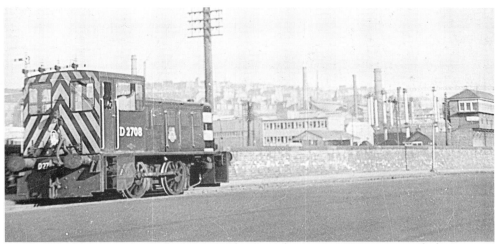

North British Locomotive Co.-built 0-4-0 225 hp diesel shunter No. D2708 pauses on the harbour lines near Camperdown Junction while a new English Electric class '4' 1Co-Co-1 diesel drops down to Dock Street tunnel with an Edinburgh train in 1961. *Author*

Metro-Cammell dmus complete their turn of duty and head through Buckingham Junction for Dundee West shed in 1961. *Author*

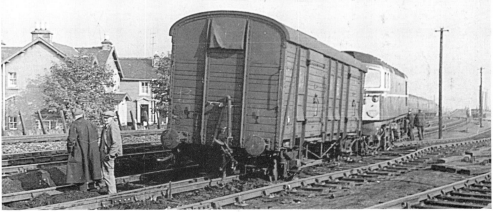

A derailed Birmingham RCW type '2' Bo-Bo diesel and van at Broughty Ferry goods yard.
Michael Smith

yards which closed with the goods depot at Lochee and the rest of the line from Ninewells Junction on Saturday 6th November, 1967. Latterly a type 1 'Clayton' diesel and finally a class '08' diesel shunter had operated a daily pick-up goods with shunting duties at each yard.

Like East station, Dundee West was allowed to run down following the relocation of the the new Arbroath to Perth services to Tay Bridge station and, when the land was required for the approach road for the new Tay road bridge, its fate was sealed. Thus one of the most striking railway station buildings in Scotland was closed from 3rd May, 1965. Dundee West station was demolished within the year, leaving all passenger services to be transferred to Dundee Tay Bridge, the cramped sub-surface station constructed for the North British which, with the general rundown in railway activity, was now able to cope with the few extra Glasgow trains.

One aspect of the remaining station was its accessibility from the main commercial heart of Dundee, never good at the best of times. Now with the construction of the approach roads for the new Tay crossing, the station was more isolated than ever. An attempt to move the country bus station adjacent came to nothing although a few buses did call for a short time. However this was short lived due to the lengthy route they had to take to the city centre. Pedestrian passengers were the most inconvenienced by having to cross a busy dual carriageway and a footbridge was constructed to accommodate them.

The opening of the Tay road bridge in 1966 landed a double blow for the railways on the Fife side of the river. It naturally provided successful competition for the service from Wormit by giving the motorist a new and speedier route to town than was provided by the ferry from Newport to Craig Pier. This competition was made complete, however when the line was severed between Tayport and Newport West to provide a new approach road from the southern end of the bridge. The final train to Tayport ran on 22nd May, 1966, a linking bus service operating until September of the following year.

Rail services continued to Wormit and Newport East for three more years, but a reduction in usage as a result of higher car ownership and the improved bus network provided by the bridge finally brought about the withdrawal of both the Newport and St Andrews trains in 1969. The last passengers travelled from Leuchars to St Andrews on 4th January and those to Newport East on 5th May, 1969 at the beginning of the summer timetable. The station buildings from Wormit were left standing for many years until being transferred and re-erected at the Bo'ness and Kinneil Railway.

Dundee station, now divested of its Tay Bridge label, was modernised fully in 1985. A £500,000 project provided a new travel centre and enquiry bureau housed in a two storey building faced with mirror glass, reflecting the architectural style of the time. The improvements were built on the site of the old Caley goods shed, to the north of the station. Having been separated from the city centre for many years, the station was provided with improved access to the town with a covered bridge from a new shopping mall in Nethergate.

The Dundee, Perth and London Shipping Company, which had provided a regular vessel from the Tay to the Thames since the beginning of the 19th century, withdrew from coastal shipping and transferred its London business to rail. The resulting three times a week dedicated overnight service departed from Sinclair Lye, adjacent to Tay Bridge station, for York Road freight terminal. Further re-organisation saw the arrival of National Carriers and the Freightliner depot at Dundee. Two cement companies established themselves in the area, Blue Circle on the site of the yard at East station and Castle near West station, the former being swept away when the East station area was redeveloped.

Invergowrie Bay Accident

October 1979 saw one of the worst accidents to occur on the lines to Dundee in the 20th century. On the 22nd of the month, the 8.44 am stopping service from Glasgow, Queen Street to Dundee left Perth with class '25', locomotive No. 25 083 in charge of five coaches, but running late and labouring under mechanical difficulties. The intermediate scheduled stops at Errol and Invergowrie were effected normally if later than scheduled, but shortly after leaving the latter station, the brakes on the leading bogie of the locomotive were found to be binding. The driver, however, decided to proceed to Dundee. The train moved forward and had reached that section of track running alongside Invergowrie Bay which formed part of the northern bank of the Tay.

One of the motors of the locomotive appeared to be on fire at this point and it drew to a standstill. The train had stopped for only a short time, when it was struck from behind by the 9.35 am Glasgow to Aberdeen express, powered by a class '47' at full speed. The impact pitched the rear two Mark I coaches of the Dundee train into the shallow water of the bay, killing both the occupying passengers of the last coach. The driver and secondman of the Aberdeen train were killed instantly, as their cab was destroyed by the impact. A further passenger died and 51 others were injured. The guard of the first train was not in the rear of the Dundee train and so escaped injury.

The signalling on this stretch of the line was semaphore and the crew of the class '47' had been alerted by both the down home signal being 'on' at Longforgan and the automatic warning system activating in the cab. In evidence to the inquiry, the guard said he saw the home signal move to 'off' (clear) as the train was slowly approaching it. The driver pulled away quickly, but the guard looked again at the signal and noted that the signal was 'a poor off', neither fully at danger nor at clear. It was the angle of inclination of the signal which was critical to the safety of the 8.44 am train and its occupants. The death of the driver of the second train meant that the explanation of events will never be known.

Final Formations

The closure of the Strathmore route in 1967, diverted all the Glasgow to Aberdeen trains through Dundee and increased the activity at Tay Bridge station. This resulted in an increase in traffic along the former Dundee and Perth line almost reducing the route over the river to second place. The need to renew track and resignal the lines through Dundee provided the ideal

Elliot junction, with the Carmyllie branch to the right near the scene of the 1906 accident.

Gerald Baxter

A Birmingham RCW-built class '27' Bo-Bo enters platform three at Tay Bridge station with a stopping train from Edinburgh, April 1982. *Author*

English Electric class '37' No. 37 156 *British Steel Hunterston* hauls an engineer's train away from Dundee, past the site of the former West sheds in October 1992. *Author*

Class '37s' Nos. 37026 and 37045 double-head an empty freight train into Dock Street tunnel from the loop line at Tay Bridge in October 1992. *Author*

An Edinburgh-bound train prepares to leave platform three at Dundee over the simplified track formation at the west end of the station. 'Sprinter' No.150 252 forms the service in October 1992.
Author

A local service to Carnoustie awaits departure from platform one at Tay Bridge station formed by 'Sprinter' No. 150 257 in 1992.
Author

A single line into the cement depot is all that remains of East station. 'Sprinter' No. 158 727 heads into Dock Street tunnel with a Glasgow train in 1992. *Author*

A ScotRail 'Express' unit No. 158 709 arrives at Tay Bridge station, platform four with a Glasgow to Aberdeen train in 1992. *Author*

opportunity in 1985 to rationalise the access from the west. All the signal cabins, those situated at either end of the station and those beyond the station limits, were closed at that time and replaced by the Dundee signalling centre housed within the new station building.

The East box had been a notorious cabin, located as it was at the eastern end of the island platform and below the Union Street bridge at the mouth to Dock Street tunnel. The smoke, damp and fumes were the blight of many a signalman's health. Dundee Tay Bridge West was at the western end of the station controlling the shunting movements from the bay platforms and the carriage cleaning sidings alongside the box. All the boxes in the Dundee district including Buckingham Junction and the central box situated near the old sheds were closed between March and April 1985.

The track rationalisation removed the carriage sidings at the western end and straightened the alignment to give an easier approach from the Perth direction while maintaining a left-hand facing junction to the bridge. Similarly track rationalisation east of the site of the old East station eased the route at Camperdown Junction to give a straighter line down the 1 in 60 incline to Dock Street tunnel. Camperdown Junction box closed in 1985 with the others in the area to be replaced by the signalling centre at Dundee.

The present level of service through Dundee is closely linked with the pattern of Aberdeen to Glasgow and Edinburgh trains. Having previously been operated by double headed type 2 locomotives including those later known as class '26' and '27', English Electric type 4 locomotives took over the through Edinburgh service when they were displaced by the 'Deltics' on the Kings Cross trains. By the seventies, Brush type 4s were in charge.

Later the Dundee to Edinburgh trains, usually dmus, were given over to single class '27s' with four coaches. There were superseded by class '150' and later '156' units. The Glasgow route depended for motive power in the 1960s on the short lived North British Locomotive Company type 2s, followed by class '26' and '27s', eventually relying upon class '47s' and their push-pull derivatives. Both routes are now worked by class '156' and class '158' Express units.

The InterCity services are operated by IC125 trains to London and the south west and overnight sleepers trains, which had run to Kings Cross, have been diverted to Euston. Freight services have now all but ceased with the closure of the Castle cement siding, there being only an engineer's train siding remaining in 1995.

Consideration has been given to electrifying the line to Aberdeen north of Edinburgh thereby further improving the quality of service to London, but cost is proving a major obstacle. Happily there are still services in three of the four directions established by the mid-19th century and the most notable feature, the Tay Bridge, still plays an significant role. Few of the other features which the Victorians created remain, save the dank Dock Street tunnel and the platform buildings of Dundee station itself. Dundee West and East have gone along with the locomotive and goods sheds. The branch line to Newtyle and its offspring to the harbour have also gone along with the north Fife lines. The city maintains the good rail connections with the rest of Scotland and Great Britain which it established in the 19th century.

Locomotives Constructed in Dundee
1833-1849

Date	Builder	No.	Name	Wheel Arr.	Driving Wheel Dia.	Cyls (in.)	Railway	Cost (£)
20.9.1883	CAR	1	Earl of Airlie	0-2-4	4' 5"	11x18	D&NR	701
20.9.1833	CAR	2	Lord Wharncliffe	0-2-4	4' 5"	11x18	D&NR	701
3.1834	DFS	3	Trotter	4-2-0	4' 6"	11x18	D&NR	
1838	KHS		Wallace	2-2-2	5' 0"	13x18	D&AR	1,012
1838	KHS		Griffin	2-2-2	5' 0"	13x18	D&AR	1,012
1838	KHS		Fury	2-2-2	5' 0"	13x18	D&AR	1,012
3.1.1839	DFS		Victoria	0-4-0	5' 0"	12x16	A&FR	1,300
18.2.1839	DFS		Caledonia	2-2-2	5' 0"	13x18	A&FR	1,300
1839	KHS		Rapid	2-2-2	5' 6"	13x18	D&AR	1,270
1839	KHS		Dart	2-2-2	5' 6"	13x18	D&AR	1,370
14.5.1839	DFS		Britannia	2-2-2	5' 0"	13x18	A&FR	1,300
2.1840	KHS		Queen	2-2-2	5' 6"	13x18	D&AR	1,370
7.8.1840	KHS	5	Wallace	2-2-2	5' 6"	13x18	GPK&AR	1,320
7.8.1840	KHS	6	Bruce	2-2-2	5' 6"	13x18	GPK&AR	1,320
1840	DFS		Albert	0-4-2	4' 6"	14x18	A&FR	1,450
1841	KHS	11	Eglinton	2-2-2	5' 6"	13x18	GPK&AR	1,320
1841	KHS	12	Portland	2-2-2	5' 6"	13x18	GPK&AR	1,320
5.1841	DFS		Princess	0-4-2	4' 6"	12x16	A&FR	1,255
3.1843	KHS	21	Burns	2-2-2	5' 6"	14x18	GPK&AR	1,386
1845	KHS	26	Mars	2-2-2	5' 6"	13x18	GPK&AR	1,390
1846	KHS	38	North Star	2-2-2	5' 6"	13x18	GPK&AR	1,530
1846	KHS	39	Meteor	2-2-2	5' 6"	13x18	GPK&AR	1,530
1846	KHS	40	Comet	2-2-2	5' 6"	13x18	GPK&AR	1,530
1846	KHS	41	Planet	2-2-2	5' 6"	13x18	GPK&AR	1,530
1846	KHS	72	Dandie (orig. Caledonia)	0-4-0	4' 0"	13x18	AR (1849)	
1847	KHS	2		0-4-2	5' 0"	15x20	D&PR	
1847	KHS	3		0-4-2	5' 0"	15x20	D&PR	
1847	KHS	4		0-4-2	5' 0"	15x20	D&PR	
1847	KHS	5	Vulcan	2-2-2	5' 0"	15x20	D&PR	
1847	KHS	6	Lucifer	2-2-2	5' 0"	15x20	D&PR	
1847	KHS	7	Dundee	2-2-2	5' 0"	15x20	D&PR	
1847	DFG		Caledonia	0-4-0			D&P&ARJ	
1847	DFG		Gowrie	0-4-0			D&P&ARJ	
1848	DFG	66		0-4-2	5' 0"	13x18	AR	
1848	DFG	68		0-4-2	5' 0"	13x18	AR	
6.1848	KCo	77	Dumfries	2-2-2	6' 0"	15x20	GD&CR	2,140
6.1848	KCo	78	Glasgow	2-2-2	6' 0"	15x20	GD&CR	2,140
6.1848	KCo	79	Carlisle	2-2-2	6' 0"	15x20	GD&CR	2,140
6.1848	KCo	80	Solway	2-2-2	6' 0"	15x20	GD&CR	2,140
8.1848	KCo	81	Afton	2-2-2	6' 0"	15x20	GD&CR	2,140
9.1848	KCo	82	Queen	2-2-2	6' 0"	15x20	GD&CR	2,140
11.1848	KCo	83	Albert	2-2-2	6' 0"	15x20	GD&CR	2,140
11.1848	KCo	84	Princess	2-2-2	6' 0"	15x20	GD&CR	2,140
11.1848	KCo	85	Nith (later Nithsdale)	2-2-2	6' 0"	15x20	GD&CR	2,140
12.1848	KCo	?						
1849	DFG		Craigie				D&AR	
1849	DFG		Carlogie				D&AR	

Abbreviations used

CAR	J. & C. Carmichael	A&FR	Arbroath & Forfar Railway
DFG	Dundee Foundry, Gourlay's	AR	Aberdeen Railway Co.
DFS	Dundee Foundry, Stirling's	D&AR	Dundee & Arbroath Railway
KCo	Kinmond & Co.	D&NR	Dundee & Newtyle Railway
KHS	Kinmond, Hutton & Steel	D&PR	Dundee & Perth Railway

D&P&ARJ Dundee, Perth & Aberdeen Railway Junction
GD&CR Glasgow, Dumfries & Carlisle Railway
GPK&AR Glasgow, Paisley, Kilmarnock & Ayr Railway

Appendix Two

Findlater's Report on the Proposed Railway between Dundee and Perth

(The following considered the possibility of building one of three proposed lines from Dundee to Perth in 1835. It reveals a little of the nineteenth century traffic and economy of the Carse of Gowrie.)

In laying the following estimate before you, I may mention that it includes every charge necessary for the finishing of the line, - following the most expensive course of the bulwarks, cuttings &c; and for furnishing the requisite machinery and furniture for putting the work in operation; and that the gross amount is fully adequate for the formation of any of the three lines.

ESTIMATE OF THE PROBABLE EXPENSE

1. FORMATION	£	s.	d.
BULWARKS, &c,-			
1133 lineal yards of bulwark, from Yeaman Shore to Magdalene Yard			
4½ cubic yards, per lineal yard at 12s., £2 14s.; but take it at £3	3,399	0	0
143 lineal yards of facing across small bay at Madalene Yard, average			
6 feet high, 2 cubic yards, per yard lineal at 12s., £1 4s. per yard,	171	12	0
939 lineal yards facing along Crescent and Binnrock lands at £1,	939	0	0
2013 lineal yards across Invergowrie Bay, at £3, average 9 feet high,	6,039	0	0
Facing opposite Mr Patton's	200	0	0
	10,748	12	0

EARTH WORK,-	£	s.	d.			
349,000 cubic yards, at 6d.	8725	0	0			
113,320 cubic yards, at 8d.	3777	6	0			
Forming road way at Kingoodie, 1100 lineal						
yards at 3s.	165	0	0			
Do. along Carse of Gowrie, 11810 lineal yards, at 4s.	2362	0	0			
Do. do. 2683 do at 6s.	804	18	0			
From Seggieden to Kinfauns,1188 lineal yards at 3s.	178	4	0			
				15,982	8	0
Total for formation				26,731	0	0

2. BRIDGES			
Culvert across burns £150 each	1150	0	0
Wooden bridges across Willowgate	4350	0	0
Drains, small culverts, &c	1330	0	0
Total for bridges	6830	0	0

3. FENCING			
3000 yards of dykes, from Invergowrie Bay to West March of			
Mylnefield, at 1s. 6d.	225	0	0
70,250 yards of dykes at 1s. 6d.	5268	15	0
Total for fencing	5493	15	0

	£	s.	d.
4. ALTERING ROADS			
440 yards at Kinfauns, at 5s.	110	0	0
440 do of dyke, at 2s. 6d.	55	0	0
	165	0	0
420 yards of road west of Kingoodie, at 3s.	63	0	0
Alterations at crossings of 13 farm roads, at £10	130	0	0
Crossing under railway in Moncrieff Island	95	0	0
Total for altering roads	435	0	0

5. LAND

	£	s.	d.
Value of the land to be occupied by the railroad, compensation surface damage, &c	11,626	15	0
Wayleaves and tenant's damages during excavation work	1,197	0	0
Total for land	12,823	15	0

6. IRON WORK

The length of the main line is 35,225 yards, requiring 140,900 yards of railway bars. These bars should contain 42 lbs. of iron per lineal yard, making   2642 tons
Besides these rails for the main way, 2250 yards of track will be required for sidings and branches in the depot, connections with and crossings for the main way at the various stopping stations along the main way, making 4500 lineal yards of railway bars. These bars should contain 36 lbs. of iron per lineal yard making   72 tons
                    2714 tons

		£	s.	d.
The price of the railway bars delivered at Dundee is £8 10s., but to include shore dues and carriage, say £9. Take therefore 2714 tons at £9		24,426	0	0
Chairs, 140,900 at 14 lbs. each, for main way	880½ tons			
4500, at 10 lbs. each for sidings	24 tons			
	904½ tons			
Waste and breakage	5½ tons			
	910 tons			
Which, at £7 10s. per ton amounts to		6,825	0	0
Turning tables, offset plates, lever switches, keys, spikes wedges, &c, &c		1,500	0	0
Total for iron work		32,751	0	0

7. FINISHING

	£	s.	d.
145,400 stone blocks, at 1s. 3d.	9,087	10	0
71,575 cubic yards of ballasting and boxing at 1s. 6d.	5,368	2	6
Boring and laying blocks, laying and finishing rails, 145,400 lineal yards, at 4½d.	2,726	5	0
10,560 lineal yards of curb stone and water channel, at 1s. 6d.	792	0	0
Larch sleepers, 10,000 at 6d.	250	0	0
Total for finishing	18,223	17	6
TOTAL FOR WORKS	101,306	7	6

	£	s.	d.
Contingencies, ten per cent	10,130	12	6
Depot ground, fittings, &c. at Dundee	5,330	0	0
Do. do. at Perth	2,320	0	0
Total for works	119,087	0	0

	£	s.	d.			
4 locomotive engines and Tenders, at £800,	3,200	0	0			
15 Passenger coaches at £60,	900	0	0			
150 waggons, at £14 each	2,100	0	0			
Couplings, tools, and other furniture for working department	213	0	0			
Total for machinery, &c.				6,413	0	0
				125,500	0	0

ESTIMATE OF THE PROBABLE REVENUE

PASSENGERS

From data derived during the last year, the number of passengers conveyed between the towns of Dundee and Perth were upwards of 145,000; besides this number, many others passed between these towns. From this, and looking to the increase of passenger traffic which has taken place where Railway communication has been opened, 300,000 through and through passengers may be safely reckoned upon - that number at 1s. each is   15,000   0   0

Conveyed intermediate distances along the line, this may be safely taken at 40,000 at 6d.   1,000   0   0

Note - Within the last twenty-five years the passenger traffic between Dundee and Perth has increased about twelve fold; at that period there was no other conveyance but the mail and a caravan, making only one trip a-day. Since 1833 the increase of passengers between these towns has been upwards of 2,500 passengers have been conveyed between these towns in one day.

PARCELS

The number of parcels now carried, at 10d. each, as ascertained from the coach and other books, is 16,000 - this number at 6d. is   400   0   0

GOODS FROM SHIPPING

The quantity now conveyed by the lighters of the Dundee and London, and Hull Shipping Companies alone being goods landed and re-shipped, amounts to about 67,500 barrels bulk, or about 8,500 tons, at a rate of about 7s. per ton. This traffic does not remunerate the London and other Companies who carry it on with Perth, from the shore-dues, and necessity of steam drags for making the passage to Perth, &c., and may therefore be reckoned upon. And considering the increase of traffic which will take place from the starting of the new steam packets to Hull, Leith, &c., 10,000 tons may safely be calculated upon; which at 3d. per ton per mile, including Railway-dues, waggonage, and haulage is   25,000   0   0

		£	s.	d.

GENERAL MERCHANDISE

There are seven regular carriers carts, and from five to seven others engaged in conveying goods to and from Perth and Dundee. These leave Dundee and Perth twice a-week, each carrying about 24cwt., at from 6d. to 10d. beside parcels. From the increased traffic which has taken place since the erection of the flax mills at Perth, Quarry-mill, and on the River Almond; and the additional number of carts thereby employed; and from the prospects of public works being extended about Perth, an increased traffic may be reckoned upon. And considering that these public works do not now avail themselves of means of water carriage, and that goods may be conveyed by the Railway at one half the present rate of cartage, and a considerable augmentation of the present amount of tonnage may be anticipated, 10,000 tons may be calculated upon at 5s.- amounting to

2,5000   0   0

COALS

Looking to the supply of this article now required in the districts proposed to be traversed by the Railway, and the probability of a new traffic being opened in this commodity along the line, 20,000 may be reckoned upon as the tonnage from this source. This however, being as yet prospective, 5,000 can only be calculated on with safety, which conveyed on an average of ten miles at 2s. 6d. is

625   0   0

FARM PRODUCE

From approximations made by Mr Young, Pitfour and Mr Deuchars, valuator, Dundee, the quantities exported from the Carse of Gowrie may be estimated at.

	£	s.	d.			
Grain, 9,500 tons, conveyed on an average of ten miles at 3d. per ton per mile	1,187	10	0			
Potatoes, 7,000 tons do. do. at 2d. per ton per mile	583	6	8			
Manure, &c. 7,000 tons do. do. at 2d. do. do.	583	6	8			
Total				2,354	3	4

STONES

During each of the years 1834 1nd 1835 about 25,000 tons of stones were sent to Dundee from the Kingoodie Quarries. The portion carted being at the rate of 2s. 6d. per load, and that conveyed by the barges about 9d. per ton. The Dundee builders gave a decided preference to the Kingoodie. stone; and state, that if the cost of conveyance was reduced, they would take double the quantity from this quarry which they now do; 40,000 tons may be safely calculated upon, which at 6d. per ton is

1,000   0   0

TONNAGES between Dundee and Bullionfield bleaching works, and mills, &c. in that neighbourhood. From the books of the Bleachfield, the annual toonage for the year appears 4,684 tons, conveyed at about 2s. 6d. per ton. From Invergowrie Mills 20 tons per week is an average; and from Gray Mill and Den Spinning Mill, 20 tons do. The traffic from these works seem to be gradually increasing, and 7,000 tons may be safely calculated upon, at 1s.

350   0   0

		£	s.	d.
Total revenue		25,729	3	4

	£	£	s.	d.
From this gross revenue there falls to be deducted,-				
1. Expences of management, maintenance, &c.	10,280			
2. Sinking fund for the renewal of engines, carriages, rails,&c. and general stock of furniture	1,000			
		11,280	0	0
Leaving amount to meet capital outlay of		14,449	3	4
Take capital at £126,000, 11½ per cent. amounts to		14,490	0	0

In conclusion, I may state, that I have in every particular availed myself of the correctest data, which could be obtained in every department, as well of the revenue as of the expense; and although the return may seem to be great for the capital embarked in the undertaking, when compared with the probable revenue of the line to Arbroath, yet this is easily accounted for. It has now been fully ascertained, that passengers form the great and profitable source of railway revenue, raised too at one-eleventh of the cost of heavy traffic, if tonnage be looked to. This being the case, the experience of every individual resident in the neighbourhood must shew him, that the number of passengers who pass along the line more than quadruple those on the line to Arbroath. While this is the case, the line now contemplated passing, as it does, through so level a country, and so rich in fertility, and terminating at Perth, the resort of so many strangers, lead me to anticipate that a handsome return will never fail to be realised for the capital embarked in carrying the present undertaking into effect.

JAMES R. FINDLATER

15, Castle Street, Dundee, October 1835

Enginemen's Reminiscences

John Soutar, Queen's Driver

In a supplement to *The Weekly News* of 5th November, 1898, when he was 64, John Soutar, perhaps one of the best known drivers in the early years of the Caledonian Railway, related his time on the railways to the reporter. During his 40 years as a driver, John Soutar spent 15 of them on goods trains between Perth and Aberdeen, five more on passenger trains between Aberdeen and Motherwell and a further 20 on the Perth to Carlisle road. He proudly claimed to have driven Queen Victoria more often than any other man in Scotland.

He began his railway life in 1851, with the Dundee and Arbroath Railway at Dundee East station, when he was 18. His first job was as goods porter, but after two months was promoted to the passenger platform, where he remained for only four more months. Soutar was then transferred to the locomotive department as fireman. 'My first driver was Willie Watson,' he related, 'There was no cleaning of the engines then. The Dundee and Arbroath had only eight or nine locomotives. Two old men were employed to clean the motion and the wheels, and the fireman had to do all the rest of the cleaning when we were on the road.

'I was fireman on the Dundee and Arbroath line for four years and five months. The first engine I fired on the Dundee and Arbroath line cost £900, the engine I am running now - *Jubilee* - cost £3,000. The Scottish Central and the Scottish Midland had a working agreement which came to an end about the year 1855. The Aberdeen and the Scottish Midland joined together to have a locomotive department of their own, and Mr Yarrow was appointed superintendent, and the engineering workshops were started at Arbroath.

'It happened that the Royal Train had to be run from Perth to Aberdeen, and Mr Yarrow had no engines suitable for the job. In this dilemma, he applied to the Dundee and Arbroath Company for the loan of two engines - No. 3 and No. 4. I was sent as fireman with No. 3 up to Forfar, to be under Mr Yarrow's instructions to run the Queen to Aberdeen. No. 4 was not used, but my engine No. 3, and a Midland passenger engine ran the Queen to Aberdeen. This was my first contact with Royalty, but I was only a fireman at the time. After the trip with the Queen I continued to run with that engine on the Dundee and Perth line.'

John Soutar was the first driver to take the Queen from Carlisle to Aberdeen with one engine, hauling a 14 coach train. In Jubilee year (1887), he once again drove an engine, named *Jubilee*, on the Royal Train. 'I had instructions from the Dundee and Arbroath people that wherever that engine went I was to go with her. Mr Yarrow was preparing some new passenger engines, and orders came to send No. 3 home. I brought her to Broughty Ferry and left her there, and went to Arbroath where I knew I would get a job from Mr Yarrow. No. 3 engine finished her course on the Blairgowrie branch. One night at the level crossing over the turnpike road she carried away the gates and the top bar went through the smoke box and damaged her otherwise.'

In 1895, he took part in the Railway Races. 'On the last day of the race I got my engine ready, and before the train came in I went up the line and sanded the rails outside the station for some distance and then I opened all the valves and let out the surplus water, and got a good head of steam up. That gave me a good start and a good start is everything. The sand made the wheels grip, and away we went like a shot, and before I was past the ticket platform I was going at the rate of 50 miles an hour.

'When we got the road at Kinnaber before the NB, one of our officials, who was on the engine, clapped me on the shoulder and cried, "That's well done, John; you've won the race." There was great excitement when the Caledonian won the race and they carried me shoulder high out of the station. That was the end of the railway race; the East Coast were fairly beaten.' After the success of the railway race one of the leading officials of the Caledonian Railway Company came up to John Soutar on the platform at Perth station one day, complimented him and said he was so much obliged to him and all the other men on that link for the service they had rendered.

Towards the end of his working life, John Soutar asked to have day working and at the time of the interview in *The Weekly News* he drove the 6.15 am local train from Perth to Glasgow and the express back, with an afternoon run to Dundee and return completing his day. He was then still in charge of No. 724 *Jubilee*.

John Anderson, Veteran of the NBR

In a second interview with *The Weekly News*, John Anderson another railwayman related his life with the Edinburgh, Perth and Dundee Railway and later the North British. When Anderson was a boy, his father's carrier business in Cupar had been badly affected by the opening of the Edinburgh and Northern Railway and the family moved to Tayport where Mr Anderson senior worked at the station on goods traffic. John Anderson entered railway service about the time of the Indian Mutiny (1857-59) when he was employed at the company's workshops at Ladybank. After gaining some experience there, he was sent to Tayport where he began to train as a fireman. During his five or six years in this job, he served his apprenticeship as a driver.

He claimed that the locomotives were very poor at that time and pretty well worn out. There were no injectors and an old hand pump was used to supply water to the boiler. 'When you got short of steam on the road,' said Mr Anderson, 'you uncoupled the train and left it standing on the line, while you ran forward with the engine and pumped water into the boiler. Then you ran back to pick up the train, which was not easy to do at times in the dark, at the risk of banging into her and doing a smash. Of course, these were goods trains.'

When the first Tay Bridge was opened, John Anderson was moved to St Andrews where he was appointed to drive trains between St Andrews and Dundee. He ran the first train over the original bridge on the first day it was opened for traffic, and also drove the last St Andrews train over the bridge on the Saturday evening before it fell. He was roused on the Sunday night at around midnight by Mr Robertson, station agent at Leuchars, who knocked on his door at St Andrews to tell him what had happened.

Some time later, a friend told Anderson that on the night the bridge fell he had been with the local gamekeeper watching for poachers at Scotscraig near Newport. In the course of the evening they had heard the voice of a woman calling for help. Running to the road which was only a field away from the River Tay, but they searched but found nothing. The following morning, the body of a woman was discovered on the beach on top of a wrecked carriage among other debris from the disaster. Anderson himself was called before the Board of Trade Inquiry at Dundee to give evidence on the speed at which the trains travelled over the bridge.

Until the new bridge was opened, John Anderson drove trains between Tayport and Burntisland, but once both rivers were bridged, he was involved in running to Aberdeen including the North British leg of the Railway Races of 1895. Like his counterpart, John Soutar of the Caledonian, John Anderson was also a driver of royalty. However, as most of the Queen's journeys to and from Balmoral were made by the West Coast route, the most significant passengers he could recall were The Prince of Wales and the King of Portugal. Mr Gladstone was a passenger when he travelled to Dundee from Edinburgh on the occasion of his speech on the McKinley Tariff in 1890.

When he was driving on the Burntisland to Tayport train at Kinghorn, he saw a man and a woman standing by the track. 'There was something between them, I thought,' he told the reporter 'but before I could think the man bolted from the woman and lay his head down on the rail. I put on the Westinghouse brake and whistled. I was scarcely two hundred yards on but I could cover that distance in two or three seconds. Just as the engine was almost touching him, the woman seized him and pulled him off the rail. I pulled up at Kinghorn and reported the occurrence to the station master. It turned out that the man had quarrelled with his wife and had tried to frighten her, but he was very near a cropper.'

Inside Dundee Central signal box in the 1960s.   *Author's Collection*

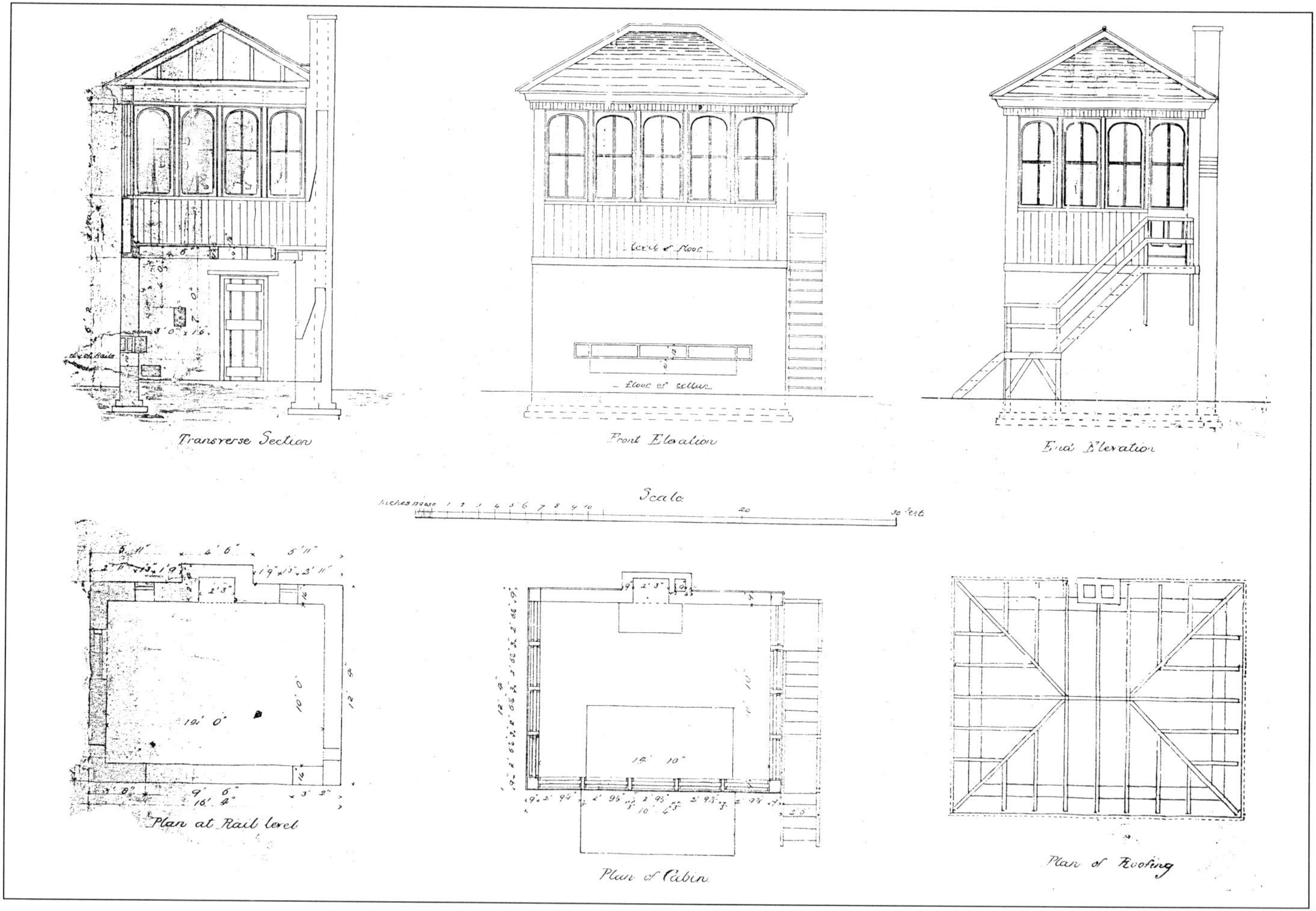

Transverse Section
Front Elevation
End Elevation
level of floor
floor of cellar
Scale
Plan at Rail level
Plan of Cabin
Plan of Roofing

Dundee & Forfar Railway Pointsman's cabin at Broughty Ferry Junction, 1870.

British Railways Board

Appendix Four

Signals and Signal Boxes

Signalling in the early years of the Dundee and Arbroath Railway was primitive compared with the present day. The company outlined its signal rules for both night and day traffic.

Signals:	Flags by day	Lamps by night

1. Line clear — Policeman to stand erect, flag in hand, no signal
2. Proceed caution — Another engine has passed on same line within ten minutes. Green flag raised
3. Proceed caution — Defect in rails. Green flag depressed
4. Stop — Red flag shown waved to and fro, Policeman facing engine
5. Stop — Seeing red light
6. Engine passed — Flag to shoulder
7. Policeman responsible for his hand lamp to be in order and trimmed
8. When a train stops at a station the Danger signal must be put up and kept up while the train is there.
   Red signal for ten minutes after passing of train
   Green signal for a further five minutes after that.
9. When a train leaves Broughty Ferry and is intended to stop at West Ferry, the Danger signal will be shown at Broughty Ferry for fifteen minutes and Caution for five minutes after that.

On the Harbour branch of the D&NR, strict conditions were laid down for traffic using the line as it was in part over public roads. The section between Nethergate and Yeaman Shore was on private property but the sections to Ward station and Dundee East station on either side of it were not. Locomotives were not permitted and passenger trains were limited to no more than three carriages, goods trains to four wagons. One hundred yards had to be left between each train. Three policemen or conductors were required for passenger trains, one, three minutes ahead of departure at South Union Street to warn of an approaching train, a second to drive the horse and a third to follow to 'superintend progress'. Only two conductors were needed for goods trains. A trumpet had to be supplied and each train had to carry four lights at night, one each ahead and behind and one either side.

On the Dundee and Perth line, signals were semaphore and were of wooden construction with two arms in slots either side. The signal was placed invariably on the left-hand side of the line as seen by an approaching engineman. 'All right' was indicated by no arms showing. 'Caution', slacken speed, by the left arm raised 45 degrees and Danger, by the left arm raised 90 degrees. If both arms were raised, then the line was blocked in both directions.

There were telegraph signals installed at Magdalen Green and Kingoodie Quarry, both of which were on the left hand side of the up line but used for the Dundee line and having only a caution signal. A further two were placed at Mylnefield and Princes Street, Perth. Engines leaving Dundee station to go to the engine shed and repair yard at Sea Braes were not permitted to pass a point opposite the large semaphore until the danger signal at Magdalen Green was on.

Signal Boxes

Co.	Location	Opened	Closed	Notes
NBR	Tay Bridge North	1/6/1878		
		1889	30/9/1929	
	Tay Bridge South	1/6/1878	1879	Fall of Tay Bridge
		1879		Open
	Newport on Tay East	1879		
	Tayport North	1879	23/5/1966	Line closed
	Tayport South		15/4/1962	
	Dundee Central	1878	28/5/1893	
		28/5/1893	14/4/1985	Dundee SC 17/3/1985
	Dundee (TB) West	1878	6/8/1899	
		6/8/1899	31/3/1985	Dundee SC 17/3/1985
	Dundee (TB)East	1878	17/3/1985	Dundee SC 17/3/1985
D&A Joint	Camperdown Junction	1878	1903	
		1903 ext. 1939	17/3/1985	Controlled from Dundee
	Dundee East Station	17/9/1893	21/5/1935	Controlled from Camperdown
	No. 2 Gates	17/9/1893	16/7/1939	Controlled from Camperdown
	Carolina Port	(?)1888	29/10/1922	
	Stannergate West	27/1/1901		
		12/7/1920	13/5/1921	
			19/10/1930	
	Stannergate East	27/1/1901	27/6/1967	19/10/1930 renamed Stannergate
	Craigie		27/1/1901	Replaced by Stannergate
	West Ferry		1/8/1917	
		1/4/1925	6/11/1925	
	Broughty Passenger	27/11/1887	Open	
	Broughty Goods	1874	2/5/1926	
	Broughty Junction	7/8/1892	19/12/1965	
CR	Invergowrie		10/10/1967	
	Ninewells Junction		8/3/1893	
		8/3/1893	9/1/1968	
	Esplanade Junction	4/5/1888	(?)1921	
	Buckingham Junction	1878	22/8/1886	
		22/8/1886	15/6/1958	
		15/6/1958	19/5/1985	Controlled from Dundee
	Dundee West		15/9/1899	
		15/9/1899	30/11/1965	
	Liff	6/3/1893	18/10/1898	
		18/10/1898	9/12/1967	Closed line
	Lochee	8/3/1893	9/12/1967	
	Fairmuir Junction	17/11/1887	9/12/1967	Auchterhouse closed 5/4/1965
	Rosemill	9/9/1892	3/8/1955	
	Barnhill	2/2/1921	7/10/1967	Closed line

Appendix Five

Private Trader Wagons in Dundee

A list of private trader wagons registered by the Caledonian Railway and operating in the Dundee area on 31st July, 1909.

Owner	No. of Wagons	Other details
Dundee West		
Johnston R. Allan & Son	4	4 Crescent Lane
J.S. Allan & Sons	8	15 Baltic Street, and 60 Foundry Lane
R.J. Anderson	1	9 Annfield Street
J. Barlow	1	1 Commercial Street
J.B. Barnes*	3	30 Commercial Street, coal merchant
J. Blackwood	3	38 Lochee Road
Wm Brown*	7	22 Barrack Street, wagons
W. Cruikshank	2	13 Arklay Street
J. Culley	2	
Charles Duncan	2	55 Victoria Road
Jas D. Ferguson	2	81 Ferry Road
Gas Commissioners	100	Gas works
J. Hill	2	50 Crescent Lane
R.N. Henderson	2	Maryfield Yard
J.S. Hood	81	Yeaman Shore & Maryfield yard
J. Lawrence & Co.	58	20 Yeaman Shore
Peter Lawson	3	16 Peddie Street
F. Lynch	2	28 Ferry Road
Muir Son & Patton*	183	26 Yeaman Shore, ran both on CR & NBR
Muir Son & Patton	28	26 Yeaman Shore, ran only on CR
D. Smart	1	18 Raglan Street
Smith Hood & Co.	9	48 Union Street
F. Stewart	2	55a Watson Street
R. Swan	1	15 Kidd Street
Taylor Brothers	30	28 Yeaman Shore
R. Taylor & Son	91	59 Yeaman Shore
J. Valentine & Son	2	Perth Road, printers and publishers
Joseph Ward	2	17 Craigie Street
J. Young	1	12 Balfour Stree
Dundee East		
C. Gray	1	40 Candle Lane
Lochee		
Cox Brothers	35	Jute merchant, also 1 tank wagon
Lee, Croll & Co.	1	Lawside Foundry, engineers
W. & A. Smith	1	242 Lochee Road
J. & A. Wooler	3	35 Camperdown Street

*William Brown was a former partner in Brown and Fyvie of the same address, which had two 10 ton wagons around 1900. These were later purchased by J.B. Barnes which in turn was amalgamated with Muir Son & Patton in 1921.

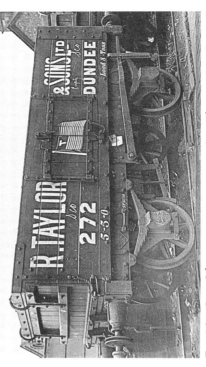

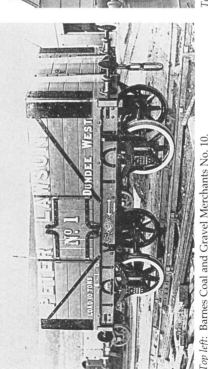

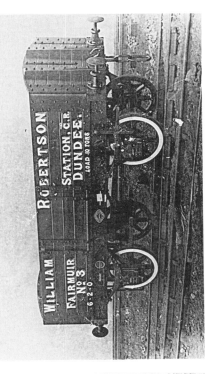

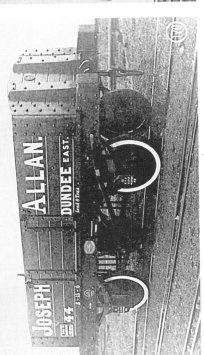

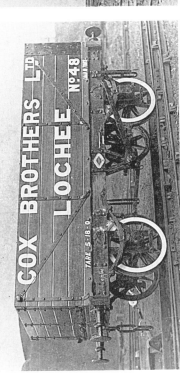

Top left: Joseph Allan, dumb buffered wagon No. 44.
HMRS/RY Pickering Collection

Bottom left: Cox Brothers of Lochee, No. 48. *HMRS/RY Pickering Collection*

Top right: Dundee and District Co-operative Coal Supply Association No. 16.
HMRS/Hurst Nelson Collection

Bottom right: William Robertson, No. 3.
HMRS/RY Pickering Collection

Owner	No. of Wagons	Other details
Lochee West		
G. Hill	2	Coal Merchant
D.B. Imrie	1	70-72 Peddie Street
A.C. Robertson	1	135 South Road
Fairmuir		
G. Edwards	5	Coal merchant
J. & A.D. Grimond	22	Jute spinners & manufacturers
J. McDonald	2	Fairmuir yard
Henry McCann	3	Dons Road
Malcolm Ogilvie	15	Jute spinners
W. Robertson	3	21 Alexander Street
George Will	53	Coal merchant
Maryfield		
H. Boase & Co.	5	Rockwell Wks (flax & hemp spinners)
Robert Brown	3	
Cargill & Co.	4	Pitkerro Road, bleachers & linen merchants
James Watson	4	98 Albert Square, & Maryfield yard
Baldovan		
Lewis Carmichael	2	Station coal merchant
Broughty Ferry		
Gas Commissioners	6	Gas works
W. Neilson	3	
D.R. Nicoll	2	55 Brown Street

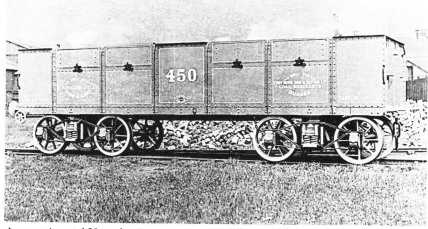

An experimental 20-ton bogie wagon No. 450 of Thomas Muir, Son and Patton.
HMRS/RY Pickering Collection

Appendix Six

Chronology

5th January, 1825	Meeting in Dundee to promote a railway to Newtyle
26th May, 1826	Dundee and Newtyle Railway Act incorporated
16th June, 1829	D&NR Shareholders meeting expresses dissatisfaction
29th May, 1830	Further Act to finance D&NR
16th December, 1831	Opening of Dundee and Newtyle from Law station
April 1832	D&NR fully opened
20th September, 1833	First locomotive arrived on D&NR
12th October, 1835	Meeting to promote a railway to Arbroath
February 1834	Harbour branch in operation
21st July, 1835	Newtyle and Coupar Angus railway incorporated
30th July, 1835	Newtyle and Glammiss railway incorporated
11th November, 1835	Report on possible Dundee and Perth railway
19th May, 1836	Dundee and Arbroath Railway Act incorporated
4th July, 1836	Further finance Act for D&NR
2nd May, 1838	Auction of the lease of the D&NR
6th October, 1838	Opening of Dundee and Arbroath Railway to Craigie
1st April, 1840	D&AR opened fully to Trades Lane
13th October, 1840	Meeting in Cupar to promote railway through Fife
January 1845	Meeting in Dundee to promote railway to Perth
31st July, 1845	Dundee and Arbroath Railway Act incorporated
31st July, 1845	Edinburgh and Northern Railway Act incorporated
October 1845	D&NR closed to regauge the track
27th July, 1846	Dundee and Newtyle leased to the Dundee and Perth
22nd May, 1847	Opening of Dundee and Perth Railway to Barnhill
2nd July, 1847	Act to widen and improve the line incorporated
17th September, 1847	E&NR opened from Burntisland to Lindores
23rd December, 1847	Junction line to Forfar railway opened in Arbroath
17th May, 1848	E&NR opened to Ferryport-on-Craig
17th May, 1848	Broughty Ferry branch opened on D&AR
2nd August, 1848	SMJR line opened from Perth to Forfar
31st August, 1848	Act leasing D&AR to Dundee & Perth incorporated
April 1849	E&NR renamed Edinburgh Perth & Dundee Railway
1st March, 1850	First service on Burntisland train ferry
9th March, 1850	Agreement to separate D&AR and D&PR
1st May, 1851	Broughty Ferry branch re-alignment opened
14th December, 1857	New station at Trades Lane (Dundee East) opened
1st November, 1860	Balbeuchley incline by-passed via Dronley
26th July, 1863	Scottish Central takes over D&NR and D&PR
14th July, 1864	Act to build Dundee and Forfar Direct Railway
7th September, 1869	John Stirling meets Dundee Councillors over bridge
15th July, 1870	North British Railway (Tay Bridge) Act incorporated
22nd July, 1871	Tay Bridge foundation stone laid
14th November, 1871	Dundee and Forfar Direct line opens
22nd September, 1877	First engine to cross Tay Bridge
31st May, 1878	Formal opening of Tay Bridge
28th December, 1879	Tay Bridge collapses in a storm
8th July, 1880	Report of Tay Bridge inquiry published

July, 1881	New Tay Viaduct Act incorporated
6th July, 1883	Foundations of new Tay Bridge begun
20th June, 1887	Passenger services begin over new bridge
6th August, 1897	Act passed to build Newburgh and North Fife line
1889	Third Dundee West station opens
27th January, 1901	Stannergate station opens
25th January, 1909	Newburgh and North Fife Railway opens fully
1st January, 1917	Passenger services withdrawn from Lochee West
2nd October, 1939	Esplanade station closes
12th February, 1951	Passenger services between Newburgh and St Fort withdrawn
10th January, 1955	Passenger services between Broughty Ferry and Kingsmuir withdrawn
1st October, 1955	Dundee (West) to Newtyle services withdrawn
9th January, 1956	Passenger services between Leuchars and Tayport withdrawn
5th May, 1958	Goods services between Newtyle and Auchterhouse withdrawn
5th January, 1959	Dundee (East) station closed
4th April, 1960	Goods services between Glenburnie Junction and Lindores withdrawn
5th October, 1964	Goods services between Lindores and St Fort withdrawn
25th January, 1965	Goods services between Auchterhouse and Fairmuir Junction withdrawn
3rd May, 1965	Dundee (West) station closed
23rd May, 1966	Tayport to Newport (East) services withdrawn
9th October, 1967	Goods services between Broughty Ferry and Kingsmuir withdrawn
6th November, 1967	Ninewells Junction to Fairmuir Junction closed
5th May, 1969	Dundee to Newport (East) services withdrawn
6th October, 1975	Passenger services reinstated to Perth via Newburgh
2nd October, 1978	Introduction of InterCity 125 service to Aberdeen
22nd October, 1979	Invergowrie Bay accident
17th March, 1985	Resignalling of Dundee area

Bibliography

Railway historians will be familiar with many of the following published sources which have inspired me to dig deeper into historical archives.

The Origins of the Scottish Railway System 1722-1844 C.J.A. Robertson, John Donald, 1983
The Caledonian Railway, O.S. Nock, Ian Allan, 1962
The North British Railway, Hamilton Ellis, Ian Allan, 1955
The North British Railway, Vols. 1 & 2, John Thomas, David & Charles, 1969 & 1975
Steam Trains to Dundee, John Perkins, Dundee Museum & Art Galleries, 1975
Dundee's Iron Horses, George McLennan Steel, Lindsay and Co, 1974
The High Girders, John Prebble, Secker & Warburg, 1966
The Tay Bridge Disaster, John Thomas, David & Charles, 1972
The Fall of the Tay Bridge, David Swinfen, Mercat Press, 1994
The Tay Railway Bridge, 1887-1987, J.S. Shipway, Institute of Civil Engineers, 1987
Railways of Fife, W. Scott Bruce, Melven Press, 1980
Tramways of the Tay Valley, Alan W. Brotchie, Dundee Museum & Art Galleries, 1965
Regional History of Great Britain Vol. 15, John Thomas, David Turnock, David & Charles, 1989
LMS Sheds, Vol. 5, The Caledonian Railway, Chris Hawkins and George Reeve, Wild Swan Publications, 1987
Dundee and Newtyle Railway, Niall Ferguson, Oakwood Press, 1995
Newtyle, A Manufacturing Village, William Murdoch Duncan, Forfar Historical Society, 1979
The Radical Laird, Charles Tennant, Roundwood Press, 1970
Crossing the Forth, Hugh Douglas, Robert Hale, 1964
The Great Road between Forth and Tay, G.P. Bennett, Markinch Printing Co.
The Railway Mania and its Aftermath, Henry Grote Lewin, David & Charles Reprint, 1968
Locomotives of The North British Railway, Stephenson Locomotive Society, 1970
Industrial Locomotives of Scotland, Industrial Railway Society 1976
Contractors Steam Locomotives of Scotland, Industrial Locomotive Society, 1990
British Locomotive Catalogue, 1825-1923 Vol.4 Bertram Baxter, Moorland Publishing Co, 1984

The work of several authors in the following magazines and journals have proved to be a valuable source of detail.

*Railway Magazine,*Vol. 25, 1909; Vol. 26, 1910; Vol. 52, 1923; Vol. 97, 1951; Vol. 104, 1958
HMRS Journal, Historical Model Railway Society
The True Line, Caledonian Railway Association
North British Railway Study Group Journal
Abertay Historical Society, Various Publications

The original documents of the various companies provide detail of company operations.

North British Working Timetables and Appendices.
British Railways Working Timetables.
Public Timetables, Special Notices etc. of D&AR, NBR, CR, LNER, LMS, BR.

Sources

My researches meant spending much time studying the material which can be found in various archives. I am grateful to the staff of these valuable sources of railway history for their courtesy and assistance.

Dundee District Library   Lamb Collection
Sandeman (later A.K. Bell) Library, Perth
Scottish Record Office   NBR & CR papers, Minute & Letter Books
National Library of Scotland   Map Room

Thanks

My sincere thanks go to the following people who gave me access to their collections of railway documents and photographs, or allowed me to use their researches and for their support and advice.

Bob Drummond, George Robin, Forbes Alexander, Harold Bowtell, Gerald Baxter, Jim Page, Allan Simpson, Michael Smith, the Caledonian Railway Association Archives and Tom McGhie.

A combination of NB (*top*) and CR arms on one post reveals the joint nature of the D&AR line at Broughty Ferry station in the 1960s.   *Michael Smith*

Index

Two Caledonian employees stand outside a permanent way hut near Magdalen Green station in the 1890s. *Dundee District Libraries*